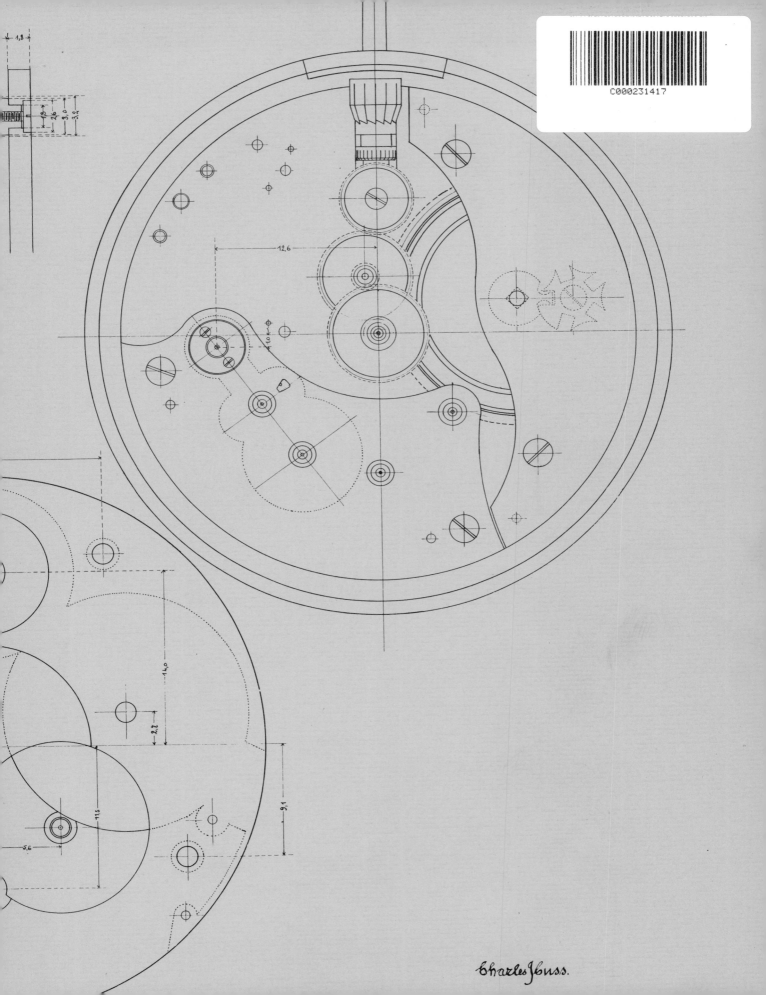

Charles Jouss.

The Camerer Cuss Book of

ANTIQUE WATCHES

The Camerer Cuss Book of

ANTIQUE
WATCHES

by T. P. Camerer Cuss

*Re-illustrated, Revised and Enlarged
by T. A. Camerer Cuss*

Antique Collectors' Club

ISBN 0 902028 33 2

Printed in England by
Antique Collectors' Club
Church Street, Woodbridge, Suffolk

Contents

Preface

This is a revised and enlarged edition of an invaluable book by the late T.P. Camerer Cuss. As far as possible all the watches originally illustrated have been re-photographed, and in some instances further views of them are included. Sixty or so more watches have also been added and there are now eight colour plates. While the original text and comprehensive glossary have been retained, the captions to the illustrations have been completely re-written and substantially enlarged to provide supplementary information to the text. A short history of Usher and Cole that has previously only appeared in a private limited edition has been included. It is an interesting glimpse at the intense competition for supremacy and the costs and processes of manufacture involved in making a high grade English watch in the Victorian era.

It was no surprise when the first edition was a resounding success, and it is sufficient to say that long before the first print was sold out the book was regarded as a standard work, and there were not enough copies to go around. T.P. Camerer Cuss was after all the most fortunate of horologists, being the fifth generation to be the head of the family firm that was founded in Bloomsbury, London in 1788. The continuous procession of watches of all kinds which passed through the workshop for restoration enabled him to obtain a vast and detailed understanding of them. Not only did he achieve an encyclopaedic knowledge, but his enthusiasm for his subject resulted in his willingness to share it with a large number of collectors. Perhaps his greatest pleasure was in imparting knowledge in the simplest terms and this undoubted talent comes through clearly in his writing. Indeed it is perhaps one of the most valuable features of the book for it reflects his daily experience: on the one hand giving advice to those already conversant with the subject and on the other hand assisting those just starting to collect.

Introduction

When planning this new edition it became obvious that because of the number of references to most illustrations they could never be placed at exactly the right point in the text. It is irritating to have to constantly turn back and forth in search of an illustration and it was felt that they would be found more readily if the two were separated.

This arrangement produced three further advantages. First it was practical to make the illustrations much larger without interrupting the flow of the text, secondly the space provided for the captions was not limited and thirdly it enabled chronological progression to be followed.

It was decided to depart from the normal practice of showing watches at actual size or smaller. Some readers may feel that enlargement distorts the objects, but it was felt that this was justified not only on the grounds of clarity, but also because it mitigates the inherent limitations of photography that can so easily destroy the full visual effect enjoyed by the naked eye, having, as it does, the advantage of three dimensional vision.

My father's clear and concise narrative has been retained. A small number of changes were necessary in the light of recent research and a few minor errors have been corrected. I have added a short section on American watches to the last chapter and a few items to the glossary. Thus my own contribution has largely been the provision of more illustrations and new captions, which I hope the reader will find a useful supplement to the text. Also included is the short history of Usher and Cole which my father published privately some years ago.

I am eternally grateful to my father for immersing me in the subject and by arranging this second edition I have had the good fortune to express some of my filial gratitude. My thanks are also due to friends who have kindly spared the time to discuss the points that I have raised with them. In particular Anthony Randall for his help with a number of technical matters and Cecil Clutton for checking some of the historical facts behind the development of the early lever watch. Dana Blackwell kindly provided some photographs and information relating to the American watch. I have been fortunate enough to have been able to draw upon some of the recent unpublished research that has been undertaken by Richard Edgcombe on the subject of *repoussé* cases.

I am most grateful to those whose watches appeared in the first edition and who have kindly made it possible for fresh photographs to be taken as well as those who have allowed me to illustrate their watches for the first time. Other photographs have been kindly provided by: The Basingstoke Museum plate no. 6; The British Museum plate nos. 2, 5, 7, 10, 14, 24; National Maritime Museum plate no. 4; The Science Museum Glossary figs. 6, 14; The Time Museum, Rockford, Illinois plate nos. 153, 158, 159; Victoria and Albert Museum plate nos. 18, 21, 28; Mr. Jürgen Abeler plate no. 1; Mr. Sam Bloomfield plate no. 165; Mr. B. Hutchinson plate no. 176; Mr. J. Kennedy plate no. 32; Count Lamberti plate no. 3; Mr. S. Leiter plate no. 37; Mr. F.C. Tufton plate no. 85.

I am also grateful to Charles Cuss for providing the technical drawing for the end papers.

Terence A. Camerer Cuss
54-56 New Oxford Street,
London WC1A 1ET
April 1976

Chapter 1

The First Hundred Years 1500–1600

Watches developed from portable clocks. Clocks were rendered portable when a coiled spring, the mainspring, was introduced to provide the driving power instead of a suspended weight.

The mainspring is, therefore, our first consideration. When it was introduced is uncertain; probably the idea arose from the use of a blade or flat spring, the 'springiness' of which was employed by the locksmith before the coiled strip of suitably hardened metal was put to use in clockwork.

Research into the very beginnings of clockwork is being undertaken afresh at the present time. The late Mr. P.G. Coole of the British Museum followed a number of lines of investigation and it may well be that much of what is still uncertain in the early history of horology will be clarified. Greater attention is now being paid to manuscripts, paintings and illuminations, and it has been established from such sources that the mainspring may have been in use by the mid 15th century, and was certainly known by 1477.

One of the earliest references to what is quite unmistakably a watch appears in *Cosmographia Pomponiae Melas* (1511), where the author, Johannes Cocclaeus, refers to the work of Peter Henlein of Nuremberg. Later, in 1730, the Nuremberg chronicler Dopplemayr wrote as follows regarding Henlein: 'A locksmith artist who gained renown through the small watch works which he was one of the first to make in the form of musk-balls at that time in use.' For a long time this was thought to indicate that Henlein invented not only watches but, by implication, the mainspring. Though it is quite clear that Nuremberg was a watchmaking centre in the early years of the 16th century, it is important to note the views now being put forward that the spring-driven clock probably had its origin, at an earlier period, in what is now Flanders and Burgandy. It is also probable that northern Italy was active in the earliest years. Though no Italian watch appears to have survived from this period, Professor Morpurgo's researches among Italian documents have convinced us that small portable clocks and probably watches were made in Italy as early as 1488. A school of watch-making existed in France by about 1525.

The portable clocks which were the precursors of the watch are drum-shaped (Pls. 2 and 3). One would have thought, therefore, that the first watches would have been similar in construction and appearance, but smaller and light enough to be worn; as Cocclaeus wrote: 'to be carried on the bosom or in the purse'. However, some of the earliest surviving watches answer the description given to Henlein's watches by Dopplemayr, for they are spherical in form. The earliest dated watch (1548) that has come to light so far has a tambour case (Pl.1).

A watch of spherical form, and dated 1551, is in the Louvre, Paris. Pl.4 shows one of a similar type but larger. Both these are by Jacques de la Garde. The Ashmolean Museum, Oxford, has an example of the German musk-ball watch; this also dates from the mid 16th century.

As might be expected, the timekeeping of these watches was quite ineffectual by modern standards, but one can easily appreciate what marvels their owners thought them — and as, in their own context, they were.

We have seen that they are powered by a mainspring. This power is delivered through a train of wheels and pinions to the escapement. An escapement performs the function of releasing the driving power step by step.

The earliest form of escapement in the light of present knowledge is the verge (see Glossary). It is not known who invented it. Before its use for watches it had already done duty for about 200 years for clocks.

The verge escapement consists of the escape wheel (driven by a pinion from the last wheel in the train), the verge itself and the balance (see Glossary). There are two pallets ('flags') located on the verge and set at about 100 degrees to each other. The teeth of the crown (escape) wheel act upon alternate pallets.

The escapement controls the release of the driving power and at the same time imparts energy — 'impulses' — to the balance to maintain it in oscillation. The balance itself controls, to a degree, the frequency with which this operation occurs.

The teeth of the escape wheel are so formed that, as the wheel rotates, each pallet is in turn pushed clear so that a tooth escapes, simultaneously impulsing the balance. This maintains the to-and-fro characteristic of the balance. At the date of which we are speaking the balance spring had not been invented, so that the interval between each alternating swing of the balance depended almost solely upon the power exerted by the mainspring and the inertia of the balance, a condition making for wear in the various parts engaged in the strife, and for erratic behaviour. It will be readily appreciated that any fluctuations in the power delivered by the mainspring affected the performance of the balance and therefore the time-keeping.

In the earliest German watches, instead of the plain wheel or balance so familiar on later watches, a bar, called a 'foliot', was used (Pl.5 and 6). This was weighted at each end, and a crude adjustment of the timekeeping could be made by altering the weights, thus altering the moment of inertia of the foliot. Another and better method of controlling the oscillations to some extent was to control the supplementary arc (see Glossary) of the foliot by making each end of the foliot bank against an upright hog's bristle, the bristle being mounted on a pivoted arm and consequently adjustable (Pl.5 and 6). The same idea was subsequently employed on the balance by the arms of the balance banking against adjustable bristles. The main endeavour to improve the timekeeping, however, was directed towards providing a more or less unvarying driving power.

A mainspring exerts a varying force depending upon whether it is in a fully wound or in a run down condition. Two equalising devices were used: the stackfreed (Pls.5 and 6) and the fusee (Pls. 3 and 4 see Glossary). The stackfreed enables a flatter watch to be made so that one may conclude that this accounts for its use in preference to the fusee by some of the 16th-century German watchmakers. Certainly the early fusee, with it theory probably only partially understood by its users, did not give results so very much better than could be obtained from the stackfreed.

Cocclaeus speaks of Henlein's watches 'going for 40 hours', whereas the stackfreed watches have a running time of about 26 hours. It is possible, therefore, that Henlein's earliest watches had neither stackfreed nor fusee, but were provided with stopwork (see Glossary). If a watch which will run for 40 hours is wound every 12 to 24, it will give a better performance because in that event only a section of the mainspring, giving a more equal torque, is being employed.

In order that the first turns of the mainspring will produce a more equal force to the subsequent turns, some power must be put on the spring; some preliminary winding-up must be done before the ordinary winding commences. The amount of this initial winding is known as 'setting-up' the mainspring; and the amount of set-up, in the pre-balance days that we are discussing, affects the time-keeping considerably. Some provision for this was made even in the earliest times on non-fusee watches; a pinion meshed with a wheel of which a small section was left uncut (as on the stackfreed watch) thus causing only a portion of the mainspring to be used effectively. The earliest set-up on the fusee watch is the ratchet and click, which was to give place, as we shall see in the next chapter, to the worm and wheel method.

From the earliest times striking, and sometimes alarum work, was incorporated. Towards the end of the 16th century astronomical indications as well as phases of the moon and calendar work became additional complications (Pl.10). In the days before printed calendars such information was useful, and to know the state of the moon before planning a night journey was a definite advantage. There was a greater chance of the date being correctly shown than the hour!

Dials had only an hour hand, the dial having hour and half-hour divisions. At each hour there was a 'touch pin' or 'feeling knob' so that the time could be told in the dark by moving one's finger across the dial (Pl.8), the steel hand was stoutly made and it suffered no damage thereby. Glasses had not yet been introduced and to protect the watch in wear either a solid cover was fitted, which had to be lifted in order to read the time, or a cover with 'windows' pierced over each hour numeral so that the tip of the hand and its position could be seen (Pl.1).

The earliest dials had a central decoration of a star or sun with twelve rays leading to the hour numerals (Pls. 4 and 5). German watches had, in addition to the twelve Roman numerals, 13 to 24 in Arabic figures engraved on an inner circle, the characteristic German 2 resembling a Z (Pl.5). At the end of the 16th century the central sun decoration began to give place to more elaborate engraving, and the tail of the hour hand was increased in length.

Judging by the very earliest watches that have survived, no great lavishness was expended on the cases. It would appear that the technical attributes were those which mattered; decoration for decoration's sake is more evident a little later. The spherical or musk ball type was shaped out of sheet copper, chiselled and engraved with arabesque and strap work, and gilded. The drum-type case was often cast with intricate patterns, worked over with a graver and then fire-gilt. Since most watches of this period had striking-work, the cases were also pierced, which enhanced the decorative effect.

Towards 1585 the German drum-shape gave place to a circular case with domed back and front covers, more elaborately engraved as well as chiselled (Pl.6). Additional forms began to appear as the century came to a close; octagonal — especially elongated octagonal — and oval (Pl.8). Around 1600 the circular watch tended to have a deep dome to the covers, the sides of the case becoming more bulging and rounded, while the most common French, English and Swiss watch, whether circular or oval, had straight sides. Watchmaking started in England, the Netherlands and what is now Switzerland, a decade or two before 1600.

Chapter 2

Decorating the Watch 1600–75

'Ah, by my Troth, Sir, besides a jewel and a jewel's fellow, a good fair watch that hung about my neck.' This quotation from Thomas Middleton's play *A Mad World, My Masters*, which appeared in 1608, shows how watches were then regarded. It is true that before 1600 watches were considered to be articles of adornment, but the next half-century is the period of the most profuse decoration of all kinds. The different crafts of the engraver, the lapidary, the enameller and the jeweller were all employed on beautifying watch-cases. This is illustrated by the remarkable inventory of Queen Elizabeth I's watches: 'Item. One clocke of golde wrought like deyses and paunseyes, garnished with little sparkes of diamonds, rubies and emorodes, and eight small pearles on the border, and a pendant acorn. Item. A watch of agatte made like an egg garnished with golde. Item. A little watch of gold enamelled with sundry colors on both sides alike. Item. A little watch of christall slightly garnished with golde, with her Ma'ties picture on it.'

The movements remained basically unaltered, although these too were given greater decoration than previously. About 1635, the click and ratchet wheel set-up (Pls. 8 and 9) began to give place to the worm and wheel system (Pl. 16), a small silvered dial — the 'figure piece' — being fixed to the wheel and a pointer fixed on the movement plate. This enabled a rather finer adjustment to be made, but for a time both methods were in use. The worm was secured to the plate by elaborately pierced and shaped supports, made of blued steel. The movement plates and the other brass work were gilded. The spring — in ratchet wheel set-up — was covered with a pierced brass decorative plate. However, improvements in timekeeping were obtained from more accurately cut and filed wheels and pinions, particularly from more efficiently shaped fusees. Fusee chains began to replace gut cord soon after 1670.

The decoration given to various parts of the movement is one of the surest means of dating a watch during a period when practically no mechanical details altered. The earliest balance cocks (see Glossary) on German foliot watches ended with a short spiral (Pl.5), later this evolved as an S. The French cock of about 1600 had a decorative pierced foot, the table being an S elaborated with a floriate design (Pl.8). English cocks of this date were pierced with scroll work and foliage and were oval in shape. Both foot and table were without a bordering rim and they were pinned to a block projecting from the plate (Pl. 12). The mainspring barrel of striking watches was engraved, and English watches were given a border of engraved foliage to the top plate (Pl. 11). All watches were now signed by their maker with a flourish, often with the city of their provenance added (Pl. 17).

Shortly after 1640 the balance-cock was screwed to the plate, and a pin or pins on its underside located and steaded it in the plate (Pl. 23). By the middle of the century, the table had been increased in size and was circular (Pl. 27). Later both foot and table of English cocks were given a rim, although, as so often happens, changes in style are over-lapped. After 1675, French and Swiss balance-cocks took the form of a bridge, being secured to the plate by two screws (Pl. 37); both the French and English forms may be found on Dutch watches.

The earliest decorated pillars were spiral in form. These were followed by round or turned columnar or baluster types (Pls. 10 and 11) and the rectangular, tapering Egyptian form (Pls. 39 and 40). Soon after 1660 the tulip-shaped pillar was increasingly used (Pls.27 and 41), and the fusee stop support given greater decoration, particularly in English watches (Pl. 31).

The typical dial of 1600-35 has an engraved landscape or figure scene in the centre and floral or human and animal figures beyond the chapter ring, which was frequently silver and applied to the gilt brass dial plate (Pl. 12). German dials also had engraved scenes and floral decoration, but some were embellished with *champlevé* coloured enamels at an earlier date (Pl. 7). Hands were steel, rather more elaborately shaped than earlier periods with the tail almost as long as the pointer. After about 1635 the chapter ring was sometimes given quarter-hour divisions.

The pendant by which the watch was hung continued to be fixed to the case so that the hole ran from the back to the front and through this a ring was passed (Pl. 12). But with the advent of the waistcoat the neck watch became a pocket watch, and its suspension accordingly altered. The pendant was generally short, with a round knob through which a loose ring was attached (Pls. 22 and 23). The fob chain was attached to the ring. The hole and the ring or bow (as it was later called) were parallel to the dial. The bow altered in shape in later years and is an aid to dating.

The first quarter of the 17th century is most notable, however, for the great diversity of shapes or forms given to the cases apart from the oval, octagonal, square or circular. Cases were made in bizarre forms such as skulls, flower buds, crosses (Pl. 14), stars, books and animals. All the watch-making countries produced these 'form' watches as they are called, but particularly Germany and Switzerland. Many cases were made out of rock crystal (Pl. 13) — frequently faceted — and other hard decorative stones such as agate. Gold cases surviving from this period are very rare and silver not common; in the main the metal used was gilt brass, although one must bear in mind that gold cases have always been subject to being melted down for their gold value. Watches of this period are not plentiful, but we have moved out of the 'museum' era and the first half of the 17th century is the favourite period for those whose taste inclines towards artistic craftsmanship.

The use of translucent and opaque coloured enamels of the *champlevé* type had begun in the last years of the previous century, and they were now to be used in greater abundance. In addition, painting in enamel began around 1630. This is of two kinds. In the first the gold case is given a smooth enamel surface which is then decorated with buds, flowers and foliage in high relief. The second method of painting in enamel is credited to Jean Toutin working in Blois in about 1630 (Pl. 18). Toutin laid down a smooth surface of white enamel on which he painted his miniature. The work was then fired. To counteract the expansion of the metal case when firing, the inside of the case had also to be enamelled. The shape of these cases can best be described as bun-shaped.

Jean Petitot (1607-91) founded a Genevan school of enamellers in about 1650. The famous Huaut family of painters in enamel (Pl. 28) also originated in Geneva, but though superlatively rich in colour, their work never achieved the refinement of execution or the delicacy of colouring of the work done at Blois. The dials of painted enamel watches were left white with the numerals in black, but frequently the centre was painted. The hands were usually of gold.

It was the advent of the enamel watch which increased the need for a protective outer case. The earliest of these were stiffened leather, but by 1650 or so the outer case had become, so to say, a part of the watch and was worn with it; the outer was made of silver or base metal, covered with leather, or fish skin. To aid the adhesive in securing the covering, pins were inserted and these were worked into a pattern: piqué work (Pls. 23 and 25). In

Stephen Thorogood, London, hallmarked 1763

Rare, English *Basse Taille* enamelled verge watch in a case of unusual construction (51mm. diam.) See plate 64.

Early French Watch Case, circa 1635

This case is of *cloisonné* enamel in relief, the bezel and back set with rose diamonds. (39mm. diam.) Enamel work of this type and date are rare.

Bovet Fleurier, circa 1835

Gold and enamel watch with bezels, pendant and bow set with split pearls, painted scene of flowers and a pair of doves. (60mm. diam.) The all steel and chrome plated movement is illustrated on plate 137.

George Graham, London, hallmarked 1739

Gold *repoussé* pair cased watch with gold matching chatelaine both with borders of symmetric design, numbered 5838 with a cylinder escapement. Gold rather than gilt metal chatelaines are uncommon. This watch commends itself from a mechanical as well as decorative point of view. (54mm. diam.) See also plate 57.

Alexander Cumming, London, hallmarked 1780

Silver gilt, quarter repeating cylinder watch. (54mm. diam.) See also plate 76. Cumming was born about 1732 and moved from Edinburgh to London where he joined the Clockmakers' Company in 1781, dying in 1814. He was appointed by the Act of Parliament of 1761 as an adjudicating expert on Harrison's timepiece. He was a Fellow of the Royal Society and wrote a number of papers on horology.

L'Epine à Paris, circa 1770

Vari-coloured gold watch, painted enamel scene. Bezel and hands are paste as are the half hour markings on the dial. In common with a good many continental watches of this period, this has a gilt metal outer protecting case, glazed back and front. (45mm. diam.) This maker's name is more often spelt Lépine. There is a normal verge movement.

Julien Le Roy, Paris, mid 18th century

Gold verge watch with green enamel case overlaid with gold *repoussé* decoration that is filled in parts with translucent green enamel and is signed G. Bouvier on the lower edge of the central group of figures. (53mm. diam.) Julien Le Roy was a celebrated maker and Clockmaker to the King. He introduced the French form of potence of which this watch possesses an example.

time it was the outer case — particularly on English watches — that received the main decoration, the case proper being left plain. Such watches are known as 'pair-case' watches.

Soon after 1625 'glasses' (albeit at first rock crystal) came into use. The glass was secured by tabs to the underside of the bezel (Pl. 16). Later, the bezel was split at the hinge, the glass inserted, the replaced hinge-pin securing the glass by tightening the bezel (Pl. 23).

A break-away from 'garnished' watches occurred in England about 1640. Whether it was just a reaction or whether it was Puritan influence one cannot say, but a type appeared — apparently restricted to this country — which was devoid even of engraving. In shape they resembled a flattened egg or sometimes they were circular (Pls. 16 and 17). Usually they were provided with a 'glass' of crystal. The surviving examples are almost without exception of silver, and the outer is also of plain silver.

There is good reason to suppose that many of the earlier decorative cases were made in Blois and exported to this country, or made here by immigrant French craftsmen. Pattern books and design sheets give us the names of some of the French and German sources from which watch dials, balance cocks, case-engravings and enamel paintings have derived.

Soon after the middle of the 17th century the round watch — recognisable as a pocket watch — became almost the universal shape. The dial was larger, protected by a glass, and where the watch had a pair-case, the outer received the decoration, the inner being usually left plain.

Decoration, however, was still very much in evidence for the next 25 years of the period under review. Very few crystal and stone cases were now made and the oval shape also fell out of favour. But form watches continued, perhaps especially in Switzerland, and the Geneva goldsmiths and enamellers were now more active than those in Blois. Some very fine engraved cases also date from this period, the design usually consisting of flowers and foliage (Pl. 23).

The *champlevé* dial — as distinct from the *champlevé* enamel dial of *circa* 1600 — began to come into fashion shortly before 1675, and the numerals, where they had been short and stumpy before, now were given greater length (Pl. 25). Quarter as well as half hour markings were general. The hands showed no great alteration except that the tailless hand was beginning to be used, and in this form it was simpler, occasionally quite plain.

Movement decoration continued; indeed in one respect it increased because the fusee stop arm was given a decorative mounting. Mechanically, the main change was that the fusee chain as opposed to gut cord was in general use, and regulation was by tangent screw and wheel (Pls. 23 and 27).

German watchmaking had been overshadowed by France after about 1620 as the Thirty Years War (1618-48) had its effect. Now as the 17th century progressed, English watchmaking came to the fore, enjoying its first golden age.

Chapter 3

The Introduction of the Balance Spring
1675–1700

The pendulum as the controller of the timekeeping of a clock had been introduced in 1657. Since that date, the watch — from the point of view of accuracy — had been its poor relation. Then, in 1675, occurred a most exciting event. The Dutch mathematician and physicist Christian Huygens achieved for the portable timekeeper what he had already achieved for the clock; he devised a practical means by which the escapement of a watch can be brought under proper control, using a spiral ring — the balance spring. Anyone who relishes an acrimonious controversy will find the story of Huygens versus Robert Hooke (and others) over the priority of the invention enthralling reading. The debate, as a matter of fact, is still likely to flare up at any time, but it has lost most of its fire except between the most avid champions.

About 150 years earlier, it had been realised that if a ship carried an accurate timekeeper, comparison of local time, as found by observation, with standard time, as shown by the timekeeper, would establish the ship's longitude. The invention of the pendulum clock at first gave hope that a solution had been found; it certainly provided (with an improved escapement) an accurate timekeeper. But a swinging pendulum on board ship presents impossible difficulties, and this hope was dashed. The Royal Observatory was founded at Greenwich in 1675 with the object of making more precise astronomical observations with the aid of accurate clocks so that 'the tables of the motions of the heavens and the places of the fixed stars' might be rectified. The advent of the balance spring offered renewed hope.

Whereas in pre-pendulum clocks and pre-balance spring watches, the period of oscillation had depended upon mechanical losses, the period of oscillation of the pendulum and the sprung balance depends upon the returning force that is proportional to the displacement. A plain balance without a spring will revolve, if set in motion, on its own axis and, of course, in the direction in which the impulse is given, until the momentum is exhausted. But if a flat spiral spring is fixed at its inner coil to the arbor of the balance, and if its outer end is secured to a stud on the movement plate or balance cock, an impulse given to the balance could cause it to travel only as far as this momentum is able to overcome the resistance of the coiled spring: the spring in the process is wound up on itself. When the resistance is equal to the impulse which has been given to the balance, the balance momentarily halts, and then is turned in the reverse direction by the energy of the spring in unwinding. The energy is more than sufficient to return the balance to its starting point, and the 'dead point' of the spring. The balance travels past this point, and the spring goes beyond the position where it would be in a relaxed state; in so doing it builds up fresh energy by unwinding against itself. This new energy then exerts itself by once again reversing the direction of the balance. The to-and-fro motion continues, with diminishing force. Finally, of course, the balance comes to rest when the initial energy given to it has been spent.

This action of a spiral spring approaches simple harmonic motion, and in the description given above, the function of the escapement has been disregarded. One action of the escapement is to impart regular impulses — impulses which are sufficient to maintain the oscillations. But what determines the time-period of the oscillations? Put as simply as possible, the time-duration of each swing is determined by the distribution of mass, the size and shape of the balance; the length, strength, thickness and material of the spring; the impulses delivered to the oscillating system; pivot friction on the balance arbor, and any interference arising from the action of the escapement.

The closely isochronous (see Glossary) property of the pendulum was appreciated in 1675. It might be thought — in fact it was for many years so thought — that the spiral spring, when applied to a watch balance, had exactly similar qualities. Hooke's Law (see Glossary) was taken to mean that the balance spring was, by its nature, isochronal, even when applied to the balance of a watch. For years watchmakers assumed that the arcs (see Glossary) of vibration, whether long or short, were performed in exactly the same time in any given spring.

Why is the point about isochronism so important? First we must remember that the timekeeping depends entirely on the time-period of the oscillations of the balance and its spring. If the speed of the oscillations increases, the escapement will work faster: the escape wheel, therefore, revolves more quickly and the rest of the train follows suit; the hands, through the motion work, will no longer register 60 minutes in a precise hour, but 60 plus the extra speed of the oscillations of the balance. Consequently, if the spring is not isochronous, and there are no neutralising factors, the watch will give an incorrect rate. For if the short arcs of vibration are performed in less time than the long arcs, any falling off in the swing of the balance, for whatever reason will result in the watch gaining. And conversely, if the short arcs occupy more time, the watch will lose.

We must remember that many factors will, and do, cause a variation in the length of arc: a variation in the motive power (due to a weakening of the mainspring); an increase of friction (due, for instance, to the thickening of the oil, or dirt in pivot bearings); any wear on working parts or inequalities in the gearing; a change in the elasticity of the spring. But perhaps most important of all is the position occupied by the watch; whether it is horizontal or vertical. It will be readily appreciated that if the watch is dial up or dial down, the effect of gravity on the balance and the escapement will differ from any of the possible vertical positions.

Watchmakers were later to realise that an improved escapement would have to be devised, as it already had been for pendulum clocks. It was also learned that variations in temperature have an effect on the functioning of a steel spring; that it loses energy or elasticity in a rise in temperature, and conversely increases in 'springiness' for a fall, resulting in a losing or a gaining rate respectively. Though Robert Hooke had propounded his law relating to springs in 1664, there were still theoretical mysteries surrounding it. Nevertheless in 1675 it must have seemed that the road was open 'to finding the longitude'. It was what we call today a 'break-through'. One can imagine how the new invention must have been discussed not only by Fellows of the Royal Society, but by men in coffee houses. Pepys records in his Diary: 'I to my Lord Brounckner's, and there spent the evening by my desire in seeing his Lordship open to pieces and make up again his watch, thereby being taught what I never knew before; and it is a thing very well worth my having seen, and am mightily pleased and satisfied with it.'

English watchmakers were the first to exploit the possibilities of the new controller (Pl. 29) and Thomas Tompion, the leading clock and watchmaker of his day, made the first attempts to turn the watch into a real timekeeper (Pl. 49). He realised that a larger and thicker watch increased the possibilities for more accurate formation and functioning of the mechanism. He was advised by Hooke on many matters and the tooth-cutting machine which Hooke invented enabled Tompion to improve his wheel trains. Tompion had acted under Hooke's instruction as regards the balance spring during the experimental period. It seems that Tompion was the first to organise his workshop on a thoroughly business-like basis. There had been sub-division of labour before his time, but he carried it a stage further. This is indicated by his numbering of the movements, balance cocks and cases, which he started in about 1680. The method of regulation by altering the effective length of the balance spring which he introduced was universally adopted, and it was used for about the next 80 years. As regulation was now done through the balance spring, the mainspring set-up was used by the watchmakers only in the initial stages of regulation, and the set-up arrangement was removed from the top plate; on balance spring fusee watches, it is found between the plates. The balance was increased in diameter. Four wheel trains with a going period of 26 hours became general.

As always, technical changes brought changes to cases and dials. Cases were now circular in form and more robust: the oval, octagonal and fancy shapes went out. Dials, as we shall see, were soon to indicate minutes, since the improved timekeeping warranted it.

The inner case on English watches became determinedly plain, outer case decoration depending mainly on tortoise-shell inlaid with silver (on silver watches); or gold or silver piqué work on shell (Pl. 39), leather, or shagreen. Engraved decoration became less common, and in many instances both cases were left plain.

This is the beginning of the French 'oignon' period: an even thicker watch than its English counterpart (Pl. 37). The cases of these were usually cast, with a shallow decoration and one can assume that many had a leather outer case although only a few seem to have survived. The oignons found today have either gilt brass or silver cases, and one can only suppose that those of gold have been the casualties of the passing years. Swiss watches of this period show strong French influence. The Revocation of the Edict of Nantes in 1685 had caused large numbers of Huguenots (many of whom were watchmakers) to emigrate to Geneva; some came with their fellow silversmiths to England.

The school of Huaut enamel painting was now at its height (Pl. 28), and movements of different nationalities are found housed in these enamel cases. In such instances the outer case is the protective one. All watches now had glasses, and by the end of the century the glass was snapped into the bezel, though the split bezel is found up to about 1705. At the same time the square hinge to the outer case gave place to one rounded off at the edges (Pl. 40).

The watch pendant of the last half of the 17th century terminated with a round knob, a loose-fitting ring passing through a side-to-side hole. About 1695 the knob was flattened and a hinged bow of oval or stirrup form took the place of the loose ring (Pls. 33 and 36). The stirrup shape sometimes approximates to a horseshoe form. Later the bow took a more distinct oval form (Pls. 42 and 46). It is from its shape at this time that it derives its name, even though in later years the plain round ring, pivoted on the pendant, came back into favour. A comparison of the bows and pendants shown in the illustrations will indicate their development.

The champlevé dial made its first appearance well before 1675, but from that date until the enamel dial came into fashion soon after 1715 (it began in France and Switzerland) the champlevé is the typical dial of the period (Pls. 36 and 39). However, watches are frequently found today which have had their original champlevé dials discarded and an enamel one substituted (Pl. 40).

The typical French or Swiss dial of about 1700 is gilt metal with chased or engraved centre and white enamel hour plaques or cartouches with the numerals painted upon them in blue or black (Pl. 37). In general, the French cartouches had blue numerals, the Genevan black. Alternatively the whole dial was white enamel, but the portions on which the numerals appeared were raised — émail à bosses.

The Dutch, whether the dial was *champlevé* or, later, enamel, were particularly fond of the arcaded or 'wavy' chapter ring (Pl. 44). Such a dial, unless the watch is unmistakably a product of Holland, will either indicate that the watch was made in England for export to Holland or that the watch is of Swiss origin.

The French Huguenot immigrants to Switzerland during the 17th century had produced a very real need for the Swiss to export. More often than not poor quality watches were produced but the fact remains they were cheap.

The ability of the Swiss to imitate and the willingness to sign a watch with whatever name was required (Pl. 59) renders it difficult to determine the quantities of both eighteenth and nineteenth century watches which were in fact produced in Switzerland. It is certain however that by the end of the eighteenth century the Dutch, Germans and Austrians had been dominated and the French industry was to some extent at least dependant on the supplies of both completed watches and unfinished movements from Switzerland. Breguet was no exception. There is no doubt the master was responsible for the designs, and his workshops for much of the finishing to his watches, but it is equally certain his contact with his country of origin was of considerable importance.

Switzerland too produced many watches, christened with the most prodigious names of England and France, but not made for resale by them. There are for instance many Breguet 'forgeries' of the most ordinary quality bearing no resemblance at all to those he sold.

The situation is more confused as high quality watches equal in style and craftsmanship to his work are quite frequently found. The irony must be that since the Swiss were responsible for some parts of Breguet's genuine work, using his name on their 'forgeries' was but half a lie.

The position is somewhat different where forgeries used English names such as Tompion and Quare. Maybe the responsibility for these rested with their fellow countrymen, but others would seem to be Swiss. As the eighteenth century progressed only the Swiss appeared to be able to meet the increasing demand. Not only were they establishing themselves abroad as both watchmakers and importers but watches were also imported from Switzerland by English, Dutch and French makers. Additionally, perhaps frustrated a little by the renown of the English watch, misspellings were frequently made of good English makers' names. There were also those that were completely fictitious and legends such as Samson and Worke were very popular. Many of these watches never entered England although quite a few carry fake English hallmarks.

These watches have been called 'Dutch Forgeries'. Although patently a misnomer, it has been suggested the Dutch were responsible for importing English hallmarked cases, and possibly dials and hands, and selling the end result as an English watch.

The position is confusing however since even in the early part of the eighteenth century work by some of those who spent part of their lives in each country have characteristics which are Swiss in origin (Duchene and Norris are examples). One might conclude that even at this date watches which approximated to English and Dutch designs were readily available in Switzerland.

The late 17th and early 18th century dials had half hour markings and the five minute divisions were marked with a 5, 10, 15, etc. The half hour markings were soon dropped and as the 18th century progressed these numerals became smaller, eventually to be discarded invariably before 1800. Up to about 1775 enamel dials had a line on the inside circumference of the hour numerals. The minute markings or strokes had bands on the inner and outer edge but during the last quarter of the century strokes and also dots without bands began to be used. Arabic hour numerals first appeared in the 1780's.

During the early part of the period, the tulip form of hour hand was most popular, together with other forms based upon it (Pl. 36). A great variety is found before the 'beetle and poker' came in around 1705 to stay for almost 100 years (Pl. 49).

The French continued with one-handed watches until after the turn of the century and the typical *oignon* has one hand, the watch being wound through the centre (Pl. 37). Two-handed *oignons* are not, however, rare.

As has been said, the normal English dial was *champlevé*, with minute divisions and hour and minute hands. However, the period 1680-1710 saw a diversity of dials which indicate that either watchmakers or their customers were not at first satisfied with this arrangement. There are at least four distinct types (described in the Glossary) which departed from the ordinary. That most rarely found is the 'differential' dial (Pl. 47), though from the point of view of reading the time it is perhaps the most practical. Also quite practical is the so-called 'wandering hour' watch (Pl. 42), which like the 'sun and moon dial' (Pl. 41) is also found on Dutch and German watches, though the latter is far more common and continued to be made in Holland well after 1700. The fourth variety is the 'six-hour' dial, and this again is rare (Pls. 29 and 32).

Changes in movement decoration also occurred after 1675, in particular to the balance cock. The table increased in size and covered the whole of the balance, which itself was larger than the pre-balance spring one. The table was given a rim, the foot at first remaining comparatively small with an irregular outline (Pl. 33). After about 1685, the pattern of the table decoration on English cocks frequently sprang from a mask (Pl. 52), shell, cherub head (Pl. 46) and, later, a design changing from floral to arabesque. A wing or streamer on either side of the junction of table and foot becomes a feature about 1700 (Pls. 35 and 46), when the foot splays-out more, follows the curve of the plate and is given a rim.

After the introduction of the balance spring, French and Swiss watches nearly always have a bridge instead of a balance cock, though the Dutch and German watchmakers occasionally followed English practice in this and other particulars. French and Swiss watches were sometimes given, around 1710, an enamelled cock or bridge (Pl. 50), a glazed hole in the back of the case making this visible. A number of silver balance bridges are found at this time.

The tulip-form pillar was the most popular type before 1675 and it continued after that date, although it increasingly gave place to the Egyptian form as the century closed, when, in addition, floral and other decorative forms (Pl. 43) appear together with the round baluster. The French continued to favour the tapering Egyptian, and where the balance bridge is silver, so, generally, are the pillars. Dutch pillars sometimes have a silver or blued-steel decorative plate superimposed on each pillar.

The so-called pendulum watch appears both before and after 1700, particularly in Holland where it enjoyed popularity well into that century (Pls. 44 and 46). A slot is cut in the balance cock table and this reveals a portion of one of the balance arms which has a disc of metal fixed to it. The oscillating balance then appears as a swinging pendulum. The pendulum cock as it was developed in Holland served to give protection to the balance, a glass being fitted over the slot, and a rim to the edge of the cock or bridge gave lateral protection: it served, in fact, as a dust-cap for the balance. The same idea, but transposed to the dial, is the 'false' or 'mock' pendulum watch, an aperture in the dial revealing the disc and giving the impression of a swinging pendulum (Pl. 43). It has been said that these watches enjoyed a fashion because of the reputation the pendulum had earned for clocks.

In spite of the new seriousness with which watches were now regarded, decoration on movements, dials and cases most certainly continued, and the quarter-century which we have just surveyed offers great interest to collectors.

Chapter 4

English Pre-Eminence;
the French and Swiss Challenge 1700—75

The lead which Tompion, Quare and their contemporaries gave the London makers before the turn of the 17th century was to be maintained over the next decades. Men like George Graham, Thomas Mudge, John Harrison and, later, John Arnold made contributions to horology which kept this country in the van of the struggle for precision timekeeping, although France began to challenge our position before the end of the period.

Apart from the improved timekeeping which the balance spring made possible, other improvements occurred around 1700. Clock-watches had been made from the earliest times. In 1676 the Rev. Edward Barlow invented the rack form of striking, which had advantages over the earlier locking plate arrangement, not least in that it made repeating work possible; this was applied at first to clocks. Barlow then devised a repeating mechanism for watches, and Tompion made a watch for him incorporating his system in about 1685. Daniel Quare, however, had also been experimenting with repeating work, and the two rivals each presented a watch before King James II for him to adjudicate as to which was the better method. The King gave his preference to Quare's on the grounds that Barlow's method required two push-pieces, one of which repeated the hour and the other the quarter, whereas Quare's only had one push-piece which operated both hours and quarters. This occurred in 1688. Repeating watches quickly took on in England, and the continental makers were soon producing them as well (Pls. 48 and 49).

Quarter-repeating watches gave the time only to the last quarter, but even before 1700 half-quarter repeaters had made their appearance; that is, in addition to repeating hours and quarters a single stroke is also sounded if 7½ minutes or more have elapsed since the previous quarter (Pl. 63).

A closer approximation to the actual time is given by the five-minute repeater; after the hours are struck, each additional stroke represents five minutes. Very few were made in the early part, but rather more in the second half of the 18th century.

The final refinement in repeating work is the minute repeater, a few examples of which are known before 1800. Thomas Mudge incorporated minute-repeating work in a complicated watch he made in about 1750 for Ferdinand VI of Spain.

17th- and 18th-century repeaters struck a bell, this being fitted into the back of the case. The sound is no uncertain one, and can cause embarrassment or awaken a sleeper if the repeater is operated at night. For this reason a 'pulse-piece' was fitted after about 1715 (Pl. 51). This is a small pin projecting from the edge of the case near the 6 o'clock position. If a finger is placed against this pin, the hammers are held clear of the bell when the watch is 'repeated', and the blows are felt by the finger and can, of course, be counted. The pin is also called a 'deaf-piece' because a deaf person can count the hours in this way.

About 1750, Julien Le Roy introduced the 'dumb' repeater, which dispensed with the bell, the hammers striking a metal block and this made a slimmer repeating watch possible. It is possible that Le Roy was anticipated by Graham in 1730, who used the dust cap as a striking block. About 1725, Matthew Stogden introduced improvements in the repeating mechanism, and this was generally adopted by English makers.

As with clock-watches (Pl. 33), the inner case (and generally the outer case as well) was pierced. The holes thus made inevitably allowed dirt to penetrate. Tompion had fitted a 'dust-ring' round the movement to protect it, but it was probably Graham (he joined Tompion in partnership in 1696) who introduced the better arrangement of the 'dust-cap' — a metal cover which fits over the movement (Pl. 51). Dust-caps were subsequently to be fitted to the great majority of English watches, whether repeating or plain. The watch could be wound and regulated without removing the cap.

English watchmaking was to receive further stimulus after 1704. In that year Nicholas Facio de Duillier (a Swiss mathematician) together with two French immigrant watchmakers, Peter and Jacob Debanfre, took out a patent (No 371) for 'An Art of Working Pretious or more Common Stones (whether Naturall or Artifical) Christal or Glass, and certain other Matters different from Metals, so that they may be employed and made use of in Clockwork or Watchwork and many other Engins, not for Ornament only, but as an Internal and usefull part of the work or Engine itselfe, in such Manners as have not heretofore been used, and that the said Art will be very beneficial to the Trade of Makeing Watches and Clocks'.

The invention was a method of cutting and piercing stones to be used as bearings for watch pivots, but Facio and his *confrères* (their name seems subsequently to have been spelled 'Debaufre') were eventually deprived of the full benefit of their patent when they applied to Parliament for a Bill to extend it. The Bill was thrown out as a result of determined opposition from the watchmakers, jewellers, diamond cutters and lapidaries, not to mention the Clockmakers Company. After Facio's ill-starred patent, English watchmakers kept the secret of watch-jewels to themselves, and jewels are found in most good English watches by 1750. At this stage, however, only the upper balance staff pivot was jewelled, this being given a diamond endstone (Pls. 49 and 51), and it is rare to find a watch with jewelled bearings for the train until later in the century.

In 1790 the Geneva Society of Arts offered a reward for a watch which had to incorporate quite usual features, but expressly excluded pierced rubies *parce qu'on les tire à trop grands frais de l'étranger'*. Continental makers used a hard steel plate called a 'coqueret' as an endstone, not having even at that date mastered the art of making watch jewels (Pl. 74). A.L. Breguet appears to have been the first to have made use of jewels on the continent.

The purpose of jewels is to reduce friction and wear. Friction has been a continuing difficulty to watchmakers. In a limited sense, it may be said to be the counterpart of the motive power because a large part of the latter is spent in overcoming the former. Variations in friction arising from bad gearing or worn bearings result in fluctuations in power reaching the escapement. This was even more important when a balance was provided with a spring, unless the spring was perfectly isochronous, an impossible requirement at this stage. This is an example, therefore, of how an improvement in one aspect (the balance spring as controller) called for improvements in other directions: the use of jewels was one of such improvements.

Lubrication of the moving parts also reduces friction. To lubricate wheel teeth and pinions would soon create more friction than it was intended to remove, as the oil would spread, collect dirt quickly and become sticky and dry through oxydisation. But it is otherwise with pivots, for it is possible to give the bearing a reservoir to hold the oil. 'Oil sinks', as they are called, were introduced by Henry Sully, an English watchmaker who spent some years in France, and in about 1715 he collaborated with the great French horologist Julien Le Roy in this matter. Sully, in fact, did much to resuscitate the ailing French watch industry. He brought sixty craftsmen from England and started a factory at Versailles. Though this undertaking was to fail, it had a lasting effect in that it appears to have rekindled French interest in watchmaking; and under Le Roy's leadership France was soon to begin to challenge England's pre-eminence. In about 1735 he introduced the adjustable potence (Pl. 65), which was a distinct improvement on the mounting of the crown escape wheel of the verge. The outer pivot hole of this wheel has an adjustable endpiece which, with the aid of a key or screwdriver, can be loosened and the action of the escapement then adjusted without dismantling the watch (see Glossary). Curiously, English makers did not adopt the screw arrangement.

As has been said, the overcoming of one difficulty often only serves to open up the vista to the next. The balance spring, though the biggest single step forward ever made in watchmaking, served also to show up the imperfections inherent in the verge escapement. An accuracy of about a minute a day was the best that could be achieved, and the rate was liable to fluctuate according to conditions.

The fact that thought was being given to a new form of escapement is shown by patent no. 344 of 1695. This was taken out by Tompion, Edward Booth and William Houghton. We have already heard of Booth under the name of Barlow, a name adopted from his godfather Dom. Ambrose Barlow, a Benedictine monk, and it will be remembered that he was associated with Tompion in the repeating watch episode. The patent describes a horizontal escapement which appears to closely resemble the cylinder while experiments reported in the 1680's might suggest the virgule.

Credit must go to Graham however for producing, in about 1726, the first practical horizontal escapement — the cylinder (see Glossary). He had already done great service to clockmaking by his invention of his dead beat escapement, and the main advantage of the cylinder over the verge lies in its absence of recoil, and owing to its property of frictional rest, any variation in impulse tends to be cancelled out. This is particularly important if the balance spring is not isochronous. For once friction was an ally of the watchmaker, though there was a reverse side to the coin; friction caused rapid wear to the cylinder itself.

It was rational enough to make the escape wheel of brass and the cylinder of hardened steel because the latter receives an impulse, or tiny blow, from each tooth of the escape wheel. But it was found that the cylinder was the first to wear even so, as the softer brass picks up grains of gritty matter and the teeth grind away the two lips of the cylinder where impulse is given. An improvement, therefore, was to have the escape wheel also of hardened steel. An even better arrangement — and an example of exquisite craftsmanship — was to make the acting surfaces of the cylinder of ruby. This was probably introduced by John Arnold in 1764. The second John Ellicott used the ruby cylinder to some extent, but it was brought to perfection by Breguet, the latter safely dispensing with the fusee and using the going barrel (see Glossary).

From 1726 onwards Graham depended entirely on the cylinder escapement. In 1728 Julien Le Roy asked to be allowed to examine it, and his request was immediately granted. Le Roy was generous in his praise of it, and adopted it himself. Since the two leading horologists of their day put such faith in the cylinder, why, we may ask, did it not supplant the verge? Firstly, it is extremely difficult to make. Jean André Lepaute wrote in 1755 that it takes a skilled man three days to make a cylinder escape wheel. Secondly — as has already been pointed out — there is the question of wear. Thirdly, it is more fragile than the verge; and finally the improvement in timekeeping over a well-made verge hardly offset the disadvantages. For as the verge has its inherent faults, so too has the cylinder: in fact, they share in one respect the same drawback as both are frictional rest escapements; the balance is at no point 'detached' or free from interference. At no point in the cycle of operations does the escapement allow the balance spring to serve its purpose as unfettered controller. Clearly, the cylinder escapement was not the answer to precision timekeeping, and the search went on.

Pierre Le Roy (son of the famous Julien) was perhaps the first man to investigate the properties of the balance spring. In 1759 Le Roy declared that the free vibrations of the spring were not exactly isochronous. This was confirmed by John Harrison. In 1766 Le Roy put forward his further discoveries by saying that 'there is in every spring, if of sufficient length, a certain length which causes all the vibrations, whether long or short, to be performed in equal time. Having found this length, if you shorten the spring the long vibrations will be quicker than the short ones; on the other hand, if you lengthen the spring the short vibrations will occupy less time than the long'. Le Roy's discovery cleared some of the mystery surrounding the balance spring, but further investigations had to be made before something approaching full knowledge was possessed by watchmakers. Even as late as 1842, Adam Thomson wrote: 'The application of the balance spring was the greatest improvement ever made in a watch . . . and now that its principle, although it may not be better understood, can be more easily applied, it offers means of obtaining time nearly equal to a pendulum'.

Only relatively minor changes occurred in movement decoration during the period we are discussing. The cylinder escapement called for a smaller balance, and this in turn meant a reduction in the size of the table of the balance cock (Pl. 63). Graham gave a solid foot to his balance cocks, and favoured plain cylindrical pillars or the baluster type, the latter style generally the most usual form in the middle of the century (Pl. 67).

Verge watches, which still far outnumbered cylinders, became noticeably of smaller dimensions, probably under the influence of the cylinders being produced by Graham, Thomas Grignion, Mudge and Dutton, and Ellicott. These mid 17th-century verges also had a smaller balance with a smaller table to the cock. As time progressed, cock decoration became less elaborate. The streamers on either side of the junction of the foot and table were omitted, the table decoration springing from a mask or head rather than from the earlier cherub or shell. The foot became narrower, and as the century progressed, was increasingly left solid, with flat engraving. French and Swiss balance bridges decreased in size for the same reasons and tended to become more oval in shape.

By 1750, enamel dials had become general, the five-minute numerals tending to become smaller as the century advanced (Pl. 69). The Dutch arcaded minute band continued to be popular in Holland or for watches intended for export to that country. 'Beetle and poker' hands, became almost standard, on English watches up to about 1800 although particularly with the decorative continental watches, elaborately pierced hands were usual (Pl. 69). Stirrup bows to pendants were most popular up to about 1750; after that date, the bow is generally of oval shape (Pl. 74).

The most common form of case decoration was a *repoussé* outer case up to about 1775, (Pls. 51, 52, 56 and 59). In the earlier part of the century, the scene — most commonly of a mythological subject — has a symmetrical frame, but after 1740 the frame is partly or completely assymetric.

Enamel painting continued (Pls. 62 and 65), but the painting itself became smaller (Pls. 71 and 74) and was often surrounded by chasing, pastes or gems, particularly after the mid-century. On some de luxe watches (not necessarily of the best quality as far as the movement is concerned) stones such as agate or cornelian were set as plaques in the case, surrounded by *repoussé* or engraved decoration.

Towards 1770, a demand arose for a flatter, more elegant watch than had been the rule.

France, and later Switzerland, were to provide for this fashion which was considerably helped by the use of the cylinder escapement, where the escape wheel is horizontal as opposed to the vertical crown wheel of the verge. J.A. Lepine further aided this fashion by the use of bridges or bars instead of the full plate movement with the balance cock or bridge on the top plate. By also dispensing with the fusee and substituting a hanging or standing going barrel, the overall depth of the movement was considerably reduced. He often used his so-called 'Lepine calibre' in conjunction with the virgule escapement, which had been invented by his fellow countryman J.A. Lepaute in 1753 (Pl. 70). The virgule (see Glossary) had no advantage over the cylinder, and was never employed in England. Indeed, English watchmakers refused to sacrifice performance to fashion, and obstinately continued to use the fusee, making the parts of a size and proportion that necessitated a relatively thick watch.

Chapter 5

The Struggle towards Precision 1775-1835

To a maritime nation, the need for a timekeeping instrument to enable seamen to discover the longitude became ever more pressing as overseas trade expanded and uncharted seas continued to beckon the explorer. In 1714, the British Parliament passed the first of a series of Acts offering reward to anyone whose method or invention should fulfil certain conditions, to be tested under the control of a Board of Longitude, the Royal Commission set up for the purpose. Among those who recommended the Act of 1714 was Sir Isaac Newton. The conditions and scale of rewards were that £10,000 would be won for an instrument or method accurate on a voyage from England to the West Indies to within one degree of longitude, £15,000 for two-thirds of a degree, and £20,000 for half a degree. This meant — expressed in terms of timekeeping — that the timekeeper should not lose or gain more than two minutes on a voyage of perhaps two months: one degree of longitude being the equivalent of four minutes of time.

It was under the stimulus of the very large awards proposed by the 1714 Act, and the subsequent Acts of 1741, 1753 and 1774, that the great improvements of the second half of the 18th century were generated. French watchmakers were given similar encouragement by the prize offered in 1720 by the Paris Academy of Science. Spain and Holland had already offered awards. Neither the ordinary verge or the cylinder escapement appeared likely to give results such as the Board of Longitude required. Pierre Le Roy had realised in 1748 that the balance should ideally be 'detached' as far as possible from interference from the escapement and the rest of the train. Furthermore, it was fully appreciated that some form of temperature compensation would be essential; a voyage to the West Indies meant that the ship would pass through regions of changing temperature. Watchmakers consequently had a two-fold task; to devise an escapement that detached, as far as possible, the balance from mechanical interference by the escapement, and to provide compensation for the changes brought about in the balance and balance spring by the effects of heat and cold.

The story of 'finding the longitude' makes fascinating reading, but it cannot be recounted here. It must suffice to say that John Harrison, after prodigious labours, eventually won the prize in 1761 with his fourth timekeeper, although he did not receive the full amount until 1773. H4 — as this famous watch is known — did not embody a new escapement that was subsequently to be generally adopted, but it did point the way, which others were to follow, towards seeing how temperature compensation (see Glossary) might be satisfactorily achieved. The escapement, in point of fact, was a modified verge with a number of refinements. The compensation was by means of a laminated bimetallic strip (Pl. 120). Harrison's own watch, made for him by John Jefferys in 1752, can be said to have been a prototype for his own prize-winning watch, and most probably was the first watch to embody a compensation curb.

Harrison had hit upon the idea of using the different coefficients of expansion of brass and steel in his gridiron pendulum to nullify the effect of temperature changes. He made use of the same idea in his compensation curb for a balance spring. He fixed the curb pins on a block at the end of a bimetallic strip of brass and steel. As brass expands and contracts more than steel for a given change in temperature (thus causing the bending of the strip), it is on the side of the strip nearest the stud. The strip is set in the watch so that for a rise in temperature the strip, in bending, carries the curb pins away from the fixed end of the spring, thereby shortening its effective length; the reverse happens for a fall in temperature.

Harrison's success inspired other makers to submit timekeepers to the Board of Longitude for trial at sea, among whom Mudge and Arnold and, later, Thomas Earnshaw were the most prominent. Mudge, although he had invented a new form of detached escapement in 1755 — of which we shall hear more — concentrated from 1771 on a remontoire escapement that proved in the end to be a blind alley as far as watchmaking is concerned.

Arnold, however, devised a form of detached escapement, the pivoted detent (see Glossary), about 1770, and in 1775 he took out a patent, No. 1113, for a helical spring and a form of bimetallic compensation applied to the balance as distinct from a curb applied to the spring (Pl.78). In 1782 his patent No. 1328 refers to the epicycloidal form of tooth that he gave to his escape wheel, and the 'incurvated' ends that he gave to the helical spring to render it isochronous. Again, the compensation for heat and cold was on the balance itself. His patent also covered his form of spring detent escapement. In the matter of the spring detent, Arnold may have been anticipated by Earnshaw, and this was certainly Earnshaw's claim.

Compensation by means of the balance does not affect the isochronal properties of the spring, and thereby obviates the chief disadvantage of the compensation curb. Pierre Le Roy anticipated Arnold in appreciation of this fact, and he had also devised a form of detent escapement some years earlier than Arnold's patent. Similarly, Ferdinand Berthoud, after a long series of experimental escapements, arrived at a privoted detent (detached) escapement. However, it would appear that work on both sides of the Channel developed independently.

Earnshaw's cut bimetallic balance and his method of making the balance, as well as the form he gave to the teeth of the escape wheel, finally perfected the marine chronometer and enabled an instrument to be made at a reasonable cost (Pl.96). It was universally adopted and has remained basically the same to this day.

These matters only concern us in so far as they bear on the development of the wearable watch; in a number of particulars they most certainly do. For instance, Harrison's maintaining power was used on fusee watches from the latter end of the 18th century until the fusee was dropped a century later. Breguet adapted the idea of a bimetallic strip on his ruby cylinder watches, giving the strip an elongated U shape. One curb pin is fixed at the free end, which is caused to move nearer to, or away from, the other pin for a rise or fall in temperature. A cut balance was used on all good quality lever watches until, in recent years, the self- compensating balance and spring of special alloys superseded it. But apart from the improvements that all watchmaking derived from the work of these pioneers in precision timekeeping, the chronometer which had been evolved had a distinguished career as a highly accurate pocket watch as distinct from a deck watch or a marine timekeeper (Pls. 81, 96, 143, 154 and 160).

We must now take a look at what was going forward in the less rarefied air of watchmaking that did not specifically have Government prizes in view, but which nevertheless was concerned with improving the watch; and particularly with finding an improved form of escapement.

In 1704, Peter Debaufre — the same man who was associated with Facio in his patent for piercing jewels — invented the escapement known by his name (see Glossary). There are a number of variants of it, but it was not used to any extent until the early 19th century when a number were made at Ormskirk in Lancashire. Such watches are usually known as 'Ormskirk watches'. The escapement is also referred to as the 'club-foot' verge. Its frictional rest, dead-beat characteristics were considered to be an improvement on the normal verge (Pl. 120). Examples to be found today are relatively scarce.

Another escapement, the origins of which lay in a period earlier than the time of its popularity, was the duplex (see Glossary). J.B. Dutertre (1715-42) invented it in its first form, but Pierre Le Roy in 1750 brought it closer to the form in which it appeared in England in 1782. In that year, Thomas Tyrer took out patent No. 1311 for a 'horizontal 'scapement for a watch to act with two wheels, being a new and very great improvement in horizontal watches' (cylinder watches). By 1800, a single escape wheel with two sets of teeth had become the norm (Pl. 99) and it was this that was now fitted to most high quality English watches, the detent and lever escapements being still at an experimental stage. It continued to be made for some time after 1845, though by then, as we shall see in the next chapter, the lever escapement at last was rapidly becoming established as the best escapement for watches. Like the cylinder and the club-foot verge or Debaufre-type escapement, the duplex is frictional rest.

The duplex escapement is not often found in continental watches. However, a variation of it was invented by Charles Edouard Jacot at Fleurier about 1830, and this made possible the mounting of a large sweep-seconds hand — that is, a centre seconds hand that moves forward at apparent second intervals. This type was exported to the Far East in large numbers, many most decoratively cased, and has become known as the 'Chinese duplex' (Pls. 136 and 137).

The Le Roys, father and son, had resuscitated the French watch industry during the middle years of the 18th century. Pierre Gregson, Romilly and Vauchez had been famous Paris makers. Lepine and Ferdinand Berthoud had made their important contributions. Finally, and most important of them all, was A.L. Breguet.

The lead that the French had wrested from their British rivals before the end of the century was not based so much on technical achievements as on grounds of fashion; with the exception, that is, of Breguet, who combined mechanical ingenuity, inventiveness and splendid execution with an elegance which has never been surpassed and seldom equalled. His work will be more fully discussed later. By 1775, a growing demand had arisen for a smaller and, more particularly, a thinner watch. By reducing the size of the crown wheel and using a shorter fusee, or alternatively by dispensing with the fusee in the cylinder or virgule escapement and the Lepine calibre layout, French and Swiss makers catered for this demand. Towards 1800 and during the early part of the 19th century, some remarkably flat watches were made (Pls. 70, 89, 112 and 140). The ultimate was reached when movements were fitted into hollowed-out coins of 100 franc size.

There is little doubt that by persisting with the fusee in their cylinder watches and refusing, on technical grounds, to make excessively flat verges, the English makers began to lose their export markets. One also suspects that the Georgian squire would have nothing to do with these continental fripperies which the elegance of the French Empire produced in the watches of the period. The omission of the bell in repeating watches, and the substitution of the wire gong by Breguet in about 1789, meant that a thinner repeater also could be made (Pl. 113).

The most popular form of decoration for these flat watches was translucent enamel laid over engine-turning (*guilloché* enamel), the front bezel and back very often surrounded with split pearls. Four-coloured gold decoration (Pl. 72) was also popular in all countries. This is combined with decoration in relief. Enamel painting often took the form of an oval plaque surrounded by engraving or opaque enamels. Pinchbeck provided an inexpensive case that was particularly popular in England. Translucent horn, painted on the underside, also gave a cheap but attractive result (Pl. 66). After 1800, black enamel inlaid on gold was a popular form of decoration on Swiss and French watches (Pl. 112). English watches relied mainly on engine-turning for decoration. Fine line engraving (*taille-douce*) became popular after about 1830 (Pl. 142).

White enamel dials were now standard, engine-turned metal dials being the alternative. On some inexpensive watches, the dials were painted with a rural, naval or military scene to appeal to countrymen, sailors or soldiers. Others had topical subjects, such as a train crossing a railway viaduct.

The beetle and poker hands only gradually went out of favour in England, and they are found up to the end of the century, after which spade hands became the most popular. A variety of hands were used on French and Swiss watches; pierced gilt, serpentine, or hands with a star or diamond-shape rectangle towards the tip, until the fine moon hands favoured by Breguet became the typical French and Swiss hands of the early 19th century (Pls. 83 and 98).

The oval bow pivoted to a flat knob on a rather long, round section pendant (Pl. 83) was usual up to about 1800 when the pendant was sometimes given a rectangular shape. Also, about that time, a spherical knob on a short pendant was introduced with a circular bow pivoted to it (Pls. 101 and 122). In the early 19th century the typical English case had a slightly convex rectangular pendant with a pivoted oval bow (Pls. 100 and 104), but the last form given to pendant and bow in all countries was the spherical knob with pivoted ring-bow. The pivoted ring continued after the introduction of keyless work.

As has been said, France and Switzerland catered for the demand for thinner watches, but they also introduced as a revived fashion the form watches of the early 17th century (Pls. 115 and 128). The difference between the forms of the earlier period and those of the later illustrate the different outlook of the two ages: the crosses, *memento mori* and the naturalistic subjects of the first contrast with the urbane and elegant materialism of the second. Watches set in finger rings were another type of form watch of the 19th century.

As France had successfully challenged England, so now Switzerland was beginning to capture the market from France, especially for 'fashion' watches. They relied more and more on the cylinder escapement, until the term a 'Geneva watch', as used in the mid 19th century, meant almost by definition a flat cylinder watch and often poor quality at that. But Switzerland was beginning to make a contribution in other directions; all we shall mention at this stage is the musical watch (Pls. 111 and 127) and the repeater watch with *jacquemarts* (Pl. 121: see Glossary). Musical watches are sometimes combined with painted enamelled dials representing a scene, against which are figures whose moving arms (for instance) give the illusion of playing musical instruments, while the watch music is being played on the comb and pinned barrel principle. This was invented in Switzerland at the end of the 18th century, and gave birth to musical snuff boxes and subsequently the musical box of the Victorian era. Switzerland's more serious contributions to the improvement of the watch will be recounted in a later chapter.

Chapter 6

The Lever Escapement

Before considering the lever escapement, it would be helpful to give some attention to what had already occurred in clock as distinct from watch escapements. After the introduction of the pendulum, an important step forward was the invention, about 1670, in England, of the anchor escapement. One of the essential differences between the anchor and the verge is that the ratchet teeth of the escape wheel of the former are cut on the periphery of the wheel and not at right angles as with the verge crown wheel. The shape of the pallets gives the anchor escapement its name. This escapement was very quickly adopted for long-case or grandfather clocks. Graham's dead-beat escapement of 1715 was a modification and improvement of the anchor escapement, the latter having recoil.

If we were to consider the escape wheel and pallets only, Graham's dead-beat clock escapement might be regarded as the immediate origin of the lever escapement for watches. The teeth of the escape wheel are pointed. The locking faces of the pallets are arcs of circles concentric with their axis. There is, therefore, no recoil during the supplementary arc. The point must be made that the clock dead-beat is for use with a pendulum and, unless modified, is unsuitable for use with a balance controlled escapement, the swing of a balance being much greater than that of a pendulum. In 1722, the Abbé de Hautefeuille published a description of an escapement which was the first attempt to use the clock dead-beat escapement in a watch, the modification being the introduction of an arm or lever, with pallets at one end, and at the other a curved rack engaging with a pinion on the balance staff. A small movement of the lever is consistent with a large amplitude of balance swing. The rack and pinion feature is reminiscent of Huygens' first balance spring watch with pirouette. Hautefeuille's invention seems to have been neglected — although Berthoud used a modification of it in his marine timekeepers — until Peter Litherland took out patent No. 1830 in 1791. After Litherland's patent a large number of rack levers (as they are called: see Glossary) were made in England, particularly in Liverpool (Pl. 97).

The rack lever escapement, like that of the verge, the cylinder, the Debaufre and its variants, as well as the duplex, all suffered interference in varying degrees from the train; hence the superiority of the chronometer or detent escapement which detached the balance except at the instant of unlocking and imparting impulse. In the chronometer escapement, the balance is 'free', or very nearly so. Ideally, impulse and unlocking take place at or near the dead point of the balance spring when these disturbing influences have least effect.

Watchmakers had appreciated the desirability of a free or detached escapement before 1740, and though one or two attempts had been made to solve the problem — apart, as we have seen, from the detent escapement — it was the detached lever escapement (see Glossary), in essence as conceived by Mudge, that finally provided the solution.

Mudge had been the pupil of Graham and eventually succeeded him. The majority of Mudge's watches employ the cylinder escapement, but in 1754 he conceived his lever escapement, and produced a drawing and later a model of it. Subsequent to this he made two or more small clocks with lever escapements, but the really historic watch, which has long been recognised as the first detached lever watch, belongs to H.M. the Queen and is kept at Windsor Castle. It was made by Mudge in 1769-70 for George III, who gave it to Queen Charlotte.

Mudge, from his own experience, had appreciated the difficulties involved. In a letter to his patron Count von Bruhl he said: '. . . it has this disadvantage, that it requires a delicacy in the execution, that you will find very few artists equal to, and fewer still that will give themselves the trouble to arrive at; which takes much from its merit.' Nevertheless, he realised the significance of his escapement, stating in the same letter: 'I think, if well executed, it has great merit, and will, in a pocket particularly, answer the purpose of timekeeping better than any other at present known.' Mudge retired from business in 1771 to concentrate on his 'hobby horse', as he refers to his marine timekeeper, declining to continue with his lever escapement for use in pocket watches. However, von Bruhl, who obviously appreciated what Mudge had achieved, persuaded Josiah Emery about 1779 to make a watch with a lever escapement, giving him access to the model made by Mudge. Emery's first lever was completed in 1782, though it differed in some particulars from the Mudge model. In collaboration with Richard Pendleton, he subsequently made some thirty lever watches, of which eleven or twelve have survived; of these, some were later converted by Emery to his own and later form of lever escapement (Pl. 79).

In both forms he favoured the 'straight line' arrangement, where the balance staff, pallet and escape wheel arbors are in line, as opposed to Mudge's right-angled layout. In the earlier form he used Mudge's arrangement of two impulse cams located on the staff on different levels, and these engaged with pallets on the lever fork which were at correspondingly different planes. In his later arrangement he used a single cranked roller on the staff which received impulse from the fork, this being in the same plane as the lever.

From about 1785 to about 1805, a number of watchmakers working in London produced experimental lever escapements. Among these were Leroux, Grant (Pl. 80), Pendleton (Pl. 90), Margetts, Perigal, Taylor and Ellicott. Pendleton, it is thought, worked for Emery. Leroux had less in common with the others than they had with each other. The differences as shown by the surviving watches of these makers strongly suggest that they were feeling their way to the ideal arrangement.

After about 1805 there is a curious ten-year gap; that is to say, it appears almost as if Mudge's statement about its 'disadvantage' as well as its merit had proved only too true, for as far as one can now judge it was not until 1814 that the lever was again on the scene, and then it would appear to owe more to the rack lever than to the work of Emery and his fellow experimentors.

It was in 1814 that the Staffordshire maker, Edward Massey, invented a form of detached escapement from which the English lever was eventually to emerge and to crystallise as that described in the Glossary. Massey's form (Pl. 107) appears in some respects as the rack lever with two highly important modifications: the pinion on the staff has been replaced by a small roller having, as a projection therefrom, an impulse pin like a single leaf of a pinion. The impulse pin acts within a square notch cut in the extremity of the lever, thus forming a fork. The fork and its notch, therefore, have taken the place of the rack. The outer slightly concave edges of the two pointed prongs of the fork serve as safety or guard pins; if necessary, they may make contact with the rim of the roller to prevent unlocking while the balance is 'detached'. When the points of the prongs enter one or other of two slots cut in the roller on either side of the impulse pin, the impulse pin enters the notch. When this occurs, the lever is moved to unlock the escape wheel and impulse is delivered. The motion of the lever is restricted by banking pins on either side of it. The balance is detached except at the moment of unlocking-impulse.

Massey's detached lever consequently was an enormous improvement on the rack lever. The safety arrangement, nevertheless, was imperfect, as should the prongs of the fork come into action to prevent unlocking resulting from the watch being subjected to a sudden jerk, friction is caused by the prongs' contact with the roller.

There are three basic variants to the Massey arrangement; the first where the impulse pin projecting from the circumference of the roller is virtually a steel pinion leaf; a second in which a jewel is held by two projections from the roller; and a third where a jewel is held by a single projection from the roller, from above. This projection from the roller, although in fact not a true crank, has caused this form of escapement to become known as the crank lever (see Glossary) or crank roller escapement. The first form, or true Massey, is rare, but the second, and more especially the last form, is quite commonly found. It was particularly popular with Lancashire makers, Robert Roskell among others producing them in Liverpool, and inscribing the plate or cock foot 'detached lever' to distinguish them from the rack lever which was still being made at that time.

It was in these latter stages of development, around 1820 or just before, that the important addition of the safety factor of draw was given to the escapement (Pls. 117, 122, 123 and 135). The lever watch made by Leroux in 1785 (the earliest watch known to have draw) can hardly be regarded as the prototype for those crank levers which possess it.

The next development, taking place around 1825, was the introduction of the table roller (Pls. 122 and 123). Here the roller may be described as a flat disc, mounted on the staff, and within its circumference and projecting downwards, is the jewel impulse pin, or ruby pin, its alternative name. The safety action is effected by a small guard pin or dart located in the lever notch: this, in the action of escapement, passes the roller through a small segment — a 'passing crescent' — cut out of the circumference of the table roller immediately in front of the impulse pin. Draw by now was recognised as indispensable.

In the second half of the 19th century, English watches of the best quality had a double roller; that is to say, a second roller, about half the diameter of that in which the impulse pin is fixed, acting as a safety roller. The action is the same as that in the single or table roller arrangement.

It is typical of the English lever — once it had become established — that the teeth of the escape wheel are pointed and inclined with the impulse plane or 'lift' on the pallets. It is also typical that the escapement is right-angled: a line drawn through the pallet and balance staffs is at right angles to the arbor of the escape wheel.

Experiment by no means ceased, however, with the advent of the crank roller. Before 1818 — within two or three years of Massey's invention — George Savage (see Glossary) invented his two-pin lever which, theoretically, was a considerable improvement since the unlocking takes place at the line of centres of the lever and the roller. Two pins on the roller serve to effect unlocking, and impulse is given by a third pin within the lever fork acting on a small slot cut in the roller itself. This same third pin serves also as the guard pin. It was thus, in a way, a reversal of the previous arrangements in that instead of the impulse pin being on the roller, and the notch in the lever, the impulse pin is in the lever and there is a very small slot in the roller. The escapement might more accurately be called a 'three-pin' lever. It required considerable skill to make, and the pins, usually made of gold, cut the steel parts on which they operated. Nevertheless, it was produced in small numbers well on into the century and by some of the best London makers.

By 1850-60 the lever watch had practically ousted the duplex and the chronometer pocket watch. The cylinder had long passed its heyday in this country, though the Swiss continued to make a cheap and commercial cylinder watch until recent times. The verge, as a tough, inexpensive timepiece, was made in England until the 1880's. During the last quarter of the 19th century and the first decade of the 20th, there was a final flowering of English watch craftsmanship, to which we shall refer again.

La Croix & Fils, Geneva, circa 1830

Gold case with a miniature of the Duchess of Sutherland and her daughter after a painting by Sir Thomas Laurence in enamel. The movement is typically Genevan with a cylinder escapement. (36mm. diam.)

Paul Bisot, St. Germain, Paris, circa 1650

Rectangular watches, particularly in gold are rare and painted in enamel of the Blois school rarer still. (41mm. diam.) See also plate 20.

Robert Grinkin, circa 1630

Both back and front covers of this watch are of cut rock crystal. The dial is of silver, while the bezels and band are of gilt metal. Grinkin was Master of the Clockmaker's Company in 1648. (28mm. wide.) See also plate 13.

Watch Case first half of the 17th century

This case is of fine quality and condition, although the movement is early 18th century. (60mm. diam.) See also plate 19.

Breguet, Paris, sold 1827

Breguet, one of the most illustrious names in horology, recognised that for everyday use there was no necessity for a watch to have two hands. (44mm. diam.) See also plate 124.

Bautte et Moynier, Geneva, circa 1820

This slim gold case is inlaid with black enamel. (44mm. diam.) See also plate 112 for the dial.

The probabilities are that the lever escapement had a separate career on the continent, and that the development in England, of which an outline has been given, was not influenced to any great extent by the French and Swiss watchmakers of the late 18th century. However, this is not to say that there was no communication between them. For instance, Ferdinand Berthoud corresponded with Mudge and visited England in 1766. Breguet made two or three visits to England between 1791 and 1795. John Arnold sent his son, John Roger Arnold, to work with Breguet. The Swiss watchmaker Sylvain Mairet came to London in the 1830s to perfect his knowledge of marine chronometers, became a friend of James Ferguson Cole, stayed five years and made fine lever watches for B.L. Vulliamy and Hunt and Roskell.

It is safe to assume that Graham's escapement and Hautefeuille's rack lever had a similar influence on the continent as they had in England; Berthoud certainly gave some attention to the rack lever, but Litherland's later rack lever seems to have had no influence at all.

A watch movement signed Julien Le Roy recently came to light which would appear to have an experimental form of detached lever. Mr. Cecil Clutton, the owner of the movement, has ascertained that it was made in the early 1770's and dozen or so years after Julien's death by his son Pierre who curiously continued to sell watches bearing his father's name.

Suddenly, in 1786, Breguet is producing sophisticated lever watches with cut compensated balance and an overcoil to the balance spring which he introduced. Like Emery, he adopted the straight line layout. He omitted draw, but from the first gave breadth to the tips of the escape wheel teeth, and subsequently used the club-toothed escape wheel, which gives divided lift. This aspect of his work had practically no influence on the English makers, who, as we have seen, favoured the pointed toothed wheel, with the lift on the pallets. The exceptions appear to be Leroux in 1785, Ellicott and Taylor, whose escapements had the lift on the tooth incline. Mairet (Pl. 140) and J.F. Cole sometimes used the reverse of the set English pattern, and employed pointed pallets as Leroux had done. Nevertheless, a few later English makers such as Glasham exceptionally used a club-toothed escape wheel with divided lift (Pl. 145).

In Paris, contemporary with Breguet, was Robert Robin, a maker with an experimental turn of mind, who produced lever watches before 1793. He was acquainted with Emery's levers, though his work does not appear to have been particularly influenced by them. But things were stirring in Switzerland. In 1786, Pouzait (see Glossary) invented a form of lever escapement which had divided lift; in this he may have anticipated Breguet. His escapement beat seconds and a fair number were made, including variants of it (Pls. 95 and 106). A curious fact about Pouzait leavers is the number of un-signed watches. Doubtless his invention had its effect in Switzerland, at least for a time, perhaps until Breguet's influence on continental watchmaking was paramount.

By the mid-19th century, the lever escapement was as firmly established on the continent as it was in England: the club-toothed lever abroad, and the pointed-toothed, or English lever, here at home. The English makers, particularly in Coventry, continued to use the fusee and full plate movement (Pls. 146 and 156), though after about 1850 the three-quarter plate (Pl. 145), and more rarely the half plate (Pl. 157), became more used. Continental makers preferred the bridged movement with going barrel. Switzerland was now gaining the supremacy and contributing her share of inventions. Above all, she was improving her methods of manufacturing and adopting machinery.

Chapter 7

Nineteenth Century Refinements;
Europe, America, and Mass Production

One of the earliest attempts to overcome the necessity of a key for winding was made in about 1752 by Pierre Caron, afterwards famous as Beaumarchais, the dramatist, whose father was also a watchmaker. He made a watch for Madame de Pompadour which was fitted into a finger ring. It measured nine millimetres in diameter. 'To render this ring more commodious', he wrote, 'I have contrived, instead of a key, a circle round the dial, carrying a little projecting hook. By drawing this hook with the nail two-thirds round the dial the ring is re-wound, and it goes for thirty hours'.

In 1820, Thomas Prest took out patent No. 4501 for 'a new and additional movement applied to a watch to enable it to be wound up by the pendant knob, without any detached key or winder' (Pls. 110 and 145). A wheel is fixed on the square of the going barrel arbor and gears with another wheel whose pinion is turned by a bevel wheel fixed to the shaft which passes through the pendant. The winding button is fixed to the end of the shaft. Prest was John Roger Arnold's foreman, and a number of watches were made by the firm with Prest's keyless arrangement. The system was only applicable to going barrel watches, and since the fusee was still enthroned in England as a necessary part of an accurate timekeeper, Prest's mechanism remained undeveloped. However, subsequently it proved to be a close precursor of keyless winding in its final form.

A successful early form of keyless winding is the type known as 'pump-wind'. The idea may have been suggested by the repeating mechanism first used by J.A. Lepine towards the end of the 18th century. The shaft, which had actuated the striking, was used to wind the mainspring in its barrel. There is more than one form of pump-winding, one of which would be more accurately described as 'pull-winding' since it is the pulling out of the pendant shaft which actually winds the mainspring (Pl. 141). The earliest patent is Robert Leslie's of 1793, No. 1790, which reads: 'A method of winding up a watch by the pendant. On the square where the key should go is a ratch; the pendant, being alternately moved in and out, turns this ratch by means of two clicks on either end of a fork fastened to the pendant.'

Edward Massey's patent No. 3854 of 1814 is the push-winding type (Pl. 107). It reads: 'The pendant being pushed in, pushes in a small pin, which causes, by simple mechanism, a rack to move forward a certain distance, and thus partially wind the watch up, by the aid of a ratchet on the fusee axle or going barrel, as the case may be. On withdrawing the pressure from the pendant, a spring returns the rack to its former place ready for a further winding up, and so on till the watch is wound up, a click preventing any unwinding'. Viner also employed a rack keyless mechanism with pump action.

J.A. Berrollas took out patent No. 5586 in 1827 (Pl. 123). This is somewhat different to either the pull or push varieties: 'The barrel ratchet, with its click and spring, which keeps the maintaining power up, is put on the barrel arbor. A recoiling ratchet is attached to, and a recoiling spring placed in, the barrel pully, and the other end is passed through the pendant, and is fastened to the impendent. The chain is not longer than to produce one revolution of the pully. To wind up the watch, pull the impendent as far out as possible; the recoiling spring will carry it back again. The operation must be repeated until the mainspring is wound up'. With all these types, the hands still required a key to set them.

An early example of a truly keyless watch has a lever action, the lever being pivoted to the mainspring arbor and projecting through the side of the case; and the hands are set by turning a milled disc (Pl. 134). This appears to have been a Swiss idea in origin (about 1835), though it was later revived in a somewhat different form by A. Burdess of Coventry in 1869 (Pl. 156). B. Haas invented a form of front cover winding in his patent No. 3945 of 1873. This was only applicable to a hunter watch; the action of opening the cover wound the mainspring. An example of this type of watch is shown on Plate 155.

The first watch which could be wound and set through the pendant was made by Louis Audemars of Le Brassus in 1838. He was followed by Adolphe Nicole in 1844 who took out the English patent No. 10348: 'Winding up watches through the handle with a knob at one end, and a bevelled pinion at the other, which takes into a wheel, which wheel takes into another fixed on to a plate, fixed by screws but capable of being moved on its axis in such a way that, if the rod be pressed in, it gears with and moves the wheel fixed on the fusee, and if the end be pulled out (it gears with) the wheels which communicate motion to the hands.'

The Swiss watchmakers Adrien Philippe (who invented the shifting sleeve form), Antoine Le Coultre, and Gustavus Huguenin contributed further improvements, the last named patenting the rocking bar arrangement in 1855, No. 2144. It was still necessary, in order to set the hands, to press down with one's finger nail a small push-piece at the side of the watch. This causes the hand-setting mechanism to become engaged. The final imrpovement, Swiss in origin, enabled the hand-setting arrangement to be brought into action by pulling out the winding button and stem into the set-hand position.

Keyless work when applied to the fusee watch, which was still the watch *par excellence* in England, was apt to be troublesome in spite of an improved form introduced by Victor Kullberg about 1869. Another arrangement was invented by W. Chalfont, but the desire for keyless watches on the one hand and the unsatisfactory nature of keyless fusee watches (unless very carefully made) on the other, doubtless speeded the departure of the fusee towards the end of the 19th century.

But it was only with reluctance that the fusee was given up. The *Horological Journal* of January, 1880, reported the first of a series of meetings under the title 'The Wisdom of Substituting the Going Barrel for the Fuzee in the English Watch Manufacture'. J.A. Lund, of Barraud and Lunds, attempted to have the best of both worlds in his patent No. 914 of 1870. This retained the virtue of the fusee movement, but provided a detachable key which was snapped into the pendant of the case, the top of the key resembling exactly the ordinary winding button: the watch therefore had the appearance of being a keyless one!

A.L. Perrelet, of Le Locle, invented the self-winding watch in about 1770. The device consisted basically of a weight pivoted in the centre of the movement. There was no banking arrangement and the weight swung through 360°, the mainspring being wound, in either direction, through the fusee. A stop was provided to prevent overwinding. Subsequently an improved system was evolved. The fusee was dispensed with and a weighted arm was pivoted eccentrically at the unweighted end. The movement of the wearer's body when walking or riding causes the weight to be jerked up and down (Pl. 130). This motion winds up the mainspring by means of a pawl fixed to the arm, which pawl engages with a ratchet wheel connected with the mainspring barrel arbor. The system is proof against overwinding by the weighted arm being locked when the watch is fully wound. Perrelet's was the first serious attempt to do away with the winding key. The hands still had to be set with a key.

Breguet produced a number of self-winding watches after 1777, and he called them *montres perpétuelles*. In 1780, Louis Recordon, Breguet's business associate in England, took out patent No. 1249 in London and the device became known as the 'pedometer wind'. Recordon was associated with Spencer and Perkins in the production of such watches. A number of other makers produced self-winding watches between 1780 and 1830, a common feature being that the pedometer weight oscillates on the circumference of the movement. The weight is kept in its normal position, against the upper of two buffers, by a weak spring. The idea lapsed until the second half of the 19th century. It was revived for a short time by von Loehr's patent No. 1473 of 1878. It was again revived, for wristwatches, by John Harwood in 1923, who took out patent No. 1576120 in 1926 (Pl. 179). His system employed a weight pivoted in the centre of the movement, each end of the weight having buffer or banking springs. The original company with which he was associated had to cease production, but the Swiss perfected the system after the last war. Harwood himself derived little benefit from his invention. It is worth noting that Perrelet's original idea of a weight or rotor swinging through 360° has finally triumphed as the best system for wrist watches.

In about 1790, Breguet invented a form of elastic suspension for the balance shaft pivots which he called a *parachute* (Pl. 124). It became almost standard practice for him to give this shockproof device to his watches, and it is curious that it was not until recent years that it has been revived.

About five years later, Breguet made his first perpetual calendar which was embodied in a watch ordered in 1783 for Queen Marie-Antoinette. The same watch had independent second, equation of time, a thermometer, and minute repeating mechanism. In addition, it was self-winding and had an 'up and down' indicator on the dial which showed the state of mainspring wind. All these appendages in a single watch give an indication of Breguet's horological genius; they are to be found on later watches by other makers.

Throughout the second and third quarters of the 19th century horological inventions continued to come thick and fast. As regards watches, a number were concerned with improvements to keyless work, improvements to the escapement (many of these fanciful), improvements to the chronometer balance and chronograph work. The chronograph is essentially an ordinary time-of-day watch with the additional complication of the stopwatch feature. A number of men contributed to its development, among whom must be mentioned Winnerl of Paris and Nicole, whose patent No. 10348 of 1844 covered 'an additional second hand capable of being stopped and moved on as required, and made to arrive and start from a given point instantaneously'. The additional wheel was carried by a cam wheel: the cam was heart-shaped and was the part which enabled the hand to fly back to the zero position The three-pressure action through the crown (winding button) of start-stop-zero was patented in 1862, No. 1461.

Strictly speaking, a chronograph by definition should have some graphic quality. A true chronograph was patented by F.L. Fatton in 1822 (no. 4645). The watch had two dials, that on the back had an 'arm' on the extremity of which was 'a little thing like a nib of a pen' containing ink. By pressing a button on the outside of the case, the nib was caused 'to descend and by an instantaneous motion to strike the revolving dial and leave a mark or dot thereon'. Fatton had worked for Breguet, who had the faculty of gathering round him men of great ability. Many of these like Fatton, Mugnier, Jurgensen, Oudin, Audemars, Ingold and Winnerl subsequently started their own businesses, often inscribing their early work *élève de Breguet*.

One of the most fascinating pieces of watch machinery is the 'tourbillon' invented by Breguet in 1795 (Pl. 165). Unless the balance of a watch is perfectly poised and positional errors non-existent, it will vary on its rate according to its position: there may be a difference in timekeeping between the horizontal and the vertical, and also between 'pendant left' and 'pendant right'. The idea of the tourbillon is to cancel out any difference there may be in the vertical positions by causing the escapement itself to revolve. The escapement assembly is mounted in a cage which is itself mounted on the arbor of a pinion driven by the third wheel, making one revolution in one minute. The arbor passes freely through a hole in the centre of the fourth wheel, which is fixed. The escape wheel pinion is carried round by the rotating cage, rolling round the fixed fourth wheel, and it drives the escapement in the normal way.

The making of a tourbillon calls for the highest skill, and no contemporary of Breguet's appears to have attempted it. In the later 19th century, however, Nicole Nielsen, whose place of business was in Soho Square, London, produced a number for Frodsham and for Smith, and their performance was quite exceptional. Fine makers on the continent, among them Girard Perregaux, also made a limited number. In 1892, Bonniksen of Coventry patented a similar system which he called a 'karrusel'. Bonniksen was born in Schleswig and came to this country at the age of 24. The karrusel is as effective as the tourbillon, simpler and more robust in construction, and less expensive to produce. (Pl. 174).

The cage or carriage of the karrusel is driven off the pinion of the third wheel which engages with a wheel — the karrusel wheel — which is screwed to the carriage. The third wheel itself gears with the pinion of the fourth wheel which is located in the carriage and drives the escape wheel pinion in the normal way. The pinion of the fourth wheel passes through a hole in the carriage bearing. The carriage rotates once in 52½ minutes.

Bonniksen's own opinion of his invention was fully justified: 'There is absolutely no mechanism in this watch which is likely to get out of order and the watch will stand as heavy usage as any watch ever produced .... It has a life time of 100 years; but to attain such venerable age bear in mind it must be cleaned every two years by a competent watchmaker, or by its maker, the charge being 15/-.'

Karrusels were produced by a number of makers under Bonniksen's patent until the First World War, among them Hector Golay, Nicole Nielsen, Usher and Cole, and Rotherham & Sons. These watches were of the highest quality. They achieved great success at the Kew Observatory Trials. A few were made with centre second and chronograph work, and in 1901 Usher and Cole produced two with fusee keyless work which gained 'especially good' certificates at Kew.

However, though a fine karrusel represents the acme of perfection of 19th-century English work, English levers with fixed escapements can be equally splendid as examples of this Indian summer of our watchmaking art. Cases, dials and hands were of unsurpassed quality (Pls. 154, 157, 164 and 178). If the best Swiss work emanating from the Valée de Joux and Geneva can justly be described as poetry, then Clerkenwell in London was producing majestic prose. But, in truth, the home trade was in a state of serious decline. Let us see why.

Subdivision of labour in all countries was no new thing in the 18th century. Watch factories had been founded in France — albeit with indifferent success — in the 1700s. But in 1776 Frederick Japy started making *ébauches* by special machinery he had devised for the work. His successful venture was taken over by his sons and the firm established as Japy Frères continues to this day. The Japy factory was the beginning of the manufacture of watches by machine tools.

In 1804, Sandoz and Trot imported machinery into Geneva for the making of watch parts. In 1840, G.A. Leschot joined the firm of Vacheron and Constantin and devised machinery which took interchangeability a stage further. He also invented tools for the manufacture of the lever escapement. The example of Vacheron and Constantin was followed by Patek, Philippe et Cie. Switzerland was on the high road to capturing the world market for the ordinary commercial watch by the new manufacturing methods.

In the Great Exhibition of 1851, where Swiss exhibits made a great impression, Rotherham & Sons of Coventry was the only English firm exhibiting watches produced by machinery driven by steam power. Clerkenwell and Coventry — then the watchmaking centres, the *ébauches* being made in Lancashire — had a few years earlier killed by their opposition the attempt of the Swiss P.F. Ingold to make watches by machine tools in England. The British Watch Company, as the venture had been called, was formed in 1843 with John Barwise as chairman of directors. Ingold was, however, well received in the United States where he left his mark; in fact, he asserted that an American company made use of his machinery after his return to Switzerland. In 1868, an American engineer called Forence Jones together with Henri Moser of Schaffhausen, harnessed the waters of the Rhine to drive watchmaking machinery in that city. The company became known as the International Watch Company.

American watchmaking was at first a small and hesitant affair. Unlike clockmakers immigrant watchmakers at first from England, but later from Holland and Switzerland, found demand for their work was very slight and spread over a vast and thinly populated continent. European methods of organised division of labour did not exist and it was necessary either to construct the entire watch or import the *ébauche* and finish it locally. It is not surprising therefore that watches were mostly imported complete ready for resale. The hand made American watch is exceedingly rare and probably owes its existence to artistic endeavour rather than any commercial consideration. Certainly Charles Fasoldt and Albert Potter the two most notable craftsmen in the second half of the 19th century moved into small batch production to make ends meet.

However the lack of established divisions of skilled labour was turned to advantage and the Americans were first to realise the real potential of mechanised mass production. The work of the Pikin Brothers in 1838 was followed by a collaboration of Aaron Dennison, Edward Howard and D. P. Davis which began production in 1853. This was the Warren Manufacturing Company which changed its name and premises a year later to the Boston Watch Company. The partnership soon failed although the factory continued and finally became the Waltham Watch Company. Howard moved on and eventually formed a company under his own name. His determination to mass produce an American high quality watch finally bore fruit.

Apart from Howard, Waltham produced the Riverside Maxiumus which was of excellent quality. Later, Elgin, Illinois and Hamilton were to make good products, but Auburndales, Waterburys and Ingersolls were never intended to be other than very cheap. The fact remains the Swiss watch was not only highly prized but it could be bought quite inexpensively. To compete, much of the American industry became engaged in cost cutting exercises which resulted in poor quality watches and financial failure. The Swiss still retained numerous craft divisions but these were now mechanised. While the American company was obliged to spread its effort over every aspect of watch making, the Swiss consisted of numerous specialists in each. The lack of traditional craft divisions in America had originally encouraged successful mechanised production by a single company but it now became a disadvantage as methods of manufacture became increasingly sophisticated. Nevertheless it is true to say that by inventing and developing the necessary machinery for mass producing parts, the American horological industry is owed an incalculable amount by today's manufacturers, not only of mechanical watches, but of other related trades.

Perhaps Sir John Bennett was, in the 1850s, the first important trade figure to issue warnings about Swiss competition. Among other reforms such as the furtherance of craft education, he advocated the employment of female labour, as in Switzerland. His views were most unpopular among the workmen of Clerkenwell as well as among the majority of his colleagues in the trade, and his warnings were not heeded. In return, Bennett was castigated for selling foreign products in his Cheapside shop.

Much heart-searching and debate was going on in the trade, as a perusal of the *Horological Journal* and of horological authors of the period makes plain. Two quotations must suffice. David Glasgow, a Vice-President of the British Horological Institute, wrote in 1885: 'Since the demand for cheaper watches on a large scale, consequent on the large number of foreign importations, watch factories have been established' at Coventry and Birmingham. 'But hitherto the attention of English watchmakers has been directed to the improvement in the quality of watches rather than to their cheapness of production, and it is greatly to be questioned whether the wholesale adoption of machinery in the manufacture would at all benefit the trade in this country.' Glasgow goes on to say how 'the good name' which English watches 'have ever borne has led to their imitation by foreign producers'. What would become, Glasgow asks, of the esteem in which the English-made watch is held 'if, instead of continuing to maintain our high position, we were to compete with the slop trade of Switzerland and America?' The remedy, he maintained, was to organise our system of manufacture, to alter and improve the plan of our movement, and to further the technical education of our workmen.

The future Lord Grimthorpe took perhaps a more realistic view. He was advocating the greater use of machinery: 'There can be no doubt in the mind of anyone who understands machinery that this is the best, as well as the cheapest way of making machines which require precision and uniformity ... The degree to which machine-making of machinery can be carried cannot be defined *a priori* ... Although labour is dearer in America than here, this machinery enables them to undersell English watches of the same quality, as the Swiss do with cheaper labour and more organisation, though with less use of machinery; and if our English makers do not bestir themselves they will lose the trade in all but the best watches ...'

Today electronics threaten even the most efficient manufacturer of mechanical watches. Much of his machinery is likely to be redundant in just a few years time although how this worldwide problem is faced remains to be seen.

ILLUSTRATED
CHRONOLOGY
OF
WATCHES

Plate 1
C.W., Nuremberg, dated 1548

The inside of the back cover of this watch bears the date 1548 and is the earliest dated watch so far recorded. Also on the back cover are the initials C.W. probably standing for Caspar Werner of Nuremberg, a contemporary of Peter Henlein. Werner is referred to by Doppelmayr (1730) in his Historical Account of the Nuremberg Mathematicians and Artists as 'a lockmaker in great repute for the small watches which he made'. The gilt metal case is in the form of a tambour, the front cover having apertures through which the hours can be seen. The gilt dial is divided into two twelve hour periods with roman numerals on the outer chapter ring and arabic numerals on the inner. The centre is engraved with twelve rays and on the outer edge are touch pins, so that time can be read in the dark from the stout (blued) steel hand. The iron and steel movement has a verge escapement with a dumb-bell foliot beneath a small S-shaped cock. Clearly visible also in the photograph is the stackfreed (see Glossary). This alternative method of evening out the power transmitted to the escapement from the mainspring was preferred by Nuremberg makers over the fusee. Reduction gearing was used as the stackfreed is required to revolve only once per winding. Locksmiths would probably find a flat spring and cam easier to construct and closer to their understanding than a fusee, and these can be more readily modified to take into account the wide varieties in character of the individual mainsprings. (56mm. diam.)

Plate 2
German Drum Clock, signed 'Phil. Imiss', dated 1554

The forerunners of the watch were drum-shaped portable clocks. These are rare and few survive outside museums. The gilt metal case of the one above is quite typical and is approximately 15mm. high. The outer circumference of the 12 hour, Roman-figured chapter ring has touch pins, enabling the owner to feel the time in the dark. A small central dial shows twelve unequal hours read from the appropriate sign of the Zodiac engraved on the main dial. In the centre of the hand there is also a disc showing each phase and aspect of the moon. The movement is of both iron and steel and the iron plates have been cut out or 'skeletonised'. This clock has also a separate alarm mechanism which can be attached, but which is not shown. (75mm. high.) *The Trustees of the British Museum.*

Plate 3
Anonymous, Italian or South German, mid-16th century

A pendant has been added later to the gilt metal case of this table clock to make it easier to carry. The dial which is marked I to XII on the outer ring and 13 to 24 on an inner ring. There is a stout single hand of steel and also touch pins so that the time could be read in the dark. The movement of both iron and steel has skeletonized plates. Note particularly the long slender early fusee. The large foliot and single footed cock are original, but with the introduction of the balance spring in the late 17th century, one was added to improve timekeeping. The Italians seem to be responsible for a fair number of early clocks, including table clocks, but it is quite often difficult to be certain where in Europe the unsigned examples were made. This is because nearly every maker was to a greater or lesser extent itinerant, and although their work might bear at least some of the characteristics of their maker's country of origin, both styles and designs were confused with cross fertilisation. This situation also applies to Italian watches and those which are distinctive enough to be identified as such are rare.

Plate 4
Portable Globe Clock, signed 'Jacques de la Garde', dated 1552

Some of the earliest surviving watches are spherical, but smaller than the clock illustrated, and there is one in the Louvre dated 1551. The fusee and gut line are clearly visible, as is the chasing and engraving on the spring barrel. The clock also has a striking mechanism and the barrel of this too is shown. The dial and hand are typical of the period. (115mm. diam.) *The National Maritime Museum, England.*

Plate 5
German, circa 1560

Some of the earliest watches were in the form of a tambour. The case is of metal casting which has then been gilded. The back and front covers are hinged lids. The band and back of the case are decorated with inhabited scrolling foliage, the pattern on the back running in a circle around a stylised floral medallion. Note that there are two chapter rings, one for twelve hour reading in Roman numerals and the other for twenty-four. The single steel hand is typical and so too are the touch pins. The movement is of both iron and steel. The extent of each swing of the foliot is controlled to some degree by a hog's bristle mounted on an adjustable pivoted arm, the tension of the main spring and therefore the power transmitted to the balance being effected by a stackfreed (see Glossary). This consists of the flexible arm extending across the top of the movement and the cam to the right of the picture. The stackfreed found only on early German work is an alternative to the fusee. This movement is not signed, but has the punch mark MB in relief. (41mm. diam.) *The Trustees of the British Museum.*

Plate 6
German, circa 1575-1600

By the last quarter of the 16th century the first faltering steps in watchmaking had been taken. This large cushion shaped watch has a gilt metal case with hinged covers. The pendant has a loose fitting ring, while there is a typical finial at the base. The dial and hand are not dissimilar from Pl. 5, but are somewhat more refined. The plates of this watch are, however, of brass, as also are the pillars, but the wheels and pinions and other parts are of steel. It has a foliot with hog's bristle regulation and stackfreed. This watch also strikes the hours; it is a 'clock-watch', and the small dial on the movement indicates the hour that was last struck. (77mm. diam.) *The Basingstoke Museum.*

Plate 7
Clock-Watch, German, circa 1575-1600

This has similar characteristics to Pl. 6, including a stackfreed. It has a silver champlevé dial, the half hour markings are in black and the quarter hour markings in translucent blue enamel; the centre with stylised foliage springing from an urn and surmounted by a bird in vari-coloured translucent enamel. This is an early example of enamel work as applied to watches. (60mm. diam.) *The Trustees of the British Museum.*

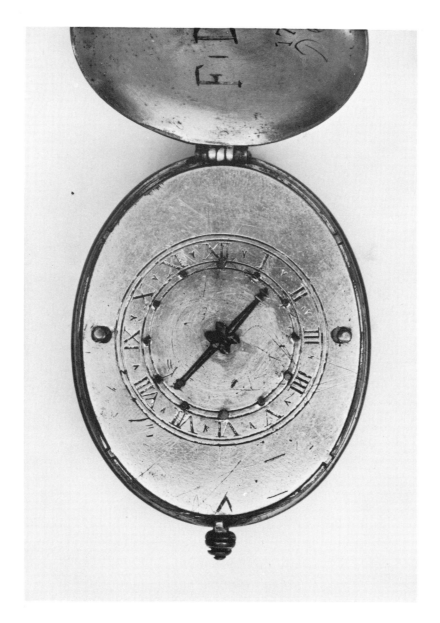

Plate 8
P. Chapelle, circa 1600

This is an unknown maker but from the general style of the balance cock and signature this watch is almost certainly French. It is a very plain watch but not untypical of the period. The case is of gilt metal and the pendant and loose ring bow and finial are of a heavy construction. The Roman figured dial has touch pins and the hour hand is plain with a long tail. The movement is not hinged to the case but it is fixed by two spring bolts which have disengaging knobs to be seen at the 3 and 9 o'clock position on the dial. The balance cock is fixed with a tenon and pin, a method of fixing which would give way to screw fixing in the middle part of the century. Note the 'S' shape to the balance cock table and the broad steel balance on which of course there is no spring. Regulation is achieved simply by a ratchet and click to adjust the initial 'setting up' of power of the mainspring. A further method of changing the going rate of pre-balance spring watches is to alter the depth between the escapement wheel and pallets. The brass movement pillars are 'columnar' or 'round baluster' and are normal for the period. (46mm. wide)

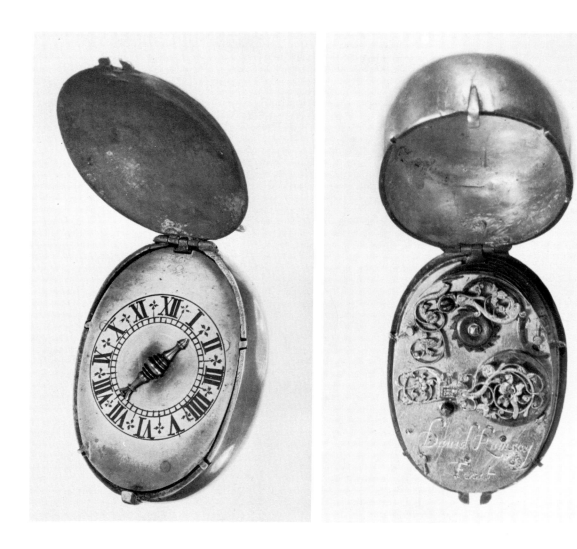

Plate 9
David Ramsay, circa 1625

This maker was Clockmaker to James I and was the first Master of the Clockmakers' Company when it was set up in 1631. The plain silver case and dial are of a very functional design and there is no finial to the base of the case. The verge movement has a three wheel train with fusee and gut. During the last quarter of the century four wheel trains were introduced when it was realised that pinions with higher leaf counts effected a smoother transmission of power. There are round baluster pillars and the potence is engraved. The clock is fixed by a tenon and pin and regulation is by the ratchet and click set up. Note that this watch has a single case; there is no provision for winding through it and the watch has to be swung out for winding. The top plate is signed 'David Ramsey, Fecit'. (28mm. wide.)

Plate 10
H. Roberts, early 17th century

The case is of gilt metal with an applied silver band. The shield of arms with helm crest and mantling inside the dial cover is probably Gurney of West Basham, Norfolk, and this very large watch was no doubt intended to be an important piece. The chapter ring is also of silver and is divided into two twelve hour periods. There are two engraved rings for the minutes and the signs of the Zodiac are represented by symbols; a gilt metal hand indicates the solar indication and the silver hand the lunar ones, thus showing their respective positions in the Zodiac. The age, phase and aspect of the moon are also indicated. The movement characteristics are normal for this date. (108mm. diam.) *The Trustees of the British Museum.*

Plate 11
Robert Grinkin, circa 1625

Typically the gilt metal case has an applied champlevé silver chapter ring and case band. The signed movement with ratchet click set up is wound through the case back, the hole covered by a small shutter. The pillars are of the round baluster variety. There are three wheels in the train, together of course with a verge escapement and a fusee linked to the barrel with a gut line. Fusees were used on watches from the earliest period except when the rare stackfreed was an alternative. Fusee chain was rarely used on watches before 1670 and those on early watches are frequently conversions from gut to chain. Grinkin was a founder member of the Clockmakers' Company and Master in 1648 and before the founding of the Clockmakers' Company in 1631, he was a member of the Blacksmiths' Company. (32mm. wide.)

Plate 12
James Vautrollier, circa 1630

The silver case has floral engraved panels, the centre panel of the dial cover is engraved showing the figure of Father Time, the back plate with Pluto and Proserpine. Note the case hinge is engraved with a cherub which was to become a very common motif on clocks towards the end of the century. The fixed pendant is parallel to the dial so that with a loose ring through the hole the watch could be suspended from a chain around the neck and laid flat on the wearer's chest. The silver chapter ring is applied to the profusely engraved gilt metal dial. The characteristics of the movement are normal for the period during which there are often no real distinguishing features between the work in England and the Continent. The top plate is signed 'Jas. Vautrollier, Fecit'; he was probably a Huguenot refugee and was a founder member of the Clockmakers' Company. His name is sometimes also spelt Vantrollier — alternative spellings are frequently found until the mid-eighteenth century. (24mm. wide.)

Plate 13
Robert Grinkin, circa 1630

Both the lid and case body are oval and are of faceted rock crystal. This type of case is particularly rare and having the original crystal rarer still. Glass substitute is frequently found. The bezels are of gilt metal.

Regulation is by worm and wheel set-up. The cock is pinned while the pillars are of narrow Egyptian form. The watch has a silver dial with floral engraving outside the chapter ring and landscape engraving within. The top plate is signed 'Robert Grinkin, Londini'. (28mm. wide.) For front view see colour plate 2.

Plate 14
C. Tinelly, Aix, circa 1635

One of the more common form watch types, although form watches of any period are rare. The case is of gilt metal with plates of repoussé gold applied to the covers, on the front the Crucifixion with the Virgin Mary and St. John on the other side, on the back the Virgin and Child. The side bands are of silver and engraved with symbols of the Passion. The gilt dial is engraved with an applied silver chapter ring and the movement is signed. (63mm. long.) *The Trustees of the British Museum.*

Plate 15
Robert Grinkin, London, circa 1635-40

This watch shows astronomical as well as astrological indications, the former generally being considered more desirable now by collectors, but astrology was of great significance when the watch was made. Both are more frequently found on clocks rather than watches and this silver cased watch is small being 38mm. in width. The inner ring of the upper dial represents the approximate dates on which the various signs of the Zodiac commence according to the Old Style Calendar, the signs being shown on the ring next to the dates. The circle of figures above the signs are the approximate sunset times for the months shown in the circle above. The outermost circle gives the date. The blued steel indicator is pointing to the fifth. The aperture on the left gives the day of the week and sign of the day. The apertures on the right give the age of the moon, the moon phase and the time of moon-set. The verge movement has a silver cock but is otherwise fairly typical of the period with a tangent screw set up (see Glossary). The watch is signed 'Robert Grinkin, Londini'.

Plate 16
Silver 'Puritan' Watch signed 'John Snow me Fecit', circa 1640

A fairly early example of crystal used as a watch 'glass'. It is held in place by tags on the underside of the bezel; this method of fixing, or similar, was used until the split bezel was introduced around 1660. The name 'Puritan' merely refers to the simplicity of the watch's appearance and is supposedly in character with Puritan austerity. The silver dial is very legible and the double-ended hour hand ensures that it can be moved with the fingers easily and without damage. The outer case affords extra protection from dust and damage, although one can assume that such cases were not always used and certainly not so many of the outer cases survive. Typically for the period the cock is pinned, and the movement has worm and wheel set up with a silver figure plate. John Snow is recorded as having made a lantern clock in 1630 and it seems that from the earliest years, in spite of the considerable variance in technique, some makers were responsible for both clocks and watches. (37mm. diam.)

Plate 17
David Bouquet, circa 1640

The simplicity of this silver watch is characteristic of the age. Note the finial to the inner case which locates in a hole in the outer. The silver dial and blue steel hand are typical. The rock crystal 'glass' is held on the underside of the cover by a rim secured with two screws. The shutter over the winding hole is a further protection against dust and dirt. The movement has no unusual features, having a ratchet set-up and pinned-on cock, the table of which is in the form of an elaborate "S". The maker was a French émigré and the movement is signed 'D. Bouquet, Londres'. He was admitted to the Blacksmiths' Company and was subsequently a founder member of the Clockmakers' Company. (30mm. wide.)

Plate 18
Goullens, Paris, circa 1640

The enamel painting covers the gold case inside and out. It is normal for enamel cased watches in the first 75 years of the 17th century to depict religious scenes. The front cover shows the Holy Family on the outside and Louis XIII on the inside. The back cover has the Virgin and Child on the outside and Cardinal Richelieu on the inside. The edge of the case is painted with scenes of the Flight into Egypt and the Slaughter of the Innocents. The movement has an early screwed-on cock. A figure plate half obscures the maker's name, which together with a balance spring was fitted some time after the invention of the latter, towards the end of the century. A partly obscured signature does not however always imply later modifications. (63mm. diam.) *Victoria and Albert Museum, Crown Copyright.*

Plate 19
Polychrome Enamel, first half 17th century

The dial and inside of front cover shown in colour plate 2. The cover illustrates the Virgin and Christ Child on her knee with John the Baptist and the back with a further enamel of the Holy Family with John the Baptist. The case band has six landscape vignettes and the inside of the upper cover and the inside of the back of the case have further landscape scenes. The movement is later, being especially made for the case in the early 18th century and signed A. Hoevenaer Arnhem. It is not uncommon for these early and rare enamel cases to contain later movements and, although a pity, generally it is not considered disasterous. (60mm. diam.)

Plate 20
Paul Bisot, St. Germain, Paris, circa 1650

Rare square Blois school enamel cased watch, the back illustrated on colour plate 2. The dial floral decoration is in delicate blue and pink, the case inside black on pale blue ground. The movement is square but otherwise standard for the period. Paintings carried out later in the 17th century by artists such as the brothers Huaut were equally fine, but bolder and the colours are harsher. Blois, a town about 100 miles from Paris, had been engaged in watchmaking from the 16th century. In about 1630 a goldsmith, Jean Toutin, developed a method of painting on enamel and his sons Henri and Jean together with Isaac Grubelin, Christoph Marlière and Pierre Chartier, established Blois as the centre of this art. The case and dial of the watch illustrated could be by Marlière or Chartier, as these men concentrated on floral designs. (41mm. square.)

Plate 21
Gold and Champlevé Enamel Watch, mid 17th century

Champlevé enamel is that type of enamel which is painted in many sections. Each section is hollowed out leaving a narrow border of metal between them. Each hollow is then filled with various colours of enamel which can be either translucent or opaque. It lends itself to flower and foliage decoration, and this example is typical. Although quite common at this time it only returned to fashion in the first half of the 19th century. As is not uncommon with decorative watches of this date, the movement has been replaced in the 18th century. The glass is held in by tags on the upper rather than under side of the bezel and this is rather unusual. (Approx. 60mm. diam.) *Victoria and Albert Museum. Crown Copyright.*

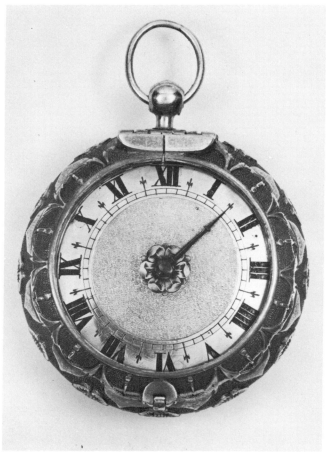

Plate 22
Benjamin Hill, London, circa 1650

Hill was a member of the Clockmakers' Company for 30 years from 1640 and was Master in 1657 and along with a few of his contemporaries he is known to have produced a number of watches in cast cases. They are quite rare and generally rather small, although this example, in the form of a seeded rose, is of average size. The movement is typical of the period, having a pinned-on cock, worm and wheel set-up, engraved potence and narrow Egyptian pillars. The dial is silver, the centre beautifully engraved with a Tudor rose, surrounded by fine matting. Note that the bezel is a fairly early example of the split variety for retaining the glass. Sophisticated case castings are currently being made mostly using genuine examples as masters and care must be taken to avoid them. The faker has a number of problems. He will either have to find a movement which is correct for date and can be made to fit his copy case (in which event he may have considerable difficulty without making slight modifications either to it or the movement, risking that these alterations may be

detectable) or make a completely new case master pattern. A genuine master used for casting will probably not be in mint condition and the copy will bear the same blemishes and one's suspicions are immediately aroused if the condition of the movement and the case are not approximately similar. The case of the watch illustrated has been modified at some time so that the movement can be wound through it and a shutter has been fitted that is shown closed. Although detrimental, it is a fact that can be used to confirm that this example is genuine! Finally the constituency of the silver used can, if practical, be analysed and, assuming that old silver has not been used, it will be radically different from a genuine example. All in all with care the modern fake can be avoided but they are certainly more sophisticated than the Viennese versions of 17th century watches produced at the end of the last century. They are merely reproductions! (44mm. diam.)

Plate 23
Estienne Hubert, Rouen, mid 17th century

A handsome silver French watch, beautifully chased and engraved and in excellent condition. The protecting leather outer case is decorated with silver pin work. The bezel is a quite early example of the 'split' type, incorporating two of the hinge knuckles. It is grooved to take the glass and closes in upon it when incorporated with the remainder of the hinge in the case. This method of fixing gradually disappeared at the end of the century. Continental movements differed very little from their English counterparts at this period. The cock, which is early to be of the screwed on variety, has a particularly elongated neck. Hubert was a maker of some note and in 1657 a John Smith is recorded as being fined ten shillings by the Clockmakers' Company for forging his name. Company rules were often abused; later in the 18th and 19th century they became ineffectual. (47mm. diam.)

Plate 24
Paul Maurin, Rome, circa 1665

A rare example of a steel cased watch with a steel chapter ring inlaid with gold chapters. The dial centre is separate, being champlevé enamel on gold; a floral background of opaque white enamel with the foliage suggested in black. The movement is wound through the back of the case and has an interior shutter operated by a pin projecting through a slot. The movement, which is signed 'Paul Maurin à Rome', is a normal verge with a tangent set up. Italian Watches are most uncommon. (50mm. diam.) *Trustees of the British Museum.*

Plate 25
Robert Seignior, London, circa 1665-70

(See colour plate 3.) Gold watches from this period are scarce, primarily because not many were made but also because of those that were, many have been destroyed for their metal. The plain gold inner case has a shutter over the winding hole while the leather outer is in crisp condition and is decorated with gold pin work in the form of an elaborated hinge. The matt gold champlevé dial has particularly large hour numerals with the quarter-hour markings close to the centre and the hour hand being short without a tail. The movement is of the highest quality for the period and it has a four-wheel train. The extra wheel allows for a higher pinion count and thus a smoother transmission of power throughout the train. It has early fusee chain and tulip pillars typical of the period and is signed 'Ro. Seignior London'. Seignior, an eminent maker, was admitted to the Clockmakers' Company in 1667. The outer case hinge has a square joint, a style which slowly disappeared after the turn of the 18th century; the inner case was made by Nathaniel Delander, one of the few early casemakers that have been identified. His mark was ND. (44mm. diam.)

Plate 26
John Fitter, Battersea, circa 1665

A particularly interesting watch which is in some respects in advance of its time. The silver chapter ring shows both hours and minutes; the steel hand indicating minutes, while Father Time revolves once in twelve hours pointing to the hours. The movement has a four-wheel train and the contrate wheel arbor is extended through to the top plate where a silver dial indicates the seconds. The indication of seconds is rare on a watch before 1700, and this example is one of the earliest known that have survived. The cock and figure plate are also of silver, while the movement has Egyptian pillars and the fusee has a gut line. The top plate is signed 'Jo. Fitter at Battersea'. In spite of the very advanced characteristics of this watch, Fitter was not admitted to the Clockmakers' Company until 1685. It was advantageous but not necessary to belong to the Guild. (47mm. diam.)

Plate 27
William Snow, circa 1670

This watch, which is signed 'William Snow in Marlebrough', serves to illustrate that provincial makers were quite capable of producing work which was in no way surpassed by their London counterparts. It was certainly not simply made to order for Snow in London and it bears some rather particular characteristics. The cock has an unusually open design which is beautifully executed and both the table and the foot are bordered, an exceptional feature at this date. Although the cock is screwed-on, curiously it is also fitted over a tenon — or block — in the plate. The steel work to the set-up is both elaborate and fine. Note the engraved potence and tulip pillars. The

leather outer case is decorated with silver pinwork and the silver dial has a matt centre with a polished silver chapter ring. (52mm. diam.) See also colour plate 4.

Plate 28
Huaut Enamelled Watch,
last quarter 17th century

The enamel is signed 'Les Deux freres Huaut pintre de son A.E. Berlin', and the paintings are both on the inside and out and around the edge of the gold case. The three Genevan Huaut brothers are by far the most renowned painters of watch enamels. Pierre, the eldest was considered the best. Jean and Amy generally worked together and this case is by them. The earliest known date for Pierre's work is 1679; his brothers continued to work after 1700. (51mm. diam.) *Victoria and Albert Museum. Crown Copyright.*

Plate 29
Henry Godfrey,
London, circa 1685

This silver pair-cased watch has an early balance spring and, more exceptionally, it has a six-hour dial. Watches with both hour and minute hands had already appeared by 1680 but they were not at first universally accepted. This watch retains a single hand yet allows for a closer reading of the time made viable with the introduction of the balance spring and the improvement of timekeeping it produced. The fine extended tulip hand revolves once every six hours, the chapter ring being marked in Roman numerals I — VI and superimposed on this Arabic numerals 7 — 12. Due to the larger spacing between the numerals the divisions between them can be legibly calibrated into two-minute divisions, and the time read to two minutes from the one hand. The balance cock table has short streamers, a decoration which became more elaborate for a

number of years before and after the turn of the century. The foot of the cock has no rim and it is small with an irregular outline. By the end of the century this foot was larger and had a rim. The silver regulator is of Tompion's form and the silver regulator disc (figure plate) is read from an arrow incorporated in the surrounding pierced gilt brass decoration. The movement pillars are individual and the top plate is signed 'H. Godfrey, London'. He was a member of the Clockmakers' Company from 1685 up to 1707. (50mm. diam.)

Plate 30
Markwick, London, circa 1685

The silver inlaid tortoiseshell outer of this silver alarm watch is illustrated in colour plate 3. The movement has a cock with an irregular border to a small foot, and an early example of a balance spring, both characteristic of the early 1680's. The divided tulip pillars however and the bold nature of the piercing and chasing of the outer case reflect the mid 17th century. Up to about 1685 Roman hour numerals tend to be bold and although there are many exceptions this is not one of them. The time of day is indicated by the steel arrow mounted on the central disc. The alarm hand is set against the arabic numerals on the disc and the alarm sounds when it points to the 12 o'clock Roman numeral. (50mm. diam.)

Plate 31
Henry Harper, London, circa 1685

The balance spring of this silver pair-cased verge watch is a fairly early example, having fewer coils and being stronger than its immediate successors. Note also the fusee chain links are larger than those found on watches just a few years later. Fusee chains were fitted to watches mostly from about 1670 while even then gut continued to be used for a number of years. They are found on watches of a much earlier date, generally because after its introduction many fusees were re-cut to take chain rather than gut line. The balance cock foot has a small and irregular border, a form which is typical of the period 1680-1685. The pillars and fusee stop are unusual, but the hand of tulip form, although particularly fine, is normal for the period. On the outer edge there is a date finger pointing to the 7th of the month in the illustration. Henry Harper worked in Cornhill and was apprenticed in 1657 and was a member of the Clockmakers' Company from 1664 and he died in 1708. (51mm. diam.)

Plate 32
Joseph Norris, Amsterdam, late 17th century

The silver outer case has an early example of repoussé work and the six hour dial is unusual (see Glossary). Note also the oval bow, a form which began to replace the simple ring at this period. Norris was free of the Clockmakers' Company in 1670 and worked in Amsterdam until 1697, when he returned to London. Travel in this way transported methods and styles from one centre to another. (51mm. diam.)

Plate 33
Nathaniel Barrow, hallmarked 1692

This gold clock watch strikes the hours on a bell housed inside the inner case. The inner case is pierced and engraved to emit the sound, as is also the outer case. Note the early pivoted stirrup bow. The notched counter wheel, which is numbered for each hour, governs the striking and is to be seen on the top plate of the movement. There are no streamers to the cock, and the foot is not bordered and has an irregular outline. There is a balance spring, and the balance arms are shaped so as to avoid the winding square. The movement is signed 'Nath. Barrow, London,' and the gold champlevé dial is also signed: the habit of signing dials was now becoming popular. Barrow was free of the Clockmakers' Company in 1660 and Master in 1689. He was said to have invented an early form of regulation (that of a worm and sector to adjust the length of the outer coil of the balance spring), but there is no real proof that he did so, although the arrangement will no doubt continue to bear his name. (50mm. diam.)

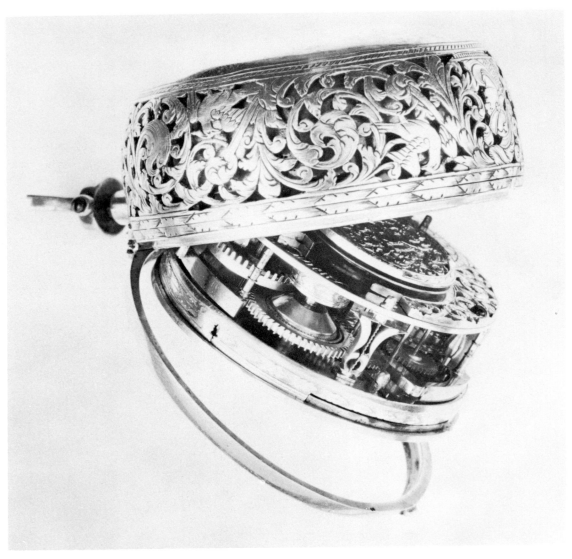

Plate 34
Wakel, Wien, circa 1700

This watch, typical of Viennese work of the period, is very English in character. The quarter repeating movement has an English type of bridge cock, while the tulip pillars were going out of fashion on English work at this date. The champlevé dial with a tulip hour hand and poker minute hand could be English, except that the arabic 2 in the form of a Z, to be seen also on the figure plate, is only found on Austrian and German work. The somewhat heavy pendant and bow is also 'un-English'. Both the inner and middle cases are pierced and engraved and the engraving on the back of the outer case is patently Continental. Both these cases are of somewhat thinner metal than one would expect on English work. Leather outers with silver pin work decoration are characteristic of the last half of the 17th century, and while sometimes it is difficult to ascertain whether or not a watch possessed one, it is safe to assume that many have been lost. The inner case of paircase repeating or alarm watches were always pierced (with the exception of some late eighteenth and early nineteenth 'dumb' repeaters), to emit sound and until about the mid-eighteenth century most outers as well. If the piercing is at all extensive on these, a third outer was fitted to exclude dust and dirt. (58mm. diam.)

Plate 35
Peter Garon, London, circa 1700

Up to the end of the 19th century eight day watches were rare and normally large. (This silver one's overall diameter is 71mm.) The cock is individual, with the foot noticeably bigger than the table, which incorporates a design of fish and birds and the streamers are in the form of birds' heads. It has a tulip hour hand, while there is a poker minute. There is a date aperture adjacent to III o'clock in the champlevé dial, which is signed 'Garon, London'. The movement is signed 'Peter Garon, London', and is number 481; only a few makers were numbering their work at this time. In spite of the fact that Garon was bankrupt in 1706, his son (also Peter) was apprenticed to him in 1713. He seems to have produced some fine watches of unusual character including differential dials as well as eight-days, both types prized by collectors.

Plate 36
Samuel Watson, London,
circa 1695

When the outer silver pair case is removed, a stop lever for the seconds hand is exposed protruding from the inner case. This lever stops and starts the movement on the balance and is an example of an early chronograph or 'pulse' watch. Sir John Floyer, the physician, is recorded as ordering the first 'pulse' watch from Watson and this is the only recorded example by him. A fine maker, he was Mathematician in Ordinary to King Charles II, and is known to have produced both clocks and watches to special order. The rest of the watch is fairly typical of the period with the seconds hand taken off the fourth wheel and both the dial and movement are signed. Note that the stirrup bow is pivoted from a circular flat topped pendant. (54mm. diam.)

Plate 37
Gosselin, Paris, late 17th century

Gosselin was Master of the Paris Corporation in 1735. 'Oignons' have rarely survived with their leather outer case, and this one still retains the gilded monogram. The cast gilt metal inner case has been beautifully finished, the dial with applied enamel cartouches with a fine steel hand, the centre engraved showing two squirrels. The movement is typical of the high grade French work of the period with silver bridge and slender Egyptian pillars, but the figure plate is particularly small. Regulation is actuated by a toothed slide which gears with a wheel under a figure plate. Movement winding is achieved through the dial centre. Only comparatively few of these watches seem to have survived with all the enamel cartouches intact. (58mm. diam.)

Plate 38
Martinus Hyllius, late 17th century

The advent of the pendulum seems to have inspired this maker to produce a quite impractical timepiece. The spherical outer case houses an inner, having gimbals so that the dial is kept in the upright position. The pendulum swings between the plates and the semi-circular bob is visible in the photograph. There is, of course, no contrate wheel or balance and the movement is wound through the back in the centre and the winding square protrudes through the case. The spherical outer case is missing, but the inner case is signed with the maker's name and 'Inventor Dresdae'. Three or four other such watches are known. (40mm. diam.)

Plate 39
Daniel Quare, London,
late 17th century

The outer tortoiseshell case is nicely decorated with silver and gold pin work, the inner case and dial being of silver. Silver pin work on shell although not particularly unusual, naturally adds interest to a watch; it is more common than silver inlay (colour Pl. 3). Daniel Quare was a maker of some note and was well known both in his day as well as to the modern collector. However, the quality of his work, the best being exceedingly fine, varies considerably, and although there are a fair number of contemporary forgeries, many from the continent, one can conclude that particularly in later years he was probably not too fussy about some of the watches and clocks that he sold. This particular watch, however, is of high quality. The movement number is 1897. (52mm. diam.)

Plate 40
Isaac Hasius Haarlem, late 17th century

This watch is typical of Dutch work of the period. The decoration, particularly the cock and movement pillars, is elaborate and the cock table is larger than most contemporary English work. The original silver champlevé dial has been replaced on this watch, probably during the period of 1720 and 1750 by the present enamel one. This was done very frequently on Dutch watches, but happily less often on French and English work. The arcaded minute band is a typical Dutch feature. Generally speaking the arches of the minute band tend to be 'flattish' on the earlier dials and increased in height as the century progressed. There is some evidence to indicate that these dials were latterly made also in Switzerland or at any rate fitted to Swiss movements signed with Dutch and English names, many of them spurious. Note the elaborate pierced gallery to the Egyptian pillars and the decorated piece to the fusee stop finger. The movement is signed 'Is. Hasius Haarlem'. The silver outer case has sloping corners to the hinges; after about 1695 the square hinge slowly lost favour, but was still used up to about 1710. (56mm. diam.)

Plate 41
Christoff Schöner, Augsburg, circa 1700

Watches with 'sun and moon' dials are quite unusual, and this watch has the addition of an early seconds hand and incorporates date indication. The sun is depicted in one half, and a moon on the other, of a disc revolving once every 24 hours, and each is visible in turn indicating the hour. The minute hand revolves round the full circumference of the dial in the normal way. An interesting feature of this particular watch is the decorative turning to the arbor of the third and contrate wheels. The pillars are of the divided tulip type. Note the use of the German form of the Arabic figure 2 on both the dial and the regulator disc. Typical of German work of this period, the filigree covers almost the entire area of the top plate and leaves only a little room for the maker's signature. Note also that the cock has a single foot in the English manner as opposed to a bridge type normal with French and Swiss work. (51mm. diam.)

Plate 42
Estienne Boisson,
circa 1700

Boisson was probably of French origin, but is recorded as working in London and although no place name appears on the watch, it is English in every respect. It possesses a wandering hour dial, an unusual type which appeared only for a few years either side of the turn of the century. The hour is shown in an aperture which moves around the semi-circular segment in the dial indicating at the same time the minutes, while the inner ring of the numerals near the dial centre indicate the quarters. The square in the centre of the dial is for setting the time. The style of the movement is quite normal, but the deep chamfered bezel of the silver case, while characteristic of the period, is a little uncommon. (57mm. diam.)

Plate 43
William Sinclare, London,
circa 1700

Watches with mock pendulums showing through the dial are not found as often as their cousins, those which simply have the pendulum showing through the balance cock on the back of the movement (see plate 46). The balance of this watch is mounted between the dial plate and the dial, and the figure plate is on the left of the mock pendulum aperture. This is 'balanced' with a small dial on the right which operates the catch of the silver case and is marked "O" for open and "S" for shut. The tulip hour hand was still quite common, but the beetle variety eventually replaced it after the turn of the century; the poker minute hand however continued in vogue into the early 19th century. The top plate is solid and is engraved as the dial, Will. Sinclare London, and numbered 78. The decorated columnar pillars are individual. Mock pendulums are most frequently found on Dutch watches. (53mm. diam.)

Plate 44
Cornelius Uyterweer, Rotterdam, circa 1705

This silver watch is a good example of Dutch work of this date; the silver champlevé dial with arcaded minute band, the mock pendulum with bridge cock, depicting a ploughing scene. The 'pendulum' is mounted on one arm of the balance and moves back and forth with its motion. The movement pillars are finely scrolled and the dial centre bears a coat of arms while the signature on the dial is broken for the date aperture. The typically Dutch arcaded minute band was later to be used by the Swiss for their 'Dutch Forgeries' (see Glossary). Dutch work, such as this example, could be of a fairly high standard, but the cases in particular never really match that normally produced in contemporary England. The hands are later. (51mm. diam.)

Plate 45
Wainwright, Wellingborough, circa 1705

This provincial watch does not differ from its London contemporaries to any real extent. The front regulator, with square and disc is a little unusual, although one would have thought that this device would have been fitted more frequently. That the watch need not be opened for regulation is a very real advantage as consequently the entry of foreign matter or damage to the movement by the owner is avoided. Dust rings (used at first by English makers) were coming into vogue, although initially they appear to have been reserved for clockwatches and repeaters. (52mm. diam.)

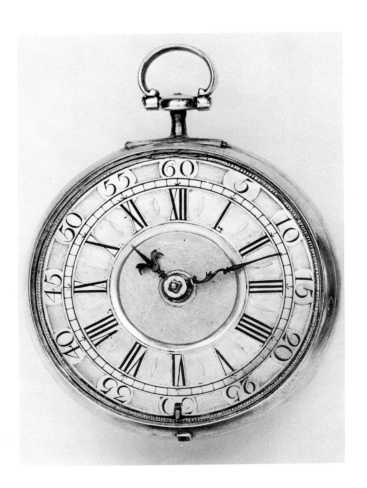

Plate 46
John Shaw, Holborn,
circa 1705

The cock has the semi-circular segment cut away to reveal a mock pendulum, a fashion which was more common for clocks, but does not of course enhance in any way the going of the watch. Note that by this stage cock foots had become very broad and table streamers can be exceedingly long. There is no figure plate, the gear meshing with the toothed segment beneath the cock in the normal way; visible behind the mock pendulum is a scale of figures as a regulation guide. The cock is engraved, 'To increase the figure will make it go faster and to decrease it slower'. The champlevé dial is not signed, but is typical of the period. This watch has a good example of an early beetle hour hand which was beginning to appear at this date, replacing the tulip form. Shaw was admitted to the Clockmakers' Company in 1682 and became Master in 1712 and was one of a number of eminent makers working in Holborn in the 17th, 18th and early 19th centuries. The dial is silver, the cases silver gilt. (55mm. diam.)

Plate 47
J(ames) Banks, Nottingham, circa 1700

The silver repoussé case depicting the Triumph of Mars and Venus, with a motto, 'Amoris tela comnium querela' is quite unusual, while the signature on the balance cock is individual, but of more significance is the dial which is of the very rare 'differential' variety (see Glossary). The centre consists of a revolving disc with the Roman hour numerals one to twelve, which rotates at a speed 1/12th less than the single poker hand which indicates both hours and minutes. Outside this disc is a decorative band depicting military emblems and the maker's signature, the minute markings being on the extremity of the dial. The case has a horseshoe bow and the bezel is uncut; the casemaker's mark is TP. The movement is fairly typical for the period, the balance cock having a broad foot and a narrow neck, while the tapering Egyptian pillars are particularly nice. Although by an 'unknown' maker, this watch is of good quality and is evidence that provincial makers can be of great interest and quite capable of producing individual work. The introduction of the balance spring some years earlier had rendered watches considerably more accurate and it was now practical to indicate the minutes on a watch dial. There was probably however some resistance on the part of the users to two-handed watches and one assumes they felt they could be confused when two hands were shown on the dial. This method of displaying time neatly overcomes their objection and, moreover, an unusual possession no doubt has its attractions! (52mm. diam.)

Frères Melly, Paris, circa 1790

The enamel of this single cased gold verge watch is after a self portrait by Rubens (43mm. diam.)

Robert Seignor, London, circa 1665

A high quality verge movement characteristic of the period, but unusually in a gold case. See also gold outer case on right and plate 25.

Outer Case, circa 1665

This belongs to the watch on the left, it is leather covered with fine decorative gold pin work in a form of an elaborate hinge. (44mm. diam.)

Dufalga, Geneva, circa 1775

The gold case is with red transluccent enamel with floral diamond decoration surrounded by a green enamel band. (44mm. diam.) See also movement plate 69.

Markwick, London, circa 1685

Pierced and engraved silver alarm watch with champlevé dial. James Markwick was succeeded by his son-in-law Robert Markham whofrequently traded as Markwick Markham. See outer case below and movement plate 30.

Recordon, London, circa 1805

Gold, repeating *grande sonnerie* striking watch signed by Recordon who was Breguet's London agent. (57mm. diam.) See also plate 101.

Charles Burges, London, hallmarked 1765

Gold verge watch with *en grisaille* enamel. Normal verge movement, white enamel dial and elaborate gold hands. (46mm. diam.)

Outer Case, circa 1685

A tortoiseshell outer case inlaid with silver is more unusual and desirable than silver pin work. This case belongs to the watch by Markwick above. Note the portholes around the circumference to emit the sound of the alarm. (50mm. diam.)

Plate 48
Claude Viet, circa 1710

Viet was a French Huguenot who joined the Clockmakers' Company in 1698 and became Watchmaker to Queen Anne. Note particularly the depth of the movement, the cock, form of regulator, signature style and provision for dial winding, all characteristics of French 'oignon' work of the period. Up to about 1685 French and English work was not dissimilar, but suddenly the 'oignon' appeared and the French industry concentrated on them almost entirely and relatively large quantities were produced until about the end of the second quarter of the 18th century. The origin of the style is obscure and really has no practical advantages over contemporary English work. This very handsome silver pair cased watch has a quarter repeating mechanism which utilises only one hammer. The hours are first struck and then the quarters each with a single blow: an arrangement that does not lead to confusion in practice, but which was not widely adopted. (57mm. diam.)

Plate 49
Thomas Tompion, hallmarked 1708

The work of Thomas Tompion has always been highly revered and there is no doubt that, particularly in his complicated work, he was unsurpassed in the late 17th and early 18th century. The dial and hands (see Colour plate 7) are of exquisite quality while the pierced outer case is typical of his design. It is of course in the movement that the quality shows best, with long slender arbors and fine pinions beautifully polished. The repeating mechanism, although of a complicated construction, is very precise and functions accurately even today. The balance cock was fitted with the original and early diamond end stone; these diamond end stones appeared only on the best quality watches after 1704. The watch number 350 follows the maker's signature on the movement back plate, underneath the cock, beneath the bell and in a cartouche at the base of the pendant on the inner case. Tompion began numbering his clocks and watches in 1680 and continued the practice until his death in 1713. Except in a few instances the number appears underneath the balance cock and on the case and very often on the pillar plate. There are many contemporary and subsequent forgeries which do not possess a number other than on the top plate. However, some have been 'improved' in recent years and numbers can now be found in all the right places, but fortunately it is often very apparent that the original dye stamp has not been employed. Forgers, too, seem to have often selected numbers that are impossibly high or out of sequence for the date of the watch, although a serial number/date check is only a test and not a golden rule. It is often assumed that if the numbers are not found in all the 'correct' places the watch is not genuine but the system is not infallible — indeed Tompion even employed the same serial number twice. This watch possesses a dust ring (covers began to be used about 1720). The movement is illustrated in colour, Plate 4. (56mm. diam.)

Plate 50
Rodet, London, circa 1715

Although apparently made in London, this watch is not of English character and is in all probability Swiss. The silver engraved case has an enamel painting of 'Greek Charity' inset on the back. Greek Charity is quite a popular subject on late 17th and 18th century enamel watches. It appears to have been first recorded by a Roman writer, Valerius Maximus, during the reign of Emperor Tiberius and is based on a story surrounding the Greek General Cimone, convicted to die of starvation in prison. His daughter succoured him on her daily visits and his life was eventually spared. The subject is often erroneously called 'Roman Charity'. The inside of the back has a further painting of a courtship scene, and the bridge over the balance has another painting, probably of General Cimone's daughter. The cock has a rim so that the balance is protected, while there is an aperture for the 'mock pendulum'. The square baluster movement pillars have silver decorated 'capitals' and the figure plate and surrounding decoration are also of silver. The dial is enamel with beetle and poker hands. (51mm. diam.)

Plate 51
George Graham, London, hallmarked 1718

This is a good example of Graham's best work with a quarter repeating mechanism. Both the inner and outer gold cases are pierced and engraved, the outer also with a repoussé scene of Hercules and Mars within the symmetrical frame. Asymmetrical frames appeared in 1737/1740 and entirely symmetrical designs were dropped. The border contains four medallion heads, a design which was popular on 17th century engraved as well as enamel cases. After 1737/1740 repoussé cases had borders, mostly consisting only of asymmetric scrolls, but occasionally a combination (generally symmetrical on their east-west sides). The movement and early dust cap are signed and the movement is numbered 445, this number also being repeated on the inside of the outer case and beneath the pendant on the inner as well as under the balance cock. The balance cock also has a diamond end stone and the foot is solid, being engraved, but not pierced. From about this date this form of cock foot was adopted by most English makers, and continued in use with little variation for the remainder of the century. The time is 'repeated' by depressing the pendant and there is a 'pulse piece' which protrudes through the cases from the movement, so that the time repeated can also be felt on a small stud. The pulse piece arm from the movement is visible just below the catch piece. Tompion's partner and successor, Graham, was a most eminent maker and inventor whose work was regularly forged by his contemporaries. He continued Tompion's method and sequence of numbering. (49mm. diam.) See also colour plate 5.

Plate 52
John Bushman, London, circa 1720

Surviving examples of silver repoussé work of this date appear to be considerably rarer than those of gold. Later in the century there were of course many watches produced of very mediocre quality and which are generally referred to as 'Dutch Forgeries' (see Glossary). This particular watch depicts the Flight into Egypt with the four Evangelists on the outside of the symmetrical frame. The champlevé dial has a date aperture and the movement is numbered 152. Although the movement is very English in character, the case is certainly of Genevan origin. Another watch with an identical case is known with a Continental movement. The hands are later replacements. (55mm. diam.)

Plate 53
George Graham, London, circa 1720

Alarm watches were made from the early 1600's, and most makers seem to have devoted a small amount of their output on them. The beetle and poker hands of this watch are particularly fine, the minute hand being cranked to clear the alarm setting square, the alarm hand setting dial showing in the aperture above 6 o'clock. There is a stop lever for the arm on the edge of the case between 2 and 3 o'clock. The alarm is struck on a bell fixed to the silver inner case, which is beautifully pierced and engraved. The silver outer case is plain, but is marked WS, as is the inner with the casemaker's stamp. The Vulliamy equation watch paper is of later date but adds interest; the wide variety of papers to be found are too often overlooked. Graham joined the Clockmakers' Company in 1695, became Master in 1722, was Tompion's nephew and died in 1751. This particular watch has a verge escapement, but after 1726 Graham invariably used the cylinder. (53mm. diam.)

Plate 54
Durand, London, circa 1735

The gold outer paircase is of an unusual design with alternate panels of polished flutes and chased decoration. The dial is signed 'Durand London', as is the movement, which is also numbered 202. The movement has a verge escapement, baluster pillars and a narrow necked cock with streamers and a table decoration that springs from a shell. Note the elegant bow and unusal hour hand. Champlevé dials continued to be used for another thirty odd years, but they were already giving way to enamel. Quarter and half hour markings on watch dials were soon to go out of fashion in favour of simplicity. They were, of course, very necessary when watches had only an hour hand. (48mm. diam.)

Plate 55
David Hubert, London, hallmarked 1737

An exceptionally fine and interesting example of repoussé work in superb condition, signed above the lower mask 'FFF'. The figure, probably of Cybele, is surrounded by a particularly loosely defined cartouche that is perhaps the earliest known example of its type. Cartouches were consistently symmetric up to 1737-40 when asymmetric designs were introduced. This case (50mm. diameter) illustrates a stylistic variant where the north and east sides are asymmetric, while the east and west sides are symmetric. The craftsman F.F.(Fecit) is possibly François Fourestier. Both the inner and outer cases are marked by the casemaker A.R., while the verge movement, enamel dial and hands are of the quality that one would expect of an eminent maker such as David Hubert, who was Master of the Clockmakers' Company in 1743.

Plate 56
Thomas Mudge, London, hallmarked 1738

Mudge was apprenticed to George Graham in 1730 and became a Freeman of the Clockmakers' Company in the same year as this watch was made. It has a cylinder escapement and bears the exceedingly early number 22, which is repeated on the inside of the inner case. The repoussé outer is possibly the earliest signed watch case by George Moser, perhaps the most eminent repoussé artist of the 18th century. Details of his life and work have been consistently recorded incorrectly. He is known to have come to London as a very young man and was married there in 1729/30. It is important to note that the scene border is of symmetric design, a style that gave way to asymmetricism in the years 1737/1740. Although occasionally combined with symmetricism, asymmetrical design took over at this date entirely. Horological historians generally have not understood that asymmetricism did not appear before this date and this is very apparent from their illustrated work. Both inner and outer cases have the case maker's mark 'IW'. It is interesting and possibly refreshing to find a watch with an outer repoussé case that does not depict scenes from classical mythology. On this case there is a figure of Britannia pointing to a shield or a medallion, which Fame is holding, on which there is a bust of a man, who is possibly Sir Christopher Wren. St. Paul's is to be seen in the background on the right and in the centre below the shield is the Monument in the City of London, commemorating the Fire of London. To the right of Britannia is the Greenwich Observatory and the design also includes telescopes and scientific emblems. The outer case also has a diamond push piece, which may be original, although many are later additions. The dial is signed 'Mudge London' and it should be noted that quarter and half hour markings are not present, features that some makers were beginning to omit at this date. (48mm. diam.)

Plate 57
George Graham, London, hallmarked 1739

This typical Graham movement is that belonging to the gold chatelaine watch illustrated in colour plate 1. The movement number is characteristically repeated on the inside of the inner case and, together with the casemaker's mark 'I.W.'. The cylinder escapement from the watch is illustrated in the Glossary. Graham is said to have invented it in 1726 but at least the germ of the idea originates with Tompion and his collaborators Barlow, Houghton and possibly Hooke. It was adopted by Ellicott and also Thomas Mudge, who was Graham's apprentice, fairly soon after its invention and it was used by most eminent English makers for the rest of the century. The Continentals were slow to adopt it, but during the 19th century the Swiss used it extensively in their mass produced watches while English makers only used it occasionally and mostly ceased to do so after about 1830. The Swiss found it had two significant advantages: it was easy to construct and could be accommodated in slim movements. Although reasonably reliable, it has all the draw backs of a frictional rest escapement. (57mm diam. with outer case.)

Plate 58
Thomas Mudge, London, hallmarked 1752

Mudge produced some really superlative watches for his more illustrious clients, but he also sold watches that although good, are of a rather ordinary nature. The movement is characteristic of the period with square baluster pillars, while the cock is nicely engraved in an asymmetric design, the table decoration springing from a mask. It has a verge escapement that was less demanding to make than the cylinder and there is no diamond endstone or dust cap. The plain gold inner case is fitted in the gilt metal tortoiseshell outer, which although not the cheapest arrangement, is indicative of a watch being produced to a price. The dial and hands are later than the rest of the watch and cannot be dated much earlier than circa 1775, both being similar in character to the watch illustrated in plate 71, while originally they were probably similar to illustration 63. Quite frequently new dial feet holes were made in the bottom plate and the old ones are left to tell the tale, but if a new dial plate has been made and the feet arranged to fit the existing movement, as in this watch, a good knowledge of the changes that took place in dial designs is required, particularly when modernisation has taken place soon after a watch has been made. The quality of the dial and hands used could well indicate that the Mudge and Dutton partnership carried out the alteration.

There exist many watches made prior to about 1800 that have been modernised in one way or another: with the introduction of the balance spring in the late 17th century, springs were fitted to watches of an earlier period and when the lever escapement came fully into its own during the Victorian era, watches particularly those with cylinder and duplex escapements, had them completely replaced or 'converted' (see Glossary). There were other changes made, including those to pendants, bows and cases, but it depends on a variety of factors how much these changes are considered detrimental to a watch. (48mm. diam.)

Plate 59
Swiss Watch signed 'J. Cater, London'
circa 1750

From the mid-18th century onwards there were a great many watches made in Switzerland and, in particular, Geneva, which were signed with makers' names that were often fictitious. It is also true that watches were made in Switzerland, sometimes in their entirety, against orders placed on them by English makers, but these were generally of higher quality and bore closer resemblance to the English style than the forgeries, which were often very poor. The outer case of this watch is very Swiss, being the unusual high relief repoussé variety that is also pierced and is backed by red silk. The overall workmanship of the case is quite good and it has been well preserved by the glazed outer protecting case. The movement has some English influence, but the bridge type cock, typical of French and Swiss work, shows that the attempt to deceive as to the origin of the watch was not very thorough. The signature does not belong to a recorded English maker. (55mm. diam.)

**Thomas Tompion,
London,
hallmarked 1708**

Side angle
view of quar-
ter repeating move-
ment, number 350.
(41mm. diam.) The dial
illustrated on colour
plate 7, see also
plate 49.

**John Arnold, London,
hallmarked 1791**

Movement
of pocket chrono-
meter, numbered $\frac{405}{704}$.
(40mm. diam.) Illustrated
on plate 81. Note the cut out
in the plate for the spring
detent, 'Z' type balance
and gold helical
hairspring.

**William Snow of
Marlebrough,
circa 1670**

The steel
work and
pierced and
engraved cock of
this movement are of
particularly fine
quality (39mm.
diam.) See
plate 27.

**Mudge and Dutton,
London,
hallmarked 1779**

Half/quarter
dumb repeating
movement from a silver
paircased watch shown in
plate 75. It is typical of the
high quality work produced
by this well known
partnership.
(39mm.
diam.)

**Dent, London,
hallmarked 1867**

A half/quarter
repeating spring
detent movement
of the watch illustrated
in colour plate 8 and plate
154 which is a fine example
of 19th century English
work. (45mm.
diam.)

**Piguet et Meylan,
Geneva, circa 1825**

The blued
steel plates of
this movement con-
trast beautifully with the
polished steel work. Some
parts are also of highly
finished silver. (48mm.
diam.) See also
plate 119.

Plate 60
Thomas Pierce, Bristol, circa 1750

Watches with repoussé chatelaines are invariably dated between 1725 and 1775. Generally speaking, repoussé work was at its best during the second quarter of the century and after about 1775 it dropped from favour. From then on watches with chatelaines were normally in enamel and these in turn were made up to about 1840. Chatelaines were rarely made of gold and, since gilt metal is not hallmarked, it can be difficult to ascertain whether or not they belong to a watch, more especially because the neo-classical scenes were often loosely interpreted. However, it can be noted that both the watch and chatelaine's cartouches in this example are symmetric on their east west sides, but are asymmetric north south. The unnumbered verge movement has a silver cock, which is a feature quite often found on watches of this date and type. It is possible that both this and indeed the entire watch is of Swiss origin. (47mm. diam.)

Plate 61
Joan Dellavos, Prague, mid-18th century

See colour plate 7 for the back of this gold watch. The maker of the verge movement is not recorded although a Johann Dellawas is and might be an alternative spelling. The enamel dial is typical of the period and the movement is wound through it in the Continental manner. The cumbersome pair case was losing popularity particularly on the Continent and the only practical means of winding a single cased watch without shutter, cuvette or double bottom (see Glossary) is via the dial. This certainly does not help the appearance and is not satisfactory as the dial can be easily chipped and the hands broken. Continentals used the single case extensively and only in the last decade of the century did they reluctantly adopt the double bottom or the cuvette as movements became slimmer. (44mm. diam.)

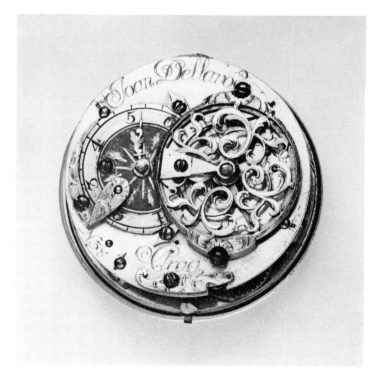

Plate 62
J.B. Baillon, Paris, circa 1750

An enamel cased verge watch with a single gold case and 'swing out' movement. The paste set hands and winding square are typical of Continental watches of the period and the painting is in reasonably good taste. In general single portraits are not so desirable as painted scenes, with or without figures featured in them, but the quality of the enamel and its condition is always paramount. The verge escapement has an adjustable potence, a refinement that was invented by Julien Le Roy as a means of moving the crown wheel teeth across the verge, thereby bringing the escapement into beat without dismantling the movement. A steel end piece on the outer pivot enables the depth of engagement to be varied (see Glossary). Jean Baptiste Baillon was a well-known maker and is listed as being maker to Queen Marie Leszinska and later to Marie Antoinette. (49mm. diam.)

Plate 63
Ellicott, London, hallmarked 1762

John Ellicott the younger worked from about 1728 until his death in 1772. He was more famous than his eminent father and was Clockmaker to the King and Fellow of the Royal Society. Much of his work has a cylinder escapement and this watch is no exception. There are other examples of his work employing this particular and handsome silver pair case, while there are a few in gold. The inner case is marked inside as well as outside near the base of the pendant with the movement number 4887. The movement is a half/quarter repeater (striking to the nearest 7½ minutes), having baluster pillars and a large diamond end stone with a cock table of asymmetrical design. Ellicott is known to have had much of his work done for him by other makers, so, although the style of this movement is characteristic and the outer case design individual to him, one cannot be certain for how much of it his own workshop was responsible. (48mm. diam.)

124

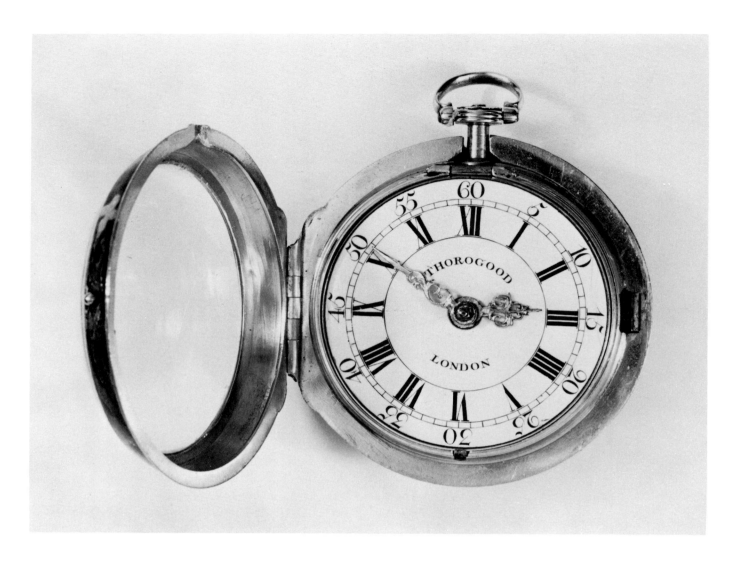

Plate 64
Stephen Thorogood, hallmarked 1763

The rare basse-taille enamel back of this watch is illustrated in colour plate 1. The style of the gold hands are similar to those found on clocks of this period, but whereas they are occasionally found on English watches from about the mid-eighteenth century, they were more popular on the Continent. The enamel dial is typical however of English work of the mid-eighteenth century, having a band on the inside of the Roman numerals which was later dropped in favour of simplicity. During the last quarter of the century there was a tendency for the outer Arabic minute numerals to become smaller and finally to disappear. It is rare to see the inner bezel omitted from a pair cased watch; this was not more often done, presumably because damage can be caused to the dial and hands when the watch is reversed for winding through the inner case. The movement is a typical verge of the period and is numbered 1627. (51mm. diam.)

Plate 65
Jean Romilly, Paris, circa 1765

Jean Romilly, along with a number of eminent makers of his day, was of Genevan origin and emigrated to Paris. This gold and enamel verge watch has a movement which is typical of a good quality Continental verge. The bridge cock has a coqueret for the top pivot of the verge balance staff. These were used on French watches from about 1735, and by 1770 they were in general use on the Continent for better quality watches. Eventually they were superseded by jewels introduced from England. The escape wheel has an adjustable potence, the movement pillars are of the baluster type, while the mechanism is wound through the dial. (43mm. diam.)

127

Plate 66
William Grant, London, circa 1765

A gilt metal pair cased watch, with the outer case covered with translucent horn painted on the underside, a form of decoration which was a popular poorer relative of enamel. The verge movement, which is numbered 209, is of good quality, although these watches rarely had movements of any particular note. Quite often the paintings are unsuccessful and dull, but otherwise they have a certain charm. The horn case is susceptible to damage and those totally without cracks are quite scarce. Painted horn decoration is found invariably on English work during the last half of the 18th century and the early years of the 19th. (48mm. diam.)

Plate 67
Justin Vulliamy, hallmarked 1772

This cylinder pair cased watch is typical of this maker's work at this period. He was active from 1730, being in partnership with Benjamin Gray until 1775, at which date his son also entered the trade. Justin Vulliamy emigrated from Switzerland as a young man and became a maker of great repute, and succeeded Benjamin Gray, who was not only his partner but his father-in-law, to the Royal Appointment. His son Benjamin retained the appointment, which remained in the family until the death of Benjamin Lewis in 1854. The dial is characteristic of his work. The minute markings are placed on the outside of the 5 minute numerals with a ring on both the inside and outside of the Roman chapters. The seconds ring and figure plate are similarly marked. The top plate is engraved 'isri' which presumably is a coded number, but which has yet to be deciphered. (45mm. diam.)

Plate 68
Robert Slater, London, circa 1775

The gilt metal case has a glazed bottom, disclosing a verge movement with a train mounted in decorated cocks and bridges and the mainspring partially revealed. These 'skeletonised' movements sometimes have an overlay with filigree work, which is mounted with paste or semi-precious stones and often has a small portrait medallion in enamel. The balance cock of this watch is signed 'Robert Slater, London', while the movement is wound through the dial. Most watches of this type are likely to be of Swiss origin. Although they are not particularly of horological significance, a comprehensive collection would generally have an example. They serve to remind us that, even in the latter part of the eighteenth century, a watch mechanism was of real interest, if not wonder. (46mm. diam.)

Plate 69
Philipe Dufalga, Geneva,
circa 1775

This high grade verge watch with
adjustable potence has a fine enamel
back that is illustrated in colour plate 3.
The bezel, hands and push piece are set
with diamonds and a further indication
of quality is the gold winding square
sleeve to protect the dial. Note the
similarity to contemporary Parisian
work. (44mm. diam.)

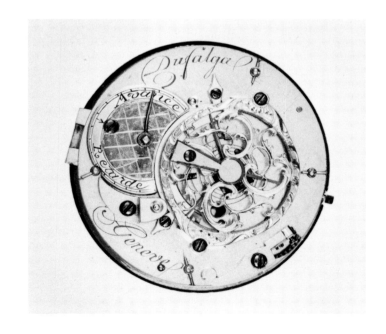

Plate 70
J.A. Lepine, Paris, circa 1775

This really high quality watch is an early example of Lepine's own calibre. The movement layout with hanging going barrel, combined with a virgule escapement, effects a very flat movement. Note the coqueret on the upper pivot of the balance staff. A pendant push opens the back and via a cuvette (shown open) the movement is wound and the hands set from the rear, leaving the dial uncluttered by a winding square. Most contemporary Continental watches had single cases with winding squares through the dial and required the hands to be set from the front — a most awkward arrangement. Virgule escapements are difficult to make, but as with the cylinder and duplex, a slim movement could be achieved. It has no practical advantage although it is quite rare and consequently of interest to the collector. The cuvette is signed 'Lepine Hger du Roy à Paris', and the case numbered 13271; the enamel back is illustrated on colour plate 5. (39mm. diam.)

Plate 71
John Arnold, London, circa 1775

Arnold (1736-1799) made this watch during his early experimental period on the detent escapement for his marine and pocket chronometers, for which he was to become famous. He was well connected in the society of the day and he was able to earn a good living by producing fine quality watches such as this. The gold outer pair case has a scene *en grisaille* (monochrome) enamel, surrounded by green and blue enamels overlaid on a chased gold background. The movement is a half/quarter repeater on a bell with cylinder escapement and diamond end stone with the signature 'Jnº Arnold London', numbered 230. Details in the dial design are normally associated with a period ten years later; the inner hour ring and minute marking bands have been omitted. (47mm. diam.)

Plate 72
Ferdinand Berthoud, Paris, circa 1775

The gold case is decorated with gold, tinted in
different colours by variation in the alloy content.
Fairly common in Continental watches in the latter
part of the 18th century, it became very popular
on English, particularly provincial, work during the
19th century. The verge movement and enamel dial
with gold hands are typical of the period.
Ferdinand Berthoud was a most eminent maker
who worked extensively on marine chronometers.
He started with Julien Le Roy at the age of 19 in
1745, having been apprenticed to Jean Henri
Berthoud — his brother. Emigration to Paris,
particularly from Switzerland, was very common.
He died in 1807. (40mm. diam.) See also colour
plate 5.

Plate 73
Richard Comber, Lewes,
hallmarked 1776

This silver pair cased watch has a differential type of dial that is occasionally found on watches from the beginning of the century, although at this date they are exceptional. Another example of this style is to be seen on plate 47 and its function is explained in the Glossary. The verge movement is numbered 347. Comber seems to have been responsible for some unusual clocks as well as watches of excellent quality, and is a good example of those talented provincial makers of special interest to the collector. The hand is of later date. (50mm. diam.)

Plate 74
Vaucher à Paris, circa 1780

This gold and enamel gem set watch, (see also colour plate 7) has a standard good quality verge movement of the period, having a coqueret and adjustable potence. Although only a timepiece, the long pendant might imply that the movement has a repeating mechanism. Both English and Continental makers often used the long pendant for their timepieces. Whether it was because they thought that it was more elegant or whether the intention was to deceive the owner's friends, it is impossible to say; perhaps it was a combination of both. The dial and movement are signed simply 'Vaucher à Paris', and there are a number of makers of this name, possibly all of Swiss origin. There is evidence to indicate that a great many watches of this period and later were wholly or partly made, particularly through family contracts, in Geneva and the Neufchatel Canton. How many 'makers' in Paris and elsewhere were simply distributors is a moot point. (43mm. diam.)

Plate 75
Mudge & Dutton, London, hallmarked 1779

This ½/¼ dumb repeating, silver paircased watch is quite typical of the high quality watches produced by this well-known partnership. Note the particularly fine enamel dial and beetle and poker hands which compare so favourably with watches by contemporary makers. Both the dust cover and movement are signed 'Tho. Mudge, W. Dutton', and the movement bears the number 1886. It has a cylinder escapement and brass escape wheel used extensively by the partnership. The pillars are cylindrical or 'columnar', the cock has a solid foot and the table a diamond endstone with a mask head near the neck. Mask heads engraved on cock tables were exceedingly popular on English watches from the latter part of the 17th century, and only passed out of fashion in the early years of the 19th century. The watch repeats the time on blocks fitted on the inside of the inner case rather than on the bell and is known as a 'dumb' repeater. The sound is a dull thud that is not particularly melodious, but it does not carry so far as the ring of a bell and can only be heard by those in the immediate vicinity of the wearer. Thus he can discover while the watch remains in his pocket whether he is late for his next appointment with the maximum amount of secrecy and the minimum amount of embarrassment. The movement is illustrated on colour plate 4. (50mm. diam.)

Plate 76
Alexander Cumming, hallmarked 1780

This half/quarter repeating movement is from the silver gilt pair cased watch illustrated in colour plate 1. Although introduced at the end of the 17th century, half-quarter repeating mechanisms were in the main only favoured in the last half of the eighteenth century and the early part of the nineteenth century. In addition to repeating the hours with one hammer and the quarters with two, an additional single stroke is sounded if 7½ minutes have elapsed since the previous quarter. There is no bell on the inner case and the hammers sound on blocks the watch is a 'dumb' repeater. It has a cylinder escapement for which Cumming introduced some minor improvements. English movements had generally become slimmer in 1780 than they were ten years earlier and cylindrical pillars had mostly replaced the square baluster variety. (54mm. diam.)

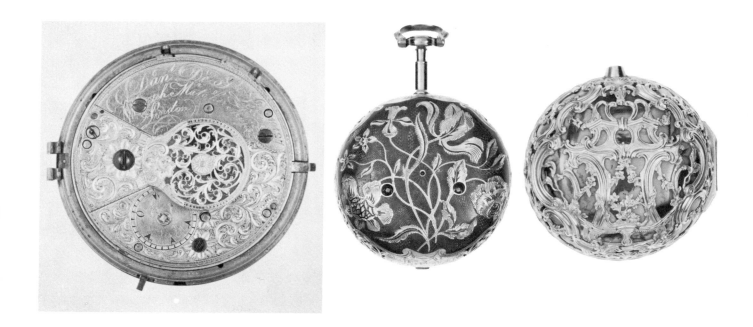

Plate 77
Daniel de St. Leu, London, circa 1780

St. Leu concentrated on the Eastern markets. The full plate movement has a verge escapement and the top plate is signed 'Watch Ma^r to Her Majesty, London' and is numbered 10127. It is also a clockwatch, a feature that seems to have returned to favour during the latter part of the 18th century, particularly for export markets and on occasions they were combined with repeating mechanisms as well. The large leather outer case is 67mm. in diameter and is overlaid with gold scroll and pin work, while the middle case is of agate overlaid with gold decoration. The inner case has green translucent enamel with gold floral decoration in relief. Agate cases are found on watches of both the 17th and 18th century, but they are rare and highly collectable. The overlaid gold work on the middle case of this watch is exceptional; note that the central portion is Chippendale in character.

Plate 78
John Arnold, London, hallmarked 1781

Arnold began making large pocket size chronometers from about 1772. His numbering system is somewhat obscure, but this with the fractional number $\frac{23}{78}$ is probably the 78th pocket chronometer he produced and was the 23rd in the series having a double T or double S balance. In his search for an arrangement to overcome the timekeeping errors that changes in temperature produced, Arnold designed a wide variety of balances and this watch (see colour plate 5. for top plate) possesses one of the rarest: a double S. It is so called because of the bimetallic strips in the form of an S that are incorporated. It was introduced in 1780, refined in 1782, but discarded in the same year in favour of the 'OZ' (a three arm plain steel balance with two exterior bimetallic curbs) which became standard until 1791. The steel balance spring is helical, Arnold having adopted the form in 1775. The escapement is a pivoted detent, being one of seven by Arnold that are recorded as remaining unaltered, the others having been changed to a spring detent which superseded the pivoted detent in the year this watch was made. The impulse pallet is of steel with a stone dovetailed diagonally into it. There is no impulse roller, but a safety roller with a crescent in it that allows an arm on the detent to enter when the impulse pallet is in the path of the escape wheel. The gold passing spring rests on an upright pin in the nose of the detent that has a straight return spring and banks against the screw. Apart from a poising error in pocket use, the principal drawback of this pivoted detent, and no doubt the reason why Arnold adopted the spring detent, was that with the light return spring acting on the detent, it was essential to oil the pivots and the point at which the return spring rubs against the locking arm. A further reason is that a greater amount of power is required from the mainspring to maintain impulse and to achieve an adequate balance arc. In time the condition of the oil changed and so did the accompanying friction, while the strong mainspring introduced unnecessary frictional wear. The silver case, large dial (60mm.) and hands are typical of Arnold's precision watches at this period and apart from the finely engraved signature and cock, there is little that is not a part of the functional design. The minute hand is screwed tight to the square and the seconds ring enters into the hour chapters. Arnold's movements were exquisitely finished and some of his balances quite remarkable and not surprisingly his watches have always been more sought after than Earnshaw's. He died in 1799, after which the business was continued by his son John Roger, who although he lacked his father's genius, nevertheless produced some excellent watches. (70mm. diam.)

Plate 79
Josiah Emery, hallmarked 1783

Thomas Mudge had first conceived the basic principles of the lever escapement in 1754, but it was not until 1770 that he gave the first watch with the escapement to George III. Emery appears to have made the next in 1782. The movement plate of this example is signed 'Josiah Emery, Charing Cross, London' and is numbered 957. The straight line lever has no draw and the steel escape wheel has teeth slotted to retain oil and the pallets are jewelled. The gold dart (safety finger) is screwed to the lever fork and the four arm balance is of unusual shape and construction and has "S" shape bi-metallic affixes. The helical hair spring has terminal curves and the cranked steel roller is pivoted in jewel holes. The construction of such an escapement required a high degree of craftsmanship and it is not surprising that such a complex design was not widely taken up. Breguet produced a much lighter and simply designed lever escapement in 1786, but comparisons should be made with levers by Grant and Pendleton, also illustrated in detail in this book (see Plates 80 and 90). Emery was responsible for about 30 lever watches and they are of course highly sought after. He was born in Switzerland in about 1725, was made an honorary Freeman of the Clockmakers' Company in 1781 and died in 1797. (60mm. diam.)

Plate 80
Grant, lever escapement from watch hallmarked 1788

John Grant was one of the early experimentors with the lever escapement, although very few watches made by him with the escapement have survived. This example is a straight line lever type and is without draw. It has a brass escape wheel with a steel lever and ruby pallets. The jewelled fork is on two planes, while the three-armed cut bimetallic balance has two flat springs above and below the balance. There are two rollers on the balance staff at levels corresponding to those on the fork, and note the passing hollow in a safety roller on the staff and the gold dart at the extremity of the lever. The escapement comes from a watch in a gold consular case with the casemaker's mark R.P., the enamel dial is the 'regulator' type similar to Emery's (see Plate 79) and Pendleton's (see Plate 90). It has gold beetle and poker hands and steel seconds hand, and the movement top plate is signed 'Grant, Fleet Street', with the number 1408. The original owner of this watch was Dr. John Ridout who died in Sherborne in 1823.

Grant became Freeman of the Clockmakers' Company in 1781, having been apprenticed to his uncle Alexander Cumming. He died in 1810 and was succeeded by his son, also John.

unnecessary from about 1806 by his son John Roger. The spring detent is according to Arnold's patent number 1328 which he took out in 1782. Arnold's spring detent is immediately recognisable, as it is fixed in a slot cut into the top plate while Earnshaw's is fixed between the plates, but there are other significant differences in design detail. A principle problem with Arnold's arrangement is that the transmission of power between the escape wheel and impulse pallet is associated with a considerable amount of friction. If these are then oiled in order to overcome the problem, the rate of the chronometer will be subject to deterioration as in time the oil both deteriorates and spreads. It will be noted that this pocket chronometer is no larger than contemporary watches with duplex or cylinder escapements. The gold case with the long pendant, enamel dial and beetle and poker hands, being a typical pocket watch style of the last decade of the 18th century, might indicate that Arnold was content that his machines could now be worn in the pocket and put to every day use. See also colour plate 4. (50mm. diam.)

Plate 81
John Arnold & Son, London,
hallmarked 1791

By 1791 Arnold had made considerable progress in the development of his form of pocket chronometer and indeed he made no significant changes for the remainder of his life. This is apparently the first surviving example with his sixth form of balance, known as the Z balance that with a few exceptions became the standard form used by Arnold, and after his death his son, and is seen in watches as late as 1818. The movement is numbered $\frac{405}{704}$. To avoid rust due to moisture, Arnold conceived the idea of using a gold alloy for his balance springs, probably around 1779, but in any event it was the standard type in use by 1784. These gold springs were finally abandoned as

Plate 82
Robin à Paris, circa 1790

The translucent blue enamel back of this gold watch is illustrated on colour plate 5. The numerals and minute markings of the dial are quite individual but the slim movement is typical of the full plate Continental verges made shortly before the turn of the eighteenth century. The white spinel set hands, bezel and long pendant and bow are normal. There were two makers of this name, both eminent clockmakers to French sovereigns. (48mm. diam.)

Plate 83
French, anonymous, circa 1792

The leaders of the French Revolution introduced the decimal system and the Republican calendar and endeavoured to popularise the ten hour day; the maker of this watch played safe by including a subsidiary twelve hour dial. The upper subsidiary dial shows the month divided into thirty equal parts, while the main dial divides the day into ten hours with 100 minutes to the hour. This system needless to say was very soon abandoned. The silver case is of the consular type, the inner dome being engraved with the French national cock, cannon and cannon balls and tricolour, while the palm tree may hint at Napoleon's Egyptian campaign. The verge movement is unsigned, and it can be wound either through the dial or through the inner back. Both the front and back bezels are hinged. Note that the design of the chapters and moon hands, although a poor relation, are not dissimilar from those which were used extensively by A.L. Breguet. (55mm. diam.)

Plate 84
Ferdinand Berthoud, Paris, late 18th century

This watch has what could be described as a 'regulator' dial. There are a good many variations, but the intention presumably was to make for easier reading of the minute and second hand. With this particular watch, however, the minutes are no easier to read, although the layout does allow the date and seconds rings to be very legible. The back of the watch is decorated with military emblems of vari-coloured gold, while the movement is a normal Continental verge of the period. (65mm. diam.)

Plate 85
Vaucher Frères, Geneva, late 18th century

A rare type of watch known as *bras en l'air*. On depressing the pendant, the hour hand rises from its 'neutral' position — i.e. where the lower twelve is shown on the dial — to indicate the actual hour. Similarly, the minute hand rises from the same neutral position to indicate the minutes shown on the left half of the dial. The name derives from those where a figure is shown on the dial, one arm representing the hour hand and the other arm the minute hand, these rising 'in the air' to indicate the time. It may seem a rather pointless arrangement, but how often does the merely odd engage the collector! The two snails which govern the distance the two racks can travel, and thus the position taken by the hands, can be seen left and right of lower centre in the movement photograph. The verge movement is otherwise normal for the period as is also the silver case. (57mm. diam.)

Plate 86
Ralph Gout, London, circa 1790

It is quite common to find the movement of watches made
for the Turkish Market signed in Turkish with the dial signed
in English. This movement is from a gilt metal, triple cased
watch with a verge escapement and an asymmetric design to
the cock with crescent moon at the neck. Gout was declared
bankrupt in 1796: a fact that might serve to indicate the
vagaries of exporting to a market that becomes unstable.

Plate 87
George Charle, London, hallmarked 1794

This watch is typical of the large and flat silver and tortoiseshell triple-cased Turkish market watches most popular with collectors; the champlevé dial is uncommon and an added attraction. The verge movement is signed 'Geo. Charle, London' and is numbered 18867. Note the continued use of beetle and poker hands, although their shape is somewhat different to those earlier in the century; the body of the poker hand being less thick and the taper not so accentuated after the first cross. The beetle wings of the hour hand are more open and turned forward and the wedged shaped head is more pronounced. (69mm. diam.)

Plate 88
Isaac Rogers, London, hallmarked 1795

Made for export to Turkey in large numbers, this verge watch has as they normally have three or 'triple' cases; an outer case of tortoiseshell with silver piqué, a middle containing the maker's watchpaper and an inner, also of silver. The bezels of the outer two cases are faceted. Frequently all three cases are in gilt metal and not silver. Broadly speaking there are three basic shapes: the small and deep, the small and slim and the large and slim variety, the last being most popular with collectors

and of which this is an example. The movement, Turkish numeral dial, beetle and poker hands are standard. Quite often they are found in near mint condition, so presumably they were considered more as treasures than timepieces by their original Islamic owners, while it is also probable that some never left this country. Sometimes they are found with a different name on the dial to that on the movement and it is most likely the same workshop produced for several makers; sometimes possibly bankrupt stock of one maker was used by another. A fourth outer case of Islamic origin is sometimes fitted. (69mm. diam.)

Plate 89
Pierre Gregson, Paris, circa 1790

Of English origin, Gregson is recorded as reaching some eminence in Paris. During the closing years of the century dials, significantly different in design to those adhered to for much of the century, were introduced, and the French in particular evolved a wide variety. Until moon hands were established at the turn of the century the French were most fond of variations of the elaborate 'Louis' type. This watch, however, has gold beetle and poker hands which were a distinctly English fashion. The movement has a going barrel with a rare virgule escapement (see Glossary) found in a few quality continental watches. It is so similar to the work of J.A. Lepine that it may have been largely made in his workshop. The gold case has an enamel back of fine quality, which is illustrated on colour plate 7. The centre is of white opaque enamel and the surrounding translucent pale blue enamel is over a beautifully engine turned or 'guilloche' ground. A deep royal blue was more popular, particularly in the 19th century, although much of the effect of the engine turned background is then lost. This watch also possesses a glazed outer protecting case, which many decorative continental watches of this period have subsequently lost. (53mm. diam.)

155

Plate 90
Richard Pendleton, London, hallmarked 1797

This watch has a straight line lever escapement and is with divided lift, but without draw. The steel escape wheel has slotted teeth the balance has a 'double S' compensation and its staff passes through the circular tail at the extremity of the lever in which gold upright pins are set, but which are not visible in the photograph. The impulse action takes place on the side opposite the lever and the impulse piece is jewelled and is on the balance staff. A passing slot is cut in the roller and the dart or safety finger can be seen in the tail. The movement top plate is signed 'Rich(ard) Pendleton, London' with the number 175. Note that the bridge balance cock is similar to Emery's, an example of which is illustrated in this book. The case is of silver gilt and the casemaker's mark is V.W.

Pendleton is generally considered to have made Emery's lever watches, and it is interesting that the case is hallmarked for the year in which Emery died. Although of course there may be other survivors, only two or three watches by Pendleton with lever escapements are known. He probably decided to concentrate on the marine timekeepers with detent escapements that he was making in collaboration with Thomas Mudge junior and others at this time. He was known to have been working from about 1780 until his death in 1808. (61mm. diam.)

Plate 91
Richard Cole, Ipswich
hallmarked 1798

This watch has an early example of, a hunter case and 'Regency' pendant. The verge movement is normal. It is signed 'Rich(ard) Cole, Butter Market, Ipswich', and bears the number 1068. A lever operating a stop start mechanism on the balance is visible on the edge of the movement in the photograph. Cole, who was the son of a local miller, was apprenticed to John Wontner in London in 1785. He is known to have sold watches by other makers including his Master's second grade products that were signed Rentnow (Wontner spelt backwards). He also made two grades on his own account, the second one signed Eloc. (58mm. diam.)

Plate 92
Richard Cole Watchpaper

Cole moved his address in Ipswich from the Butter Market to Cornhill in about 1799 and this paper is from about this date. The local jail is behind a somewhat dwarfed figure of Father Time on the left and the market cross is on the right with the estuary beyond. Cole's son, also Richard, was apprenticed to him in 1823, and it was he who, together with Joseph Usher, set up the well known firm of watch and chronometer makers Usher and Cole in London in 1861.

Plate 93
English painted horn, circa 1800

The rustic simplicity of the outer case of this watch is not without character. Topically the 'redcoat' appears to have a French peasant well within range. The movement is contemporary but does not belong to the gilt metal paircase. It is Genevan (Ls De Lacorbiere & Compe) and wound through the dial, while the inner case back has a hole for the same purpose. (48mm. diam.)

Plate 94
Ralph Gout, circa 1800

Gout patented this watch with a pedometer and saddle case in 1799, the patent number being 2351. The verge movement is signed, 'By the King's Letters Patent No. 49, Ralph Gout London'. The upper dial gives hours and minutes and the large central hand the seconds. The three subsidiary dials in the lower portion record the number of paces; that on the right registering up to ten; the middle up to one hundred and that on the left up to one thousand. The stem passing through the pendant and bow is linked to the hook on the upper part of the saddle case by a cord (shown lacking). The motion of the horse causes the watch and outer case to jerk up and down and the stem moves on the pace recorder through a ratchet system. Ralph Gout was declared bankrupt in 1796, but was obviously back in business by 1799. He presumably considered that the verge escapement was well able to stand up to a cross country chase! (220mm. long.)

Plate 95
'Breguet à Paris', circa 1800

From the style of the dial and case this watch cannot be dated any earlier than about 1800 and by this time Breguet no longer used 'à Paris' with his signature. Indeed this watch cannot be regarded as being of 'Breguet' quality, but it is very interesting nevertheless. Jean Pouzait (1743-1793) invented its rather unsatisfactory form of the lever escapement in about 1786. It has divided lift which was first introduced by Pouzait but the safety action can be troublesome. Moreover it has a very large slow beating balance, the inertia of which is easily upset. It is of gilt brass with four arms. The full plate movement has a three wheel train with a fusee and chain and an escape wheel planted in the centre of the movement with thirty teeth standing up from its plane. The notch of the lever is clearly visible in the photograph and on the upper prong or exit side the safety pin is located. This pin acts on

the outside edge of the safety ring mounted on the balance in one direction and passes through a slot in it, and acts on the inside edge in the other direction. The steel impulse pin is also mounted on the balance and this plays within the lever notch. The balance staff has a steel end piece, and there is no jewelling. The silver single case has a reeded band with the casemaker's mark $\frac{CH}{G}$ and is numbered 18361. Pouzait was certainly an interesting maker and is thought to have worked for Breguet. (60mm. diam.)

The helical balance spring and bimetallic balance with wedge-shaped weights are typical of Earnshaw's work at this date. In varying temperatures the bimetallic rims of the balance having free ends move the weights to and from the balance axis, thus increasing or decreasing the moment of inertia of the balance sufficiently to compensate for the effects of heat and cold upon both the balance spring and the balance itself. The weights can be moved around the rims so that their effect can be altered. Two timing screws are provided, one at each end of the balance arms, which moved outwards, tend to make the watch lose. Also typical is the engraving on the movement and like Arnold's chronometers includes the claim 'Invt. et Fecit': he was adamant that he had invented the detent escapement. (59mm. diam.)

Plate 96
Thomas Earnshaw, London,
hallmarked 1801

Collectors will probably always attach greater value to a watch by John Arnold than a contemporary one by Earnshaw, but if Earnshaw worked in his shadow, it is not to say that the watches are not of considerable excellence. This gold watch numbered 626 is characteristic of his work, while the style of the case and dial (see colour plate 6) are classic English workmanship of the period. The movement has Earnshaw's form of spring detent escapement and this is illustrated in detail in the Glossary. There was considerable acrimony between Arnold and Earnshaw as to the question of who invented the spring detent escapement, although there are significant differences of detail in design between the two escapements. It is now generally accepted that Arnold has the stronger claim, but it was Earnshaw's form with slight, although essential modifications, which was finally adopted as standard and is still being manufactured today.

to about 1830 with other Liverpool makers including Robert Roskell.

The style of the silver case, dial and gilt hands of this watch are typical of the last decade of the 18th century and the first couple of years of the 19th century. Note that the seconds hand revolves once round its ring every fifteen seconds. The watch is wound through the back of the inner case in the normal way. The movement is signed and numbered 2229, while the cock foot and table with diamond end stone are both solid with 'patent' engraved on the former. Note Bosley's form of regulator with the index scale engraved on the movement top plate, and the adjustable slide introduced by Litherland shortly before the turn of the century so that the depth of the rack into the pinion and the pallets into the escape wheel could be adjusted. This slide is visible on the top pate, partly obscured by the balance rim. The small arm protruding from the movement through the inner case acts on the escapement lever to stop the watch. (55mm. diam.)

Plate 97
Litherland & Co. Liverpool,
hallmarked 1802

This watch has an example of the rack lever escapement (see Glossary) that Peter Litherland patented in 1791, although an earlier escapement embodying the same principle was invented by the Abbé de Hautefeuille in 1722. The very early rack levers had 15 tooth escape wheels but very soon a 30 toothed escape wheel was fitted. Litherland died in 1804 and a return to the 15 toothed wheel was made about this date. As the century progressed 30 toothed wheels (more desirable to the collector) were used only infrequently. Litherland watches are signed in a variety of ways — up to 1800 'P. Litherland & Co', 'Peter Litherland & Co.', or just 'Litherland & Co.', thereafter up to his death the alternatives 'Litherland' and also 'Litherland, Whiteside & Co.', appeared, the latter style of signature continuing up to about 1813. Afterwards from 1816 to 1876 the firm was Litherland, Davies & Co. The rack lever was popular up

Plate 98
Breguet, Paris, sold 1st October, 1802

This is an example of one of Breguet's more expensive and larger 'montre a tact' watches. The gold case has touch pieces on its edge corresponding with the position of each hour. The platinum hand on the cover is turned until it meets with resistance at which position the time can be read in conjunction with a corresponding touch piece. This type of watch was invented by Breguet between 1796 and 1800 and continued to be made with a wide variety of detail up to about 1834. They were certainly not necessarily cheaper than repeaters but simply an alternative: the advantage is that the approximate time can be

ascertained without any repeating sound while the watch remains in the user's pocket, thus avoiding possible embarrassment with others. A more accurate reading of the time can also be made by a small silver engine turned dial visible through the back cover that has a 'secret signature'. This is less than 3mm. in length and just visible in the photograph on either side of 12 o'clock. Using a pantograph Breguet introduced his secret signature in about 1794 and it is to be found on most of his work from that date on, although it has quite often been lost from metal dials that have been cleaned. 'Secret signatures' not executed by Breguet are to be found, some of which are very well done and thus they are no guarantee of a watches authenticity. Typically this watch has a ruby cylinder escapement, 'parachute' shock proofing, a compensation curb and still retains its short gold chain and ratchet winding key that has a hand set square in its head. Breguet introduced this type of key fairly early on in his career, the purpose of which is to prevent a watch being wound in the wrong direction.

Only a few of Breguets original sales documents, which were started in 1794 have survived. From 1808 he sold watches with numbered certificates and these or their copies certainly assist in authenticating a watch. (64mm. diam.)

Plate 99
Thomas Reid, Edinburgh,
hallmarked 1804

At the end of the eighteenth century and the early years of the 19th, both the detent and lever escapements were rarely used and for all intents and purposes most British makers used the Duplex for their best watches. This watch is of no exception but it is also unusually large. The large seconds ring and bold seconds hand, combined with a balance stop mechanism used for setting the watch to the nearest second (the arm of which is visible on the top plate), emphasize that the watch was expected to keep good time. The dial is very legible, with a good early pair of gold spade hands, the hour with a 'heart' head. Spade hands first appeared in the closing years of the eighteenth century. Initially they were fine and slender with a small

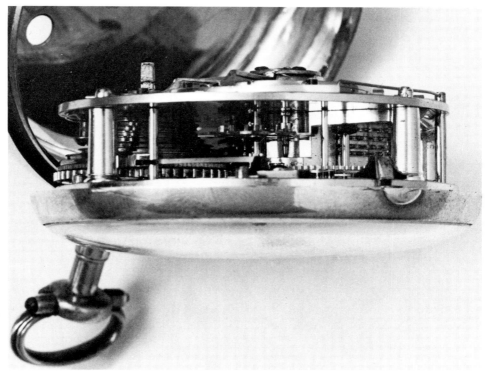

head only on the hour hand, but as the 19th century progressed both tended to become bolder and the minute hand shaped. Sometimes combined with contemporary matching dials, they are frequently found fitted to watches of a much earlier date. The escapement has a ruby roller, the three arm steel balance has timing screws with a diamond end stone and the index plate is of silver. Maintaining power is fitted so that there is no fall off of power and therefore no variation of timekeeping while the watch was being wound. Reid's work is quite often individual and he wrote a number of treatise on horology. (65mm. diam.)

Plate 100
Thomas Earnshaw, London, hallmarked 1809

Thomas Earnshaw's name is of course immediately connected with his work on the marine chronometer, but, like the Arnolds, he also made watches without detent escapements. As the 19th century progressed he made a good many box chronometers, but he also made an increasing number of pocket watches of high quality with a variety of escapements. Along with most of his contemporaries he did not consider the lever escapement at this date and the duplex was used in the best English watches for domestic use. He was rarely content to make a watch without some form of compensation and as can be seen in the photograph, this has bimetallic strips in the form of a pair of tongs. At the extremity of these tongs are

curbing pins embracing the outer coil of the balance spring, while at the other end the tongs are attached to an index. Experiments with bimetallic compensation curbs generally ceased by 1840. Earnshaw introduced the method of fusing brass and steel together for bimetallic compensation; previously they had been riveted or soldered together. The white enamel dial has arabic numerals which came into vogue from shortly before the turn of the century, although they never succeeded in becoming so popular as Roman. The figures are a little particular being placed radially from the centre of the dial. The steel moon hands were more popular on the Continent and are of course to be seen on most of Breguet's work. The heavy high quality gold single backed case (maker W.M.) has a 'Regency' pendant, while the dust cover and movement are signed 'Thomas Earnshaw, London', with the number 3155. Earnshaw, who had a long life and did not die until 1849, worked, along with a number of his contemporaries, in the Holborn area of London where there is a street named after him. (49mm. diam.)

Plate 101
Recordon, London, circa 1805

The gold engine-turned case with hinged cuvette and ribbed band has a round pendant that came into vogue shortly after the turn of the century along with the 'Regency' type. The silver dial has an engine-turned centre and outer edge, the chapters being engraved on the polished ring, and the moon hands are of steel. The overall appearance is in fact identical to

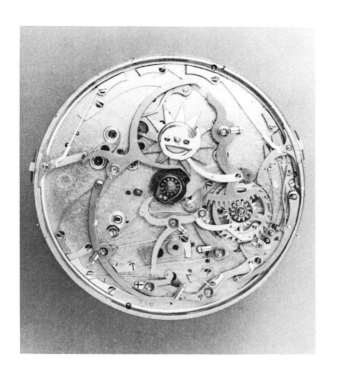

watches that were produced by A.L. Breguet at this time. This is not surprising as Louis Recordon was not only Breguet's London agent, but was also Swiss by birth and the movement also bears many characteristics of Breguet's work, and it is very certain that the ebauche if not the entire watch was imported from him. It has a ruby cylinder escapement and is a repeating clockwatch which strikes not only the hours but also the hours at the quarters (*grande sonnerie*). The striking mechanism is discharged to repeat the time to the nearest quarter by the depression of an unusual counter sunk push piece located at the top of the pendant. The solid balance has three arms, the compensation curb is according to Breguet's principle, and the dial plate is stamped 250. The entire watch is of the highest grade; ruby cylinders were only fitted to high grade watches and a *grande sonnerie* feature is unusual particularly at this date. Recordon succeeded Josiah Emery, another Swiss, and his early work is signed, 'Recordon late Emery'. Watches bearing his name can either be English or Continental in character. (57mm. diam.) (See colour plate 3).

Plate 102
Lord's Prayer watch paper, circa 1815

A wide variety of watch papers are to be found, but the very centre of this is most unusual. The Lord's Prayer has been written freehand in full and covers an area about the size of a finger nail. It is from a watch signed 'Barraud', who were a well-known family of watch makers during the 18th and 19th centuries. There would appear to be a signature below the prayer which could read E. Barraud. Elizabeth was the wife of F.J. Barraud.

Watch papers were placed between the inner and outer of pair cases to prevent them from rattling and damaging one another. From the late 18th century they often served as advertisements for both makers and repairers.

Plate 103
English, Anonymous, hallmarked 1812

This is a good example of a windmill dial. The painted scenes on these watches never seem to be quite realistic or to scale, but if they are un-damaged and well drawn, with good colouring, they are considered worth while for a generally representative collection. The sails of the windmill are mounted on an extended arbor of the contrate wheel and jerk round in a rather hesitant fashion. Sometimes the sails revolve around a marked band and indicate the seconds. The silver case has a 'Regency' pendant that was in vogue from about 1800 to 1840 and the movement is a typical English verge of the period. (56mm. diam.)

Plate 104
John Bowen, China Long Vill,
hallmarked 1813

The English verge movement is fairly normal for the period as is also the silver pair case, but note that this watch has a 'Regency' pendant, which with a few exceptions, together with the type as in Plate 101, succeeded the long pendant at the turn of the century. The painted enamel dial is typical of its type, showing 'redcoats' and a castle; a revolving disc beyond the doorway in the castle wall simulates soldiers marching past and adds to the watch's interest. This type of watch was most popular in the provinces. (55mm. diam.)

Plate 105
Robert Pennington, London, hallmarked 1815

Pennington (1780-1816), a successful chronometer maker was one of a team set up by Thomas Mudge junior to make marine timekeepers according to his father's design. He is sometimes confused with another member of the team, Richard Pendleton, but otherwise there is no reason for this except perhaps the similarity of their names. This watch was primarily made to be used as a deck watch and possesses its original box. The silver double bottom case contains a movement that bears no decoration at all and is simply signed together with the number 162 which is repeated on the swivelling brass lid of the box. The spring detent escapement is of Earnshaw's type, there is a steel helical balance spring and the two arm bimetallic balance is an early example where screws have replaced brass weights. The balance is provided with threaded holes around its circumference so that the screws can be moved backwards and forwards from the free ends. This arrangement renders it far more easy to adjust the watch for temperature compensation, as particularly on pocket chronometers it was found that weights could not be easily moved accurately and it is more important than for a marine chronometer that the balance is poised.

Pennington is credited with the introduction of the use of screws to replace weights. There are many early pocket chronometers which have had a later balance fitted: those watches made prior to about 1815 that have balances with compensation screws rather than compensation weights must be approached with some caution. (Watch 54mm. diam.)

177

Plate 106
Swiss, Anonymous, circa 1815

The escapement of this watch is an interesting variant of a Pouzait type lever, but without draw (see Glossary). The movement is a Lepine calibre with hanging going barrel and four wheel train. The large five arm gold balance has steel end pieces to its staff, and there is a start/stop whip mounted in the plate that acts on the circumference of the balance. The escape wheel, which has twelve upright pins, is steel, as is the lever. There are two upright pins mounted on the lever and the impulse piece plays between them. The safety roller is beneath the impulse piece on the balance staff. This escapement beats seconds as does the steel seconds hand. The sunburst hour and minute hands are of gold and so are the joints of the plain silver case which is stamped AD and numbered 28677. There was no necessity for this escapement to have jewels, which was a positive advantage particularly on the continent where the art of making them was not far advanced. Makers were still feeling their

way in the construction of lever escapements and apparently only a few were aware that without draw no lever escapement could be particularly accurate when a watch was used in normal wear. 'Sunburst' hands in various forms were used throughout the 19th century, generally by Swiss makers. (56mm. diam.)

Plate 107
Waight, Birmingham, hallmarked 1816

In 1814 Edward Massey took out a patent (number 3854) for both a lever escapement and a push pump winding mechanism and this watch features both. A satisfactory keyless winding mechanism had yet to be invented and a watch which could be wound without a key was of course immediately attractive. Massey's arrangement was very simple; when depressed the pendant operates a rack linked to a ratchet on the fusee arbor and when withdrawn the rack is returned by a spring. The process is then repeated until the watch is wound. The development and the application of the lever escapement in England had almost totally ceased around the turn of the 18th century and not until Massey (1772-1852) produced a form which was not only reliable but simple to construct, did it return to favour. Initially it had one significant failing and that is that not until about 1820 was draw introduced. Even then many escapements lacked draw as presumably its significance was not fully appreciated and makers were reluctant to give up the dead beat characteristics of a drawless lever. However with some slight modifications to the roller and safety action, English makers such as Waight, largely relied on Massey's form of lever escapement until the industry died out in the early 20th century. Pouzait had first used draw on the Continent in 1786, and Breguet took it up again around 1812. Apart from him, continentals were as reluctant as their London counterparts to use the lever when it was fully established in Liverpool. Certainly Savage's 'two pin' had a very meagre following in London. Few watches survive signed Massey, but he appears to have made his escapements for other Liverpool makers who at first used rack lever ébauche. The heavy engine turned case, gold spade hands, gold dial and full plate movement are typical of the period. (48mm. diam.)

Plate 108
Charles Viner, London, hallmarked 1816

Viner was responsible for two types of watches, both of which are normally found in generally representative collections. One is his alarm watch of which this is an example and the other his pull wind (see Plate 141). This watch has a nice heavy silver engine turned hunter case with a reeded band, the casemaker's mark being J.M. The matted silver dial forms a good background for the polished gold raised numerals and gold serpentine hour and minute hands. The alarm hand is also of gold and is set through the button in the pendant. The full plate verge movement numbered 350 has a solid cock, engraved 'Viner Patent' and the index on the top plate is engraved 'Royal Exchange & New Bond Street, London'. There is a flat steel balance with a sapphire endstone and a gong for sounding the alarm. Hunter cases came slowly into fashion from about 1800 and half hunters seem to have followed soon after. There are a fair number of hunters that have been converted into half hunters having had the centre portion of the front cover cut out and a glass fitted while later in the century chapter rings were added as well: these alterations are generally discernible. Heavy numerals and serpentine hands were introduced around this date, being most popular with Liverpool makers and both continued up to about 1840, but came back into vogue towards the close of the century. Viner became a member of the Clockmakers' Company in 1813 and was a Liveryman between 1819 and 1840. (54mm. diam.)

Plate 109
Samuel Smith, Coventry, hallmarked 1816

This maker's name is immediately associated with the patent number 3620 he took out in 1812 for an extraordinary form of attached lever and this watch has an example of the escapement. The five toothed escape wheel is vertical and at right angles to the lever pallets on the arbor of which there is a wheel mounted which engages with a pinion on the balance staff. The arrangement allows the balance to

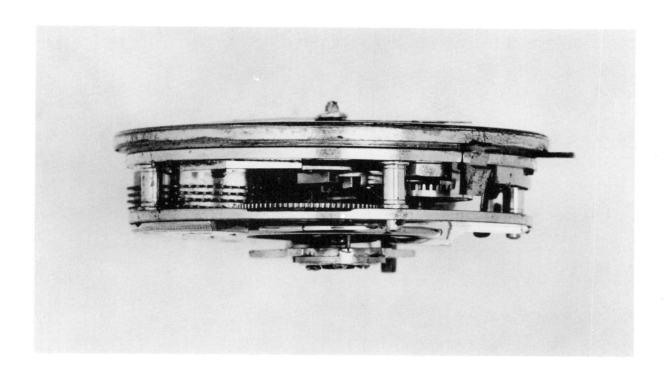

vibrate slowly in an arc of more than one turn and the watch to beat seconds. This escapement possesses a great deal of friction that could not be conducive to good timekeeping, but it must be remembered that a lever with detached characteristics was not fully appreciated while at the time a seconds beating watch was fashionable. The silver hunter case engine turned with ribbed band is well made, but the appearance of this and the standard enamel dial and spade hands give no clue to the remarkable movement: watches having 'Patent' on the dial are often of no particular note. It seems that no one else bothered to take up Smith's invention, but he continued to make these watches for some years. This example is numbered 178. (55mm. diam.)

**J.A. Lépine, Paris,
circa 1775**

The gold
case of this
enamel watch is
particularly slim and
well made for the period.
It contains a movement of
Lépine's own calibre with
a virgule escapement.
(39mm. diam.)
See also plate
70.

**Thury, Geneva,
circa 1840**

Gold
and enamel
pearl set watch
with a miniature of
Queen Victoria. It
has a keywind
cylinder move-
ment. (36mm.
diam.)

**Robin, Paris,
circa 1790**

Gold and blue
translucent enamel
watch set with white
spinels. (48mm. diam.)
The movement is a typ-
ical late 18th century
verge: the unusual
dial is shown on
plate 82.

**John Arnold, London,
case hallmarked 1781**

A move-
ment from an
early chronometer
with the maker's own
rare double 'S' balance.
(60mm. diam.)
See plate 78.

**James Ferguson Cole,
hallmarked 1821**

A silver
duplex watch of
individual character
and high quality and a
very early example of
this maker's work.
(56mm. diam.)
See also plate
116.

**Berthoud, Paris,
circa 1775**

Gold single
case with fine
enamel dial and
elaborate gold hands
typical of the period.
(40mm. diam.) See
plate 72 for the
four coloured
gold back.

**Blois Enamel Watch
Case, circa 1650**

The
most rare
and sought after
form of early painted
enamel. The religious
scenes on both the in-
side and outside of
the case are typi-
cal. (32mm.
diam.)

**George Graham,
London,
hallmarked 1718**

This
maker
continued
Tompion's number-
ing sequence and the
number of this gold pair-
cased quarter repeat-
ing watch is 445.
(49mm. diam.)
See also plate
51.

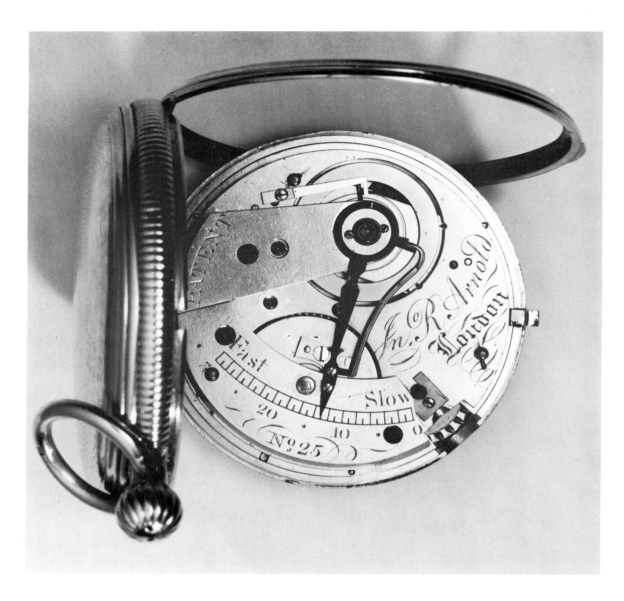

Plate 110
J.R. Arnold, London, hallmarked 1820

The first successful form of keyless winding was patented by Thomas Prest in 1820, the patent number being 4501. Prest was Arnold's foreman and was a highly skilled watchmaker who worked on many of Arnold's finest pieces. The disadvantage of this keyless mechanism is that in England the fusee was considered to be part of an accurate timekeeper and the system is only applicable to watches with going barrels. Another disadvantage is that the hands still need to be set with the key. Although not a great number were made, they were produced for a good many years by Arnold and his successors and there are examples dated from the late 1850's. This example is in a gold engine-turned case (casemaker T.H.) with ribbed band and a button of small early form. The gold matted dial with raised gold numerals is shown removed, but note the hands particularly the minute which Arnold seems to have favoured in much of his work. The escapement has a ruby cylinder with a brass escape wheel, with the plain steel balance being sunk through the top plate, with its lower

pivot in the pillar plate. Cylinders, with ruby as opposed to steel shells, were fitted to better quality work by many makers and are preferable, since they are liable to less wear and friction: they were probably introduced by Arnold senior in 1764. There is a compensation curb and large index with its scale engraved on the barrel bar. The movement is signed 'Jno. R. Arnold, London No. 25' and 'Patent' is engraved on the flat balance cock. (52mm. diam.)

Plate 111
Swiss, anonymous, circa 1820

Almost all musical watches date from the first four decades of the 19th century and they are largely Swiss in origin. A great many are unsigned and of those that are, the signature that appears on the inner dome is invariably that of the retailer rather than the actual manufacturer. Of these retailers a fair number are well known Paris 'makers'. They mostly have quarter repeating mechanisms and gold engine-turned cases with ribbed bands. The quality of both the movements and the case vary considerably and often the tone of the music is poor and the melody obscure and or indecipherable. Sadly a good number have passed through the hands of watchmakers who have caused considerable damage to mechanisms which they have not understood, and it seems that those examples of mediocre quality, because they have given the most trouble, have had the worst treatment. Often these watches have rather dull dials and possibly the most attractive are those of gold with

applied enamel numeral plaques; the taille douce engraved centre of this one is particularly unusual. Normally music pins are on a disc mounted below the music spring, but this watch has the rare feature of a pinned cylinder of the type generally found in musical boxes (the engraved cover for it is shown removed). Everything else is standard: the music plays at each hour or can be released at will by a small knib piece in the case band; there is a cylinder escapement, and the quarter repeating mechanism is operated through the pendant. (57mm. diam.)

Plate 112
Bautte et Moynier, Geneva, circa 1820

This is a slim gold and enamel watch, the back of which is illustrated in colour plate 2. The main feature however is the jump hour aperture in the silver engine turned dial. The hour which is indicated in the window at the normal 12 o'clock position changes at each hour. The movement is standard Genevan work of the period with cylinder escapement. These watches are not particularly common and did not remain in fashion long and the vogue ceased around 1840. They are quite often found with quarter repeating movements in plain gold engine turned cases. (44mm. diam.)

aperture and the regulator arm with crescent background for front regulation. The movement also incorporates one of Breguet's less practical innovations: the hour hand only flirts from one hour to the next when the full 60 minutes of that hour has passed. The 'jump hour' feature that can cause much initial confusion to the owner is found in many of Breguet's repeaters. As can be seen from the photograph, the normal hand motion work is dispensed with, the hour hand being on a wheel linked directly to another on the hour snail star wheel, the ¼ snail turning the star one tooth in the usual way. Since they are directly linked, the hand jumps at the same time as the star wheel. (44mm. diam.)

Plate 113
Breguet, Paris, 1821

Breguet was one of the earliest users of the lever escapement and by 1786 he introduced his own version which was radically different and in many ways superior to contemporary versions. It was not however until about 1812 that he angled the pallet locking faces to give draw to the lever. The lift was divided between the pallets and wheel teeth, which were also drilled for oil retention. He frequently used a counterpoised long lever arm and a double roller safety action with the smaller roller being made part of the balance staff. It is a pity from the collector's point of view that much of this most elegant escapement is placed beneath the dial. At this date Breguet used the lever escapement for all his better class watches and was producing a movement layout which also resulted in a slim and elegant timepiece. There is a single gong on which is sounded hours and quarters operated via a slide in the case band. It is interesting to note that such was the control of Breguet over the watches that were produced in his workshop, that his repeating mechanisms are never particularly melodious as he became increasingly deaf. The dial view photograph shows the gold wheel for the dial date

Plate 114
F.J. Lompeje, Vienna, circa 1820

This gold form watch is in the shape of a mandolin. The table is set with split pearls on a scarlet enamel background, while the reverse is decorated with foliage and has a musical score on a blue ground which has a hinged cover to reveal the watch dial. The movement is a verge with a bridge cock, and as seems quite frequently the case with form watches, is by a Viennese. (67mm. long.)

Plate 115
Austrian or Swiss, Anonymous, circa 1820

This gold case is in the form of a 'cello and is covered with red translucent enamel. The reverse has a musical score entwined with foliage, which opens to reveal a vignette together with a white enamel dial and a bridge cock verge movement. Watches were put in cases of various forms from the beginning of the 17th century, but they were not at all common until the second quarter of the 19th century. Musical instruments seemed to be the most popular, but it takes some perseverance to collect examples of the wide variety that were made. (72mm. long.)

Plate 116
James Ferguson Cole,
hallmarked 1821

This is a very early example of the work by a most interesting maker, who is sometimes known as the 'English Breguet'. As can be seen from the illustration, Cole (1798-1880) produced highly individual work even at the beginning of his career. The partial bridge movement has some continental influence, but the overall style is very individual. The escapement is a standard duplex but Cole used a wide variety and developed many of his own, some of which are highly impractical. The silver case is normal except that the inner dome is lipped so that it closes inside rather than outside the case flange. It is signed, as is the movement, James F. Cole, London with the code number 'dl'. The fine enamel dial is stylistically more similar to watches of the third quarter of the 18th century rather than those currently in vogue, but note the five minute markings are characteristic of his early work. The blued steel moon hands reflect Breguet's influence, but the steel seconds hand with gold central boss is very English. (56mm. diam.) See also colour plate 5.

193

Plate 117
Robert Roskell, Liverpool, hallmarked 1824

This watch can be described as a transitional three-quarter plate movement, the balance being countersunk into the top plate. The lever escapement has a Massey type 'crank' roller and has draw, while the plain gold balance has three arms and a diamond endstone. Note that the index finger is cranked to rise up onto the regulation scale engraved on the top plate. The top plate is also engraved, Robt. Roskell, Liverpool with the number 37689. The case is of silver with gold bezels, hinges, pendant and bow; a mixture that was in vogue in the early part of the 19th century and used occasionally throughout it. The movement swings out of the case once the front bezel has been opened and the dust cover is hinged with a fly catch. Robert Roskell was responsible for a large variety of watches which are signed with the address both from Liverpool and London. He worked from 1798 to 1830 and favoured vari-coloured gold dials and cases with bands of stylised floral decoration. A view of the dial is on colour plate 8. (47mm. diam.)

Plate 118
Robert Roskell, Liverpool, hallmarked 1824

Generally of small size (approximately 42mm.), these gold keywind watches were mostly made by Liverpool makers between about 1820 and 1840. The dial, principally of yellow gold, has a red, green and white gold border (see colour plate 8), while the case has bezels, pendant and bow of heavy stylised floral decoration and an engine turned back. The gold spade hands are typical, although fleur de lis, serpentine and moon styles were also used. The full plate lever movement has an early form of roller fitted, but generally speaking they are of no special interest to the collector. Lever escapements are most common but the verge, duplex and cylinder are also found.

Plate 119
Piguet et Meylan, Geneva, circa 1825

This handsome and high quality watch has the advantage of having an attractive as well as a mechanically interesting movement. The movement is partly skeletonised with blued steel plates, and nearly all the other parts are polished steel or silver. The quarter repeating mechanism is of polished steel, and is mounted on the top plate rather than behind the dial where it is normally found. The double wheel (steel) duplex escapement is rare, and this too

is clearly visible . . . how often is it that the interesting features of a watch are hidden from view! The repeating work is operated by depressing the pendant in the gold case, which is nicely engine-turned. The advantage of using the duplex escapement is that there is virtually no recoil and the sweep seconds hand is to all intents and purposes 'dead beat'. I.D. Piguet and P.S. Meylan are recorded as working in conjunction with Louis Audemars between 1811 and 1828. Audemars made *ébauches* for Breguet. (55mm. diam.) See colour plate 4.

Plate 120
David Forster, Dublin, circa 1825

This large (62mm. diameter) and rather strange movement is not of particularly good quality, but is of some interest. The maker has employed a bi-metallic compensation curb, a Debaufre-type escapement and a curiously small uncut three arm balance, from which presumably he expected an above average degree of accuracy. The straight bi-metallic compensation strip has a screw adjustment some two-thirds down its length. Brass and steel expand with temperature by different amounts and, when fused together, the free end will curve left or alternatively right, thus changing the effective length of the balance spring in curb pins at the free end. The type of escapement employed, when well made, can be really quite reliable and although invented at the beginning of the 18th century, it had a revival at Ormskirk, Lancashire in the early part of the 19th century.

Plate 121
Swiss, Anonymous, circa 1825

These quarter repeating automation watches are known as 'Jacquemarts'. When the pendant is depressed, the figures on either side of the dial *apparently* strike the bells in unison with movement gongs. 'Jacquemart' has a number of derivatives — the Latin Jaccomarchiadus implies a 'man in a suit of armour' while belfry lookouts were called 'Jacks'. The figures on this particular watch are certainly not wearing armour, but are typical of those found, although there is a large variety. Rarer than a two figure Jacquemart is the three figure variety, and this watch has a cherub beneath the 6 o'clock numeral also appearing to strike a bell. It follows immediately after the main figures when the quarters are struck and the third movement gong is provided. Some Jacquemarts have an enamel background (often blue) to the striking figures and unlike this example none of the repeating mechanism is visible. They were produced in fairly large numbers from about 1800 to 1840 and like musical watches they are often unsigned or signed by retailers. The cases are normally gold and engine turned and the movements have mostly verge escapements. (55mm. diam.)

Plate 122
A. Camerer & Co., London, hallmarked 1826

There is no reason why this watch could not be put to everyday use but both the bezel and back perimeter are set with split pearls. It would thus require delicate handling for damage to be avoided and could be described as a 'semi-decorative' watch. The case back is beautifully engine-turned with only the central portion plain. Watches with enamel backs demand even more care and indeed the collector must be wary of examples where the enamel has been so damaged that it has been totally removed. Those with translucent enamel backs invariably have engine-turned backgrounds, which can be similar to those which were never intended to be enamelled. The movement of this watch has considerable continental influence, being of the bridge type with hanging barrel. The escapement however is a right-angled English lever, with a table roller, gold balance and diamond endstone. The barrel cover is signed A. Camerer & Co., Bloomsbury with the number 1612. There are gold spade hands and a gold dial, both typical of the period. Andrew Camerer started the firm in 1788 and after a variety of partnerships it became Camerer Cuss & Co. (44mm. diam.) See colour plate 8.

Plate 123
William Cribb, London, hallmarked 1828

Joseph Berrollas took out a number of patents of which the keyless winding mechanism of this watch is number 5586 of 1827. A length of chain similar to fusee chain encircles a pulley and ratchet mechanism attached to the barrel. A cap in the head of the pendant is pulled outwards bringing the chain with it in a most alarming fashion. When released both the cap and chain are drawn back to the movement and the process is repeated until the watch is wound. This watch has a gold single case (maker J.B.), gold dial and gold waisted moon hands. It has an early example of the three-quarter plate movement lay out and is signed, Willm. Cribb, Southampton Place, Russell Square, No. 553. Continental makers were

now in general constructing bar movements but English makers were only infrequently attracted to this type of lay-out. They continued to make full plate movements for many years but slowly they took up three-quarter and half plate designs, which not only resulted in a slimmer watch, but were easier to adjust and repair. The right-angled lever is with draw, the gold balance has a table roller and a diamond endstone while the escape wheel is capped jewelled. William Cribb is recorded as working in Coventry and London from about 1816, he died in 1876. The main aim of most patentees is of course to have the invention widely used and although in this case unsuccessful, Berrollas was no exception. (48mm. diam.)

Daniel Delander, London, circa 1710

This gold, repoussé, paircased clockwatch (numbered 112) has a verge escapement, an unusual solid cock table with early diamond endstone and a gold champlevé dial of the highest quality. Note the finely engraved dust ring. (58mm. diam.) Delander was a journeyman of Thomas Tompion's and this watch certainly bears his influence.

Thomas Earnshaw, London, hallmarked 1801

This gold paircased pocket chronometer has the maker's own form of detent escapement. (59mm. diam.) See plate 96.

Sylvain Mairet, London, hallmarked 1846

This watch was made for retailers Hunt & Roskell and their name is on the dial. The male key winds the watch through a hole disclosed by a shutter in the case back and sets the hands by a square in the centre of the minute hand. Mairet was a pupil of Breguet and worked for a while in London. (42mm. diam.) See plate 140.

Allamand and Mangaar, London, circa 1765

Watches with Bilston enamel cases are unusual. Occasionally they were made as dummies and contained no movement, but this one has a typical English verge of the period. (45mm. diam.)

H. Capt., Geneva, circa 1820

A gold watch with inlaid enamel with an unusual scolloped edge to the case. It has a typical cylinder movement. (37mm. diam.)

English Anonymous, hallmarked 1835

The standard English lever movement is unsigned, but the enamel work is of good quality. Watches with matching enamel fob were mostly made between 1790 and 1840. (43mm. diam.)

Plate 124
Breguet, Paris, sold 1827

Although sold some four years after Breguet's death, this watch bears all the Master's influence in both character and quality. He initially adopted the single hand for his 'souscription' watches, as he realised that many people required only an approximation as to the time, and that with one hand a dial could be designed to be read to fairly close limits — in this case five minutes. A single hand also appealed to his desire for simple yet elegant forms. The dial centre is beautifully engine-turned setting off the gold hand to its maximum advantage. In the 12 o'clock position there is a window where the date is shown on the gold disc, while there is a further aperture below the dial centre indicating the position of the regulator and a simple plaque below this is signed Breguet. The platinum case band is ribbed while the gold engine turned back has a hole in the centre through which the male key winds the movement. The other end of the key has a smaller square which is pivoted and

can be folded into the main body and this if inserted into the hole used for winding will set the hand. The same end of the key is used for setting the date through a hole in the case band, and also regulate the watch through a hole in the back at the 6 o'clock position. Thus the watch could be wound and all the adjustments made without opening the case, and it enabled Breguet to design one which could be exceedingly difficult for the owner to open and possibly tamper with the movement. The movement is characteristic with Breguet's own form of ruby cylinder in which the cylinder (of ruby) extends beyond the bottom staff pivot, which is carried by a slender steel arm about which a cylinder may revolve. The escape wheel with triangular teeth is mounted below the dial. The top pivot of the balance staff has Breguet's parachute suspension; a shock resisting device which takes the form of a flexible spring which is looped to allow for horizontal as well as vertical movement. It is interesting to note that Breguet considered the cylinder escapement as quite satisfactory for normal purposes long after the lever escapement was established. (44mm. diam.) See colour plate 2.

Plate 125
Du Bois et Fils, hallmarked 1828

The top plate is engraved 'I.H. London', but this watch is Swiss and not of English manufacture. The case is of silver gilt with engine-turned back, ribbed band, pendant and bow, and is also probably of Swiss origin, being hallmarked on entry into England. The full plate movement has a fusee with a seconds beating debaufre type escapement. The large gilt brass balance has a staff with an integral pinion — a 'pirouette'. The contrate wheel is placed in the centre of the movement while the two parallel crown wheels of four teeth face inwards and act on a steel pallet whose arbor carries a wheel gearing with the pinion on the balance staff. The pallet arbor also carries the 'mock pendulum' showing through the window in the dial. There is a small lever in the side of the case which operates a stop that acts on the balance

and is visible in the photograph. Peter Debaufre was a member of the Clockmakers' Company between 1689 and 1722, although he originated from Paris. His escapement with slight modifications was revived at various times, particularly in the 19th century, but it has all the drawbacks associated with frictional rest escapement. Nevertheless it is an interesting and collectable arrangement. (56mm. diam.)

Plate 126
Henry Whitehead, Old Park, Salop, hallmarked 1828

The movement of this silver pair cased watch is a typical English verge of the period. The dial however has a quaint missive around the perimeter, 'Keep me clean and use me well and I to you the truth will tell'. Fleur-de-lis hands, originally a continental design, became popular with some English makers during the 19th century, and were fitted to some of the high quality watches towards the end of the century. (58mm. diam.)

Plate 127
Swiss Musical Watch, Anonymous,
circa 1830

This is typical of the gold musical watches made in fairly large numbers between about 1820 and 1840. It has a quarter repeating mechanism, cylinder escapement, and gold dial with applied enamel plaques or 'cartouches'. Gold dials are considered more desirable than those in plain enamel. The music combs are situated on the dial side of the bottom plate while the pins are set on both the top and bottom of a disc mounted below the musical mainspring. A small train of wheels terminating in a governor regulates the speed the mainspring unwinds. Recognisable tunes with a good tone are the most sought after; if the 'Marseillaise' or 'God Save the Queen' are played, so much the better. Sometimes the plate is signed beneath the combs by the tuner. The movement designs are satisfactory enough and not unduly complicated, but the quality is not particularly good and many appear to have given trouble to repairers who have not fully understood them with the result that some are to be found in deplorable condition. The gilt brass couvettes are often unsigned or signed by a retailer. The case backs are normally engine turned, but sometimes they can be so thin that, in common with some poor quality late 19th century Swiss repeaters, they can be squeezed like an oil can. In this condition they let in a considerable amount of dust and dirt and should be avoided. However a good musical watch can be a great pleasure to own and those of small calibre are rare. (55mm. diam.)

Plate 128
David Gide, Paris, circa 1830

A gold form watch in the shape of a dolphin, where the scales are enamelled in black and red. The side is hinged to reveal the dial, while the movement is a typical verge of rather ordinary quality, with a bridge cock often found in a form watch. (47mm. long.)

Plate 129
Haidar, Persia, circa 1830

Watches that were made in Persia are uncommon and very individual. The Persian numerals are engraved on the silver dial anticlockwise and the steel hands also travel anticlockwise. If this is not confusing enough one needs in order to set the alarum: (a) wind the alarum spring and rotate the alarum hand

until alarum rings (b) note the difference in time between the hour indicated by the alarum hand and the time shown (c) set alarum hand this number of hours in advance of the time at which one wants to be roused. The engraving on the dial translates 'Made in the capital; made by my master' and the maker's name is engraved on the back also in Persian. Note the unusual layout of the cylinder movement. (59mm. diam.)

Plate 130
Stor, Micallef a Malte, circa 1830

This watch is not Maltese, but is of Swiss origin. The case is of gilt metal with paste set bezels and has a typical Swiss enamel painting of the period. Swiss enamel paintings at this date were generally only of mediocre quality, although the colouring and scene depicted on this watch is quite pleasant and the condition is good. The full plate cylinder movement has the rare feature of a pedometer winding mechanism, sometimes called 'montre perpétuelle'. The mainspring is wound as the weight mounted on the top plate bounces up and down as the wearer moves. Is it generally accepted that pedometer winding watches were invented by A.L. Perrelet in about 1770 after which they were made by Breguet and others, but never in any quantity. They are of course forerunners of the automatic mechanical wrist watch. (46mm. diam.)

Plate 131
Bronikov, Russia, circa 1830

Only a limited number of pocket watches were ever made in Russia and most seem to have been made almost entirely of wood and bone. This example, with a cylinder escapement, certainly celebrates the carver's art! Russia has made no contribution to horological science, but has been responsible for commissioning some fine pieces, particularly in the 19th century. Fabergé imported his movements from Switzerland and Switzerland made watches for other Russian vendors signed to order. (45mm. diam.)

Plate 132
Robert Roskell, Liverpool, hallmarked 1832

This watch has J.A. Berrolla's rather particular form of repeating work, patent number 3174 of 1808. The button in the pendant is turned clockwise to strike the hours. This will have moved it away from the case, and on turning it back anticlockwise into the case, the quarters will be sounded. Although by 1832 there were watches that repeated either by the depressing of the pendant or by a slide in the band of the case, this watch has the very great advantage of allowing the user to govern the speed at which the time is struck. The heavy gold case with cuvette is engine-turned as is also the dial centre, the raised gold numerals being on a mat gold chapter ring. The blued steel serpentine hands are quite unusual, although quite typical of Liverpool work; so indeed is the movement, numbered 10030, which has a rack lever escapement. Robert Roskell sold a large number of watches and his company seems to have continued after his death in 1830. The quality varied a good deal although this is an example of his best work. (54mm. diam.)

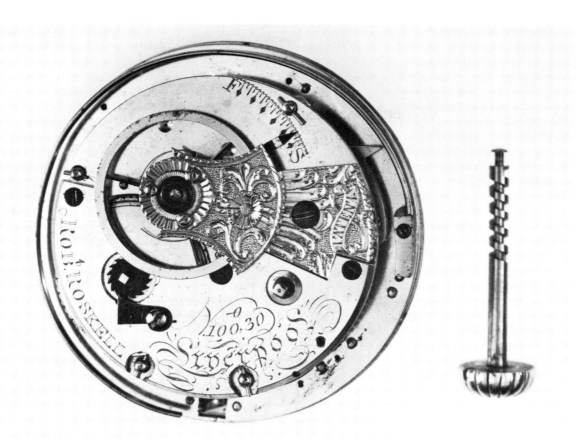

Plate 133
S. Humphreys, Tarporley, hallmarked 1834

A silver pair cased verge watch with an example of an enamel painted 'Speed the Plough' dial. English watches of this type and date are generally large and sometimes exceedingly heavy although they do not have to have country scenes painted on the dials to fall into the general category of 'Countrymen's' watches. It was certainly not a feature of horological excellence, but judging from the number of very heavy watches there must have been a market requirement for them. The movement plates can be exceedingly thick and the movement alone can weigh in excess of five ounces. We are told that country folk judged the quality of the watch by its weight and would pay for it accordingly! (60mm. diam.)

Plate 134
Swiss, Anonymous, circa 1835

This is an unusually slim and elegant example of a type of quarter repeating watch of Swiss origin which was produced in fairly larger numbers through to the third quarter of the 19th century. The cap in the pendant is pulled out and twisted half a turn and a cam is then engaged with the repeating mechanism which strikes when the cap is pushed downwards. The gold case is deeply chased and engraved on the back and the centre has inlaid floral enamel. See colour plate 8. The engraved silver dial is eccentric and has steel moon hands. The movement is typical of the period with ruby cylinder escapement but it has an added unusual feature, for instead of it being keywind, there is a lever protruding from the side of the case pivoted on a ratchet mechanism on the mainspring arbor. An up and down movement of this lever winds the mainspring, while the hands are set with the milled disc mounted in the centre which projects through the inner back cover. Some 30 years later a very similar arrangement was patented by Burdess of Coventry, an example also being illustrated in this book (see Plate 156). (45mm. diam.)

Plate 135
Robert Barrow, Farnworth, hallmarked 1839

Occasionally English makers used the club toothed lever escapement when invariably, as in this watch, they were right angled. The escape wheel is of steel, the gold balance has three arms and a diamond endstone, while the impulse roller is the type that is sometimes erroneously called a 'crank type' (Glossary). The three-quarter plate movement is signed with the maker's name, numbered 32, and engraved 'Improv'd detach'd lever'. Note the dust cover that is hinged to the side of the movement, a form which was common around the second and third quarters of the 19th century. The gold case (not shown) is characteristic of Liverpool work with a band, pendant and bow of stylised foliage in relief. The dial is gold of two colours and is also chased with stylised floral decoration. (46mm. case diam.)

which has an enamel scene illustrated on colour plate 7. It is of a lion hunt, but on some examples the hunt is of tigers, while on others there is a painting of flowers and occasionally together with doves. A few have gold cases which of course are more desirable. There are some, often in silver, without enamel backs that were manufactured after 1864 when the company ceased. The dial and hands of this watch are normal; they invariably have centre seconds hands which on those watches with 'Chinese' escapements apparently show nearly 'dead beat' seconds. (60mm. diam.)

Plate 136
Bovet, Fleurier, circa 1840

This is a type of Swiss watch made from about 1830 that is commonly known as a 'Chinese duplex'. Although quite a few remained in Europe they were made primarily for export to the Far East and as a result they are sometimes signed 'Bovet, London', when the city's trading contacts were used. Strictly speaking 'Chinese duplex' refers to the escapement, invented by C.E. Jacot, as a variation of the duplex with double locking teeth resembling a fork (see Glossary). Not all these watches have the escapement and this example has a standard duplex, but otherwise it is typical, having both plates and skeletonised movement bridges profusely engraved. The case is of silver gilt with split pearls on the bezel and bow, as well as on the perimeter of the case back

Plate 137
Bovet, Fleurier, circa 1835

An example of this maker's best work produced primarily for the oriental market. The enamel back of the gold case is illustrated in colour plate 1. The escapement is a standard duplex and the movement, although it is made entirely of steel and chrome-plated brass, has similar characteristics to the more commonly found 'Chinese duplex' watches that have profusely engraved gilt brass plates. The cap in the 'Regency' pendant operates a fly spring releasing the inner dome. William Ibury and his son who satisfied the same market, had addresses in London and Fleurier, but later also set up in Canton. (60mm. diam.)

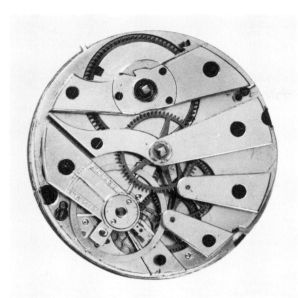

Plate 138
Anonymous Geneva movement, circa 1840

This flat 'bar' movement with going barrel and cylinder escapement is largely machine made. There are no other jewels besides the ruby end stone, while the dial plate is counter sunk to reduce depth. These were produced in large quantities in various sizes. One cannot visualise that they were ever intended to be very accurate timepieces and certainly today, unless they have had very little use, they are not at all popular with watch makers and are mostly totally unreliable. The case and dial are however in good condition and the design of the engraving is pleasant and well executed. (40mm. diam.)

Plate 139
S. & A. Meylan, Geneva, circa 1840

The second quarter of the 19th century threw up some rather obscure and quite scarce keyless winding mechanisms; this is a particularly complicated example. The flat cap in the pendant pulls the rack bar that is engaged directly with a disc mounted on the mainspring arbor with ratchet teeth cut into a portion of it. This winds the mainspring through a click system. The cap is returned into the pendant by means of a short linked chain which passes round a pulley and a subsidiary spring barrel, (clearly seen between the balance cock and pendant in the photograph) that is wound when the cap is pulled out. Unlike Viner's system and others a key is not required to set the hands, the cap when turned rotating them when a sliding knib piece in the case band is operated to engage the motion work. The club toothed lever escapement is well finished and the balance is cut and bimetallic. The lever arm is unusually long and is counterpoised in a manner used by Breguet and frequently found in Genevan work of this period and later although by this date it had been found that the design in practice had no significant advantage, except perhaps to make the escapement more attractive. As can be seen from the photograph an arm extends from the centre of the lever above and between the pallets over the escape wheel with open 'butterfly wings' at its extremity. The gold back is engine turned while the white enamel dial has thin roman numerals and moon hands, characteristic of the somewhat weak design of much of Swiss work of the last three quarters of the 19th century. (44mm. diam.)

Plate 140
Hunt and Roskell (Sylvain Mairet) London, hallmarked 1846

This is an exceptionally elegant watch to which no illustration can do real justice. The bottom plate is numbered 277 and is stamped with the initials of Sylvain Mairet, a Swiss watchmaker and a pupil of Breguet who lived in London for about five years and who worked for Vulliamy and Hunt and Roskell. At the top of the gold engine turned dial there is a gold disc in an aperture showing the hours against a fixed steel hand, while the subsidiary dial to the left of the centre indicates the minutes and that to the right the seconds. The temperature (fahrenheit) is indicated in the lower segment and to the right of this there is a regulator index with Hunt and Roskell's signature in a corresponding segment to the left. The movement has Mairet's special form of lever escapement that has pointed pallets with all the lift on the escape wheel teeth in which there are channels for oil retention. The notches for the lever fork are lined in gold and the balance is bimetallic. Note the almost semi-circular groove cut into the plate beneath the dial which contains the bimetallic curb which together with a rack, pinion and coiled spring affects the fahrenheit dial temperature indication. The movement is remarkably flat, being only 4mm. in depth and the entire watch is therefore exceedingly slim. To help to this end there is a male key (see colour plate 6) for the watch to be wound through the back of the gold case and the hands are also set with it by a square through the centre of the minute hand. The highly unusual fixed pendant is characteristic of Sylvain Mairet's work, the bow having secret joints some 2mm. on either side of the pendant enabling it to swivel at right angles to the case.

There are a few other watches by Mairet which appear at first glance to be similar, but although of good quality they have simple movements with cylinder escapements, and are not of the same degree of excellence. This watch formerly belonged to Mairet's descendant the late Philip Mairet. (42mm. diam.)

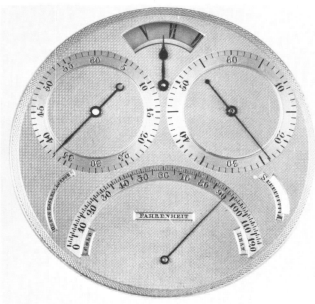

Plate 141
Charles Viner, hallmarked 1848

Of the wide variety of keyless watches other than those with a rotating winding button, Viner's pull wind watch is the most numerous. The flat cap set in the pendant winds when it is pulled outwards, and it has to be pushed back manually. The hands are set from the back with a key on the square extension of the centre wheel arbor. The movements have going barrels with Genevan stop work, they have diamond endstones, are jewelled to the third wheel and the escapements are generally duplex. The movements are signed in a variety of ways, this being signed on the barrel cover 'ChaS. Viner, 82 Old Broad Street, Royal Exchange' and the number 5011 is on the foot of the balance cock and London engraved on the dial plate. They are slim and this watch has a gold single case with an engine turned back. It has a gold dial with an engraved centre and a subsidiary seconds dial in the 3 o'clock position, but the moon hands are of steel. See colour plate 8. They more frequently have enamel dials which are very thin and often cracked in consequence. The Genevan stopwork, which is clearly visible on the top of the barrel cover consists of a six sided star, in the form of a Maltese Cross, the end of one arm being convex while the remainder are concave. On the barrel arbor there is a disc with a finger in the form of a tooth set in it, shaped so that as the watch is wound, this flirts each star until the convex arm butts. The use of Genevan stopwork adds weight to the general impression that this watch is at least in part of Swiss origin. Charles Viner was apprenticed in 1802 and was a Liveryman in the Clockmakers' Company and is recorded as working up to 1840. The company continued after his death. (47mm. diam.)

Plate 142
Anonymous, Swiss, circa 1850

Fine line engraving known as *taille-douce* was used occasionally on the cases of 19th century watches normally of Swiss origin. Although more frequently found on dials, it is on both the front and back covers of this gold hunter. When one considers the large amount of garish enamel work emanating from Switzerland during the last half of the 19th century, it is possibly surprising that *taille-douce* engravings are nearly always in good taste. The movement of this watch is of no great consequence and is a typical 'bar' type with a club tooth escapement. (46mm. diam.)

Plate 143
Litherland, Davies and Co., Liverpool, circa 1850

In 1849 John Hartnup designed the balance to be used in conjunction with detent escapements and it was considered for a few years mostly by Liverpool makers. Otherwise this movement is standard. The top plate has a fractional number $\frac{137}{4352}$. Although Hartnup's balance has some theoretical advantages, it was not widely used and then mainly on marine chronometers: they are rarely found on watches.

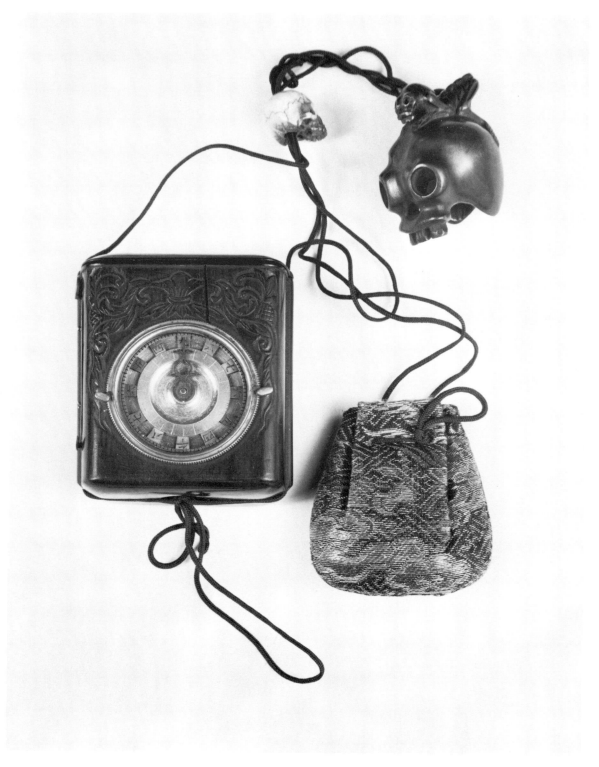

Plate 144
Japanese, circa 1850

Japan produced a number of verge watches during the middle part of the 19th century, the movements of which are rather crude compared to European watches of this date. The wooden cases are well carved and this watch has a pouch and skull netsuke (pronounced

neski) en suite. The Japanese method of telling the time originated from China and was based on the natural day which commenced at dusk. The period from dusk to dawn was divided into six equal divisions and similarly from dawn to dusk. Of course the length of each period varied depending on the time of year, so the hour plaques are made so that they can be moved accordingly. The fusee movement is circular with plates at each end and the top plate has a bridge cock for the horizontally mounted balance. (62mm. long.)

Plate 145
J.R. Arnold, Chas. Frodsham, London, hallmarked 1851

Experiments were not at an end by the mid-19th century and the set form of English lever did not crystallize until a little later, but nevertheless the escapement of this watch is unusual having the lift divided between the pallets and escape wheel. The three-quarter plate movement with a going barrel is signed 'J.R. Arnold. Chas Frodsham, 84 Strand London' and numbered 7172. The winding mechanism is a late example of Prest's keyless work; the white enamel dial has gold spade hands that need to be set with a key. The gold case is engine turned with a ribbed band. The partnership between John Roger Arnold and Dent lasted for ten years up to 1840, while on Arnold's death in 1843 the business was taken over by Charles Frodsham. Many collectors like a watch that can be used in daily wear and that is also sufficiently unusual to be a collector's item — this is an example. (46mm. diam.)

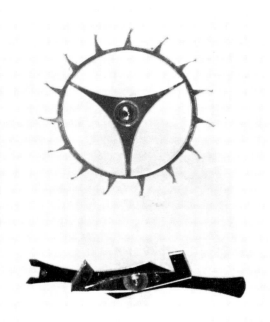

Plate 146
Thomas Yates, Preston, hallmarked 1851

Many watch collectors have an obscure attraction to interesting movements hidden by very unprepossessing exteriors. Yates might have had them in mind when he took out patent number 11443 in November 1846. This provides for a half second dead beat English lever with a balance vibrating at a very slow rate. Most watches before the last quarter of the 19th century have wheel trains and escapements designed so that the balance beats 14,400 times per hour. Yates decided that this was not necessarily conducive to good timekeeping and designed a 7,200 train with radically altered gear ratios and a heavy balance. Most examples appear to have plain balances, but this one is bi-metallic with large gold screws. The full plate movement with 'Liverpool' jewels is numbered 1742 and the cock is engraved 'patent'. The gold case is engine turned and the white enamel dial has spade hands and a dead beat sweep seconds hand. Having no draw the escapement can easily be affected by shocks. The arrangement for everyday wear could never have been particularly satisfactory, but the very high standard of finish and overall interest of the movement is quite enough to satisfy a collector. (45mm. diam.)

Plate 147
Dennison Howard & Davis, American, circa 1855

This watch, part of a series numbered from 1001 to 5000, is an example of the first practical model produced by this partnership and was made while it was trading under the name of the Boston Watch Company at Waltham, Massachusetts. As can be seen from the photograph, it bears a general resemblance to English watchmaking of some years earlier. The button in the pendant is simply for opening the hunter case and the going barrel is key wound. It has a lever escapement and although some have compensated balances this has a plain one fitted. The dial is white enamel with Roman figures and there are spade hands. The watches the company was producing owed much to Aaron Dennison's influence, and were not to Edward Howard's liking: in 1857 he left to set up his own company. However they certainly represent the first successful American watches produced in any quantity. (18 size — 44.86mm. movement diam.)

Plate 149
E. Howard & Co., American, circa 1859-60

Plate 148
Appleton, Tracy & Co., American, circa 1858

The Boston Watch Company failed in 1857 and for a couple of months its watchmaking assets were owned by Tracy Baker & Co. which then became Appleton Tracy & Co. The watches were produced in various grades, but they bear much resemblance to those produced by the original partnership of Dennison Howard & Davis, in the same factory at Waltham, Massachusetts. The full plate keywind movement has a lever escapement and plain uncompensated balance. It is a hunter which is opened with the depression of the pendant button. The white enamel Roman figured dial has blued spade hands. (18 size — 44.86mm. movement diam.)

Edward Howard, disenchanted with his partnership with Dennison, set up his own company in 1857 and designed a watch more to his liking. This design was very advanced and the overall quality better than other contemporary American watches that were produced in any quantity. The elliptical shape to the gap in the split top plate is one of three varieties to be found in early Howard watches. The other two are straight gaps — one broad, the other very narrow. This keywind watch possesses a mainspring arrangement patented by George Reed in 1857 that did away with the lower portion of the barrel, the spring simply resting in a recess in the pillar plate. Although maintaining power needs to be incorporated, it has the advantage that, when the mainspring breaks, the teeth in the wheel train are not damaged, since the pillar plate receives the shock. The club toothed lever escapement, with single roller and the split compensated balance, is well finished. (18 size — 44.86mm. movement diam.)

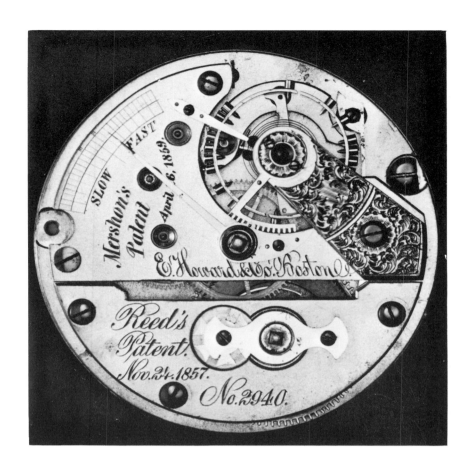

Plate 150
E. Howard & Co., Boston, circa 1862

This high grade lever movement, with bimetallic balance, incorporates Mershon's patent regulator. This ingenious regulator, devised by a jeweller in Ohio, was fitted by him to various imported watches, but also incorporated by Howard on his own. There is a rack fitted to what would normally be the index, which is linked to a regulator arm, that is pivoted around the central hand setting lever, with the result that considerable movement of the arm along an index will produce only a slight movement of the rack and the watch could thus be regulated closely with considerable ease. Examples of this form of regulation are highly sought after by American collectors. The movement also incorporates Reed's mainspring arrangement. (18 size — 44.86mm. movement diam.)

Plate 151
Tremont Watch Company, Boston, circa 1865

Aaron Dennison was the principal force behind the Tremont Watch Company which was set up in 1864. At Waltham Massachusetts he had had great difficulty in making every part of the watch and, unlike Edward Howard, he began assembling watches using Swiss parts. There were no significant design changes and the movements were keywound with going barrel, lever escapement and a cut bimetallic balance and can be compared to plate 148. In 1866 the company's name changed to Melrose Watch Company, but Dennison left in the same year and the company failed in 1868. (18 size — 44.86mm. movement diam.)

Plate 152
E. Howard & Co., Boston, circa 1865

Howard found that, although satisfactory, the layout of his early model incorporating Reed's and Mershon's patents was unnecessarily complicated. This simplified example was very popular during the 1860s in spite of the fact that, with Reed's barrel, no keyless winding mechanism could be fitted. It was not until 1868 that Howard patented a barrel which he incorporated with J.H. Gerry's stem wind arrangement: movements incorporating Reed's barrel were discontinued in 1871. (45mm. movement diam.)

Plate 153
Charles Fasoldt, Albany, New York, circa 1865

Fasoldt was born in Germany in 1818 and moved to New York in 1849, where he soon began making a small number of highly individual watches. In 1861 he set up a small factory in Albany and continued making a small quantity of high grade watches until about 1878. This watch possesses an escapement that he patented and called a chronometer, but it is in point of fact a double wheeled lever escapement. In principle this consists of a small escape wheel giving impulse in one direction and a larger wheel giving impulse in the other, with locking accomplished by a third pallet acting on the larger wheel. The micrometer regulator is in principle similar to the type used by Howard and patented by Reed in 1865, but it avoids the somewhat uncertain movement of the curb pins inherent in Reed's system. The dial, hands and gold hunter case are good, but they do not have any particular distinguishing features. However Fasoldt's movements were far and away superior in design, quality and finish to their American contemporaries, and together with those of Albert Potter, which are mostly somewhat later, they demand today the highest respect on an international scale.

**Pierre Gregson, Paris,
circa 1790**

Gold and translucent blue enamel, the movement with going barrel and virgule escapement (see Glossary). The virgule escapement was only used on high quality watches by the more eminent French makers of the period. (53mm. diam.) See also plate 89.

**Justin Vulliamy, London,
circa 1780**

The inner gold case and white enamel dial with diamond set hands belong to the outer paircase shown below. This watch has a typical Vulliamy movement with a cylinder escapement which is numbered "uon". (45mm. diam. including outer case.)

Outer Case, circa 1780

This outer paircase belongs to the watch by Justin Vulliamy above. It bears an enamel of the Prince of Wales cypher, Vulliamy having inherited the Royal Patronage from his father-in-law and partner Benjamin Grey. (45mm. diam.)

**Joan Dellavos, Prague,
circa 1750**

The enamel painting is of Venus blindfolding Cupid. The case is of gold, the verge movement is normal, but see also plate 61. (44mm. diam.)

**Thomas Tompion,
hallmarked 1708**

Gold quarter repeating watch of the highest quality, numbered 350. Tompion had a separate number series for his repeating watches. (56mm. diam.) See also plate 49.

**Vaucher, Paris,
circa 1780**

The gold case has an enamel portrait, possibly of Princess de Lamballe, surrounded by garnets and zircons. (43mm. diam.) See also plate 74.

**Bovet, Fleurier,
circa 1840**

The enamel scene is on silver gilt with split pearls. Primarily made for Eastern markets. (60mm. diam.) See plate 136.

Plate 154
Dent, London, hallmarked 1867

The firm of Dent, started by E.J. Dent (1790-1853), sold many high grade watches throughout the Victorian era. In 1830 Dent went into partnership with John Roger Arnold and ten years later, shortly before Arnold's death, he started up on his own. This watch has the quite unusual combination of a repeating mechanism with a spring detent escapement. The movement is illustrated in colour plate 4, while the case and dial are illustrated in colour plate 8. Note the helical balance spring, the diamond endstone and the bimetallic

balance as well as the keyless mechanism. The winding mechanism is engaged when the push piece in the case band between 1 and 2 o'clock is depressed; a small knib piece at 12 o'clock engages the hand set mechanism but only when the hunter cover is open. The half/quarter repeating mechanism is operated by a slide also in the band. The white enamel dial and spade hands are normal. It has only been in the fairly recent past that watches such as this have been fully appreciated by collectors, although no doubt watchmakers have admired them very much longer. There are more complicated examples of English work at this period, but it is of a standard that is rarely surpassed. (54mm. diam.)

Plate 155
Louis Frederic Lebet, Swiss, circa 1880

Even during the second half of the 19th century there were still interesting attempts made to have a watch wound other than by a stem winding button. This gold watch indeed could be regarded as automatic in so far as the action of the hunter cover opening and closing winds the mainspring. The principle was patented in 1873 by Haas, and Lebet presumably considered it practical, although it must also have had attractions as a novelty.

The hands are set by a small button in the side of the case that is revealed when a slide is moved. The movement is typical of high grade Swiss work of the period; note all pivot holes in train are jewelled. The balance is bimetallic and the escapement is a Swiss club tooth lever and the movement is engraved with two medals of the Paris Exhibition of 1867. Swiss makers tended to favour slender moon hands at this time, while their English counterparts preferred the spade variety. (52mm. diam.)

Plate 156
A. Burdess, Coventry, hallmarked 1875

Adam Burdess took out patent number 2286 for the lever winding and hand setting mechanism of this watch in 1869. Keyless winding, via a rotating button in the pendant, had been established for some considerable time, but one must assume that Burdess considered that it had significant drawbacks or his arrangement had significant attractions as a gimmick: it could only have been marginally cheaper to produce. The winding lever protrudes from the edge of the movement through the inner dome of the double bottom case. It acts on the mainspring arbor with a ratchet mechanism and, when moved up and down, the mainspring is wound. To set the hands the bezel is opened and a toothed wheel protruding from the edge of the case is linked with the minute wheel for adjusting the hands. This full plate 15 jewelled movement is signed 'A. Burdess, Coventry' and is inscribed 'Patent' with the number 8524. It has a normal lever escapement with cut bimetallic balance, sapphire endstone and silver regulation scale that is screwed to the plate. Burdess used white enamel dials, spade hands and engine turned cases either in gold or more frequently in silver, with gold joints, of which this is an example. It is interesting to note that a similar winding mechanism was used on an anonymous Swiss watch that can be dated around 1835 and illustrated in this book at Plate 134. (47mm. diam. including case.)

Plate 157
Geo. Edwards & Son, hallmarked 1877

English makers still preferred to use the fusee on their better watches when their continental counterparts had generally long since disposed of it. One of the drawbacks to the fusee is that the chain can be broken more easily than a mainspring: an up and down indication on the dial of this watch shows when it is close to being fully wound. It has also an additional safety feature of a small pin protruding from the bezel at the 4 o'clock position which allows the watch to be wound only when the hunter cover is open. Watches with a fusee and an up and down of this date are often associated with a freesprung balance, but in this instance there is a normal regulator and arm. In spite of their high quality this grade of Clerkenwell watch can be found with a variety of names upon them, many of which are of no particular note. Conversely always, but particularly in the late 19th century, a vendor's reputation is no guarantee of a watch's excellence. Although rather plain in appearance many late 19th century English watches exude the feel of quality, are often very dependable even today and consequently they lend themselves admirably to everyday use. Note that the movement layout of this watch is half plate (see Glossary). (54mm. diam.)

Plate 158
Albert H. Potter & Co., Geneva, circa 1877

Potter was born in the United States in 1836 and emigrated to Switzerland in 1876, having previously made his name with a very limited number of fine watches. This watch, made soon after his arrival in Switzerland, incorporates the safety spring barrel he patented before leaving the United States in 1875 (number 168581). The first wheel in the train is mounted on the mainspring arbor and is free to turn. A small pawl, fixed to the edge of the barrel, rotates the wheel unless the mainspring breaks turning the pawl in the wrong direction. In this event the pawl is so constructed that it will then not rotate the wheel. The watch also possesses improvement on the spring detent escapement where the unlocking friction is much reduced by an unusually large active radius of the passing spring. As one would expect, the watch has bimetallic balance, helical hairspring and keyless winding. The general layout is quite individual and the finish exceptional. Potter and Charles Fosoldt are perhaps the two most outstanding American watchmakers.

Plate 159
Benedict & Burnham Manufacturing Co., Waterbury, circa 1880

D.A. Buck devised a version of the duplex escapement that was incorporated in a movement which housed the mainspring in the back of the case and which rotated the movement and the minute hand on its arbor once per hour. The dial is partially skeletonised and the chapter ring is of paper, while the case is of nickel. The watch was produced to meet the large public demand for a cheap watch and it was sold for $3.50. Such was the length of the

mainspring, that bitter complaints were heard from owners that the watch ran down quite as fast as it could be wound up! However the watch was an immediate success, the factory expanded, and there was an almost immediate change of name to the Waterbury Watch Company. It was designated series A and as improvements followed in rapid succession, W was reached after some ten years. Needless to say the long wind model was abandoned after about two years with the introduction of series E. (52mm. diam.)

Charles Viner, London, hallmarked 1848

A typical Viner pull wind watch, the gold dial with engraved centre is characteristic of the period. (47mm. diam.) See plate 141.

Robert Roskell, Liverpool, hallmarked 1824

The case of this watch is both silver and gold, the body and band being of silver. The movement is a transitional three-quarter plate with lever escapement. (47mm. diam.) See plate 117.

Hector Golay, English and Swiss, hallmarked 1902

The largely Swiss movement has been fitted with an English case, dial and hands. The watch has minute repeating, perpetual calendar, chronograph and moon phase mechanisms. (57mm. diam.) See plate 173.

Robert Roskell, Liverpool, hallmarked 1824

A full plate watch with fusee and lever escapement. Note the four coloured gold dial and decorated case, both popular with Liverpool makers. (42mm. diam.) See plate 118.

Record Watch Company, Tramelan, Switzerland, circa 1900

A silver 'sector' watch inlaid with niello. The winding button is opposite the bow. (58mm. diam.) See plate 168.

A Camerer & Co., London, hallmarked 1826

The engine turned gold case has split pearl bezels. The bridge movement has a gold balance, diamond endstone and lever escapement. (44mm. diam.) See plate 122.

Anonymous, Switzerland circa 1835

A particularly slim gold and enamel repeating watch with lever wind mechanism. (45mm. diam.) See plate 134.

Charles Frodsham, London, hallmarked 1920

A gold minute repeating watch of high quality produced at a time when the industry in England had all but passed into oblivion. (57mm. diam.) See plate 178.

Dent, London, hallmarked 1867

This watch has the quite unusual combination of a detent escapement and a half/quarter repeating mechanism. (54mm. diam.) See both colour plate 4 and plate 154.

253

less and less in watches as the 19th century came to its close, as it was found that in practice the lever escapement was easier to make, less delicate in wear, and could be made to produce results that were quite as good. Its one advantage, a more constant rate, assured its continued use in marine chronometers. (52mm. diam.)

Plate 160
K. Zimmerman, Liverpool, hallmarked 1881

This watch has a typical English late 19th century spring detent escapement with a helical balance spring, diamond endstone and bimetallic balance. There is an up and down indication below the 12 o'clock position, a feature that was fitted primarily to high grade fusee watches in order to indicate the state of wind of the mainspring. Not only was it to remind the owner that the watch needed to be wound, but it also showed him when to take care not to overwind. The subsidiary dial at the 9 o'clock position is unusual, particularly for this type of watch. This dial can be set independently of the main time of day hands and can be used for example to indicate the time in a different time zone. Note the large movement jewel and the cast stylised decorated floral case band, both features of Liverpool work. Detent escapements were used

ment sizes using the letters of the alphabet to denote them, beginning with A as one inch with steps of 1/16ths of an inch for each succeeding letter. Thus the N engraved on the plate immediately above the barrel indicates the size of 14/16ths inches. The micrometer whiplash regulator is according to Reed's patent 49154 of 1865. Fasoldt invented a somewhat similar form of regulator about the same time, the general principle of which was adopted later by many Swiss makers, including Patek Philippe, for their high class work.

Plate 161
E, Howard & Co., Boston, sold 1889

The dial, hands and case in this illustration are from a different watch from the movement, but both illustrations are typical of watches produced by Howard in the 1880s. As the case is a hunter, the keyless pendant and bow are at the 3 o'clock position. There is considerable variety of detail to the nickel plated movements produced by Howard for the collector to assimilate, and the six figure serial numbers indicate only a part of this variety. Below the serial number in the illustration, a deer is engraved, which Howard used to denote that the watch was adjusted for both temperature and position. An engraving of a horse would show that the watch was adjusted for temperature only, and a hound, that the watch was unadjusted. He produced a large number of move-

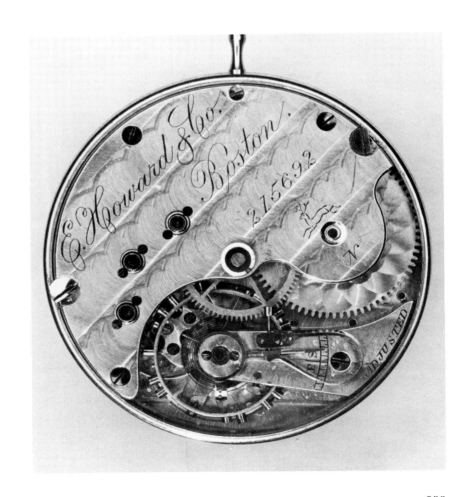

Plate 162
J.L. Audemars, Switzerland, circa 1890

This maker made approximately four of these highly complicated watches, one of which was exhibited in the Paris Exhibition of 1889. The movement with Swiss lever escapement has three mainsprings and is required to carry out a large number of complicated functions and its design, let alone its construction, could only have been carried out by someone with brilliance, skill and an amazing amount of application. It has minute repeating, *grande sonnerie* striking and split chronograph mechanisms. Below the dial 12 o'clock position

there is a rare form of fly-back date hand, which takes into account leap years (known as a perpetual calendar) with the year shown within the semi-circle. The time of day, together with the month, is indicated by the subsidiary dial to the left of the dial centre. To the right is a second pair of time and day hands (to be set independently of the first) also with day of the week indication: at 7 o'clock the phases of the moon, at 5 the age of the moon and at 6 a Reaumur temperature scale. Above this last there is a one-fifth second dead beat hand (an arrangement patented by the maker), together with normal seconds indication. Needless to say the case is of gold and the overall quality of the watch is excellent. J.L. Audemars was almost certainly one of Louis Audemars' seven sons. (59mm. diam.)

Plate 163
Swiss, circa 1899

These are known as 'mysterious' watches as the dial area is entirely of glass and the watch can be seen through. The hands are rotated by glasses driven by the movement, which is located immediately below the pendant. A Christmas competition in 1899 offered this particular watch as a prize for guessing the right number below 20,000. A Joseph Mason won out of 111,235 entries and his winning number 14,779 is crudely scratched on the plaque. These watches were only made for a fairly short time, but were produced in reasonable quantities and, as can be gathered from the competition, they must have caught the public's imagination. (52mm. diam.)

Plate 164
Usher & Cole Clerkenwell, London, hallmarked 1890

Usher & Cole finished many watches and they sold them mainly to the trade signing them to order and only occasionally does their name appear. Indeed there are some instances where third parties were involved and then the watches were numbered, but left unsigned. In common with other 'makers' they were more strictly speaking 'finishers'. The *ébauche* of this watch was made by Joseph Preston & Sons of Prescot, Lancashire, while the casemaker was Thoms and the dial maker Willis. Indeed all the other parts were 'bought in' and outside specialists did much of the finishing. However the most important aspect, that of springing, was done 'in the house'. The fusee keyless movement of this watch has a double roller lever escapement and jewelled to the centre wheel. There is an overcoil balance spring, diamond endstone and minute repeating, perpetual calendar and moon phase mechanisms. The engraved case is unusually of 22ct. gold and weighs 5.10oz. troy. The watch was expensive in 1891 and sold for £110: English perpetual calendars that have, as is usually the case, other complications are amongst the most highly sought after watches from the end of the nineteenth century. (57mm. diam.)

Plate 165
Girard Perregaux, circa 1890

This keyless watch that has a one minute tourbillon with a detent escapement is an example of Swiss workmanship at its very best. The three parallel bridges are of gold and the whole train is jewelled including the barrel, the cover of which is engraved, 'Girard Perregaux, Patented March 25th 1884'. Unlike many Swiss watches attention has also been paid to the case which is well chased and engraved, of good weight and fine construction. The makers made only a small series of these and they are highly sought after. In essence the tourbillon is an arrangement whereby the entire

escapement revolves normally once a minute, but occasionally longer, with the purpose of ironing out the effects of positional (vertical) errors. It was invented while Breguet was in Switzerland between 1793 and 1795 and was fitted by a variety of makers, both on the continent and in England since that date. Occasionally they are badly constructed and are in watches of poor quality but, otherwise the skill that was required to make them deserves our constant admiration. (58mm. diam.)

Plate 166
L. Leroy & Cie, Paris, circa 1900

This large keyless, hunter watch was entered for time trials in Besançon and it obtained the gilt award medal shown. The gold case is so well made and soundly constructed that at first glance the watch could be English. The bar movement is Swiss made and is of the highest grade with a club tooth lever escapement and jewelled to the centre wheel. Note the ratchet toothed winding. The medal is recorded as being designed by Duvivier, engraver to the Paris Mint and first struck to be a reward to meritorious students of a short lived government sponsored Paris factory between 1786 and 1789. The aphorism, 'Le temps a pris un corps et marche sous nos yeux', is a quotation from Delille. (54mm. diam.)

Plate 167
Swiss Anonymous, circa 1900

Beetle form watches can be disconsertingly lifelike, particularly as far as the underside is concerned, the legs and thorax being made to the minutest detail. The watch is of gold with red translucent enamel wings, the engine turned ground producing various shades of colour. Form watches of this type are nearly always of high quality and set with diamonds. (58mm. long.)

Plate 168
Record Watch Company, Tramelan, Switzerland, circa 1900

These 'sector' watches were made over a fairly short period, but in reasonably large quantities. At the end of each hour, the minute hand returns smartly to zero, as does the hour hand when twelve hours have elapsed. The silver case is inlaid with niello, a form of decoration which was popular at this time, while the design is of Art Nouveau character. These were no doubt intended to be novelty watches, but judging from the condition of examples to be seen, many have been well used. Niello is a black composition of lead, copper silver and sulphur which was used to decorate silver and gold work from the Middle Ages into the 20th century. (58mm. wide.) See colour plate 8.

Plate 169
A.M.T. Rosskopf, Switzerland, circa 1900

A typical example of a wide range of cast nickel chrome cases that were produced in Switzerland at the end of the 19th and the beginning of the 20th century. They depicted most commonly, trains, cars, motor cyclists and cyclists. Part of their charm is the fact that these are decidedly dated. This particular example has 'AMT Rosskopf Panthere Patent' between the tracks. The movement has a form of pin lever escapement first introduced by G.T. Roskopf in 1867; as on this occasion, his name was sometimes plagiarized. These watches are now enjoying a renewed life in so far as the Swiss are currently manufacturing almost exact copies in fairly large quantities. (50mm. diam.)

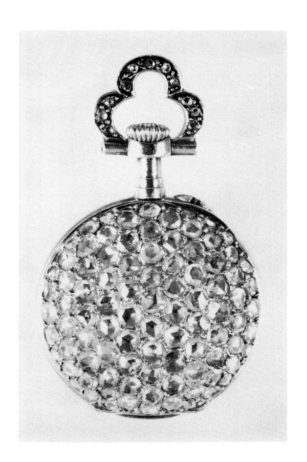

Plate 170
Swiss Anonymous, circa 1900

Watches of small lady's size are sometimes found with lapel brooches en suite. This example is of exceptionally high grade and studded with diamonds, but there are many that, even when enamelled or set with semi-precious stones, are often of rather ordinary quality. They are mostly of Swiss origin and, except for the better examples, they have cylinder escapements. This watch has a standard Genevan bar movement with a lever escapement and keyless winding mechanism. Keywind watches continued to be made at least to the turn of the century and long after the more expensive keyless winding mechanism was established. The dial of this watch is according to fashion, being slightly opaque and having arabic numerals; the 'Louis' style hands are of gold. (23mm. diam.)

Plate 171
The American Waltham Watch Co., Massachusetts, circa 1900

This 'Riverside Maximus' was made by the eventual successors to Dennison, Howard & Davis and is considered as being one of the highest grade American watches ever produced in quantity. All parts of the keyless wound 23 jewel movement are well finished, while elaborate decoration to the nickel plating is most impressive. There is a bimetallic

compensated balance, club tooth lever and micrometer regulator. The gold case, dial and hands are characteristic of both Swiss and American watches at the turn of the century, but the inclusion of bands between the minute markings together with five minute numerals, is something of a throwback to the 18th and early 19th century. A comprehensive list of collectable American watches is quite outside the scope of this book; the Waltham Companies alone produced some 34 models divided into over 360 different grades. (16 size movement — 43.18mm.)

Plate 172
Camerer Cuss & Co., London, hallmarked 1901

English as opposed to Swiss split second chronographs are not common. The two seconds hands start together when the button is depressed, one of them stopping when the side push piece in the one o'clock position is in turn depressed, the other hand continuing until the winding button is again operated. If the side push piece is then operated the 'split hand' will catch up with the main seconds hand and the two can then be returned to zero by the winding button. Below the 12 o'clock position there is a minute recording hand which flirts over one minute after every revolution of the seconds hand. The subsidiary seconds hand above 6 o'clock is independent of the stopwatch mechanism and cannot be stopped or started. The gold case has an inner dome and is marked by the casemaker, F.T. (Thoms), the 'egg shell' or off white dial was made by Willis, while the blued steel hands were made by Hood. The three-quarter plate free sprung English lever escapement has a double roller and an overcoil balance spring. There is a diamond endstone and the right-angled lever escapement has capped jewels. This watch is typical of high grade Clerkenwell work at the turn of the century and the movement plate is signed Camerer Cuss & Co., with the address 56 New Oxford Street, London and it is numbered 1902. Even in the 17th century there were high degrees of specialisation with individual parts of the watch being made by specialists. Indeed some parts were made in the rough or 'grey' by one person and passed through several hands before the component was completely finished. Records however of these specialists are sketchy, but a fair number of them are known particularly from the latter part of the 19th century. (53mm. diam.)

simple month indication. The quality of Swiss perpetual calendars vary considerably, but not as much as simple calendar watches that were frequently made to really very ordinary standards. This movement is however of a very high standard and has moreover been fitted with an English case and dial. The calendar is set through the bezel by levers at 7 and 11 o'clock positions. (57mm. diam.)

**Plate 173
Hector Golay, London,
hallmarked 1902**

The high grade movement of this watch is Swiss but the case (Thoms) and the dial (Willis) and hands are English. See colour plate 8. The lever escapement is an English type, but the regulator has a micrometer adjustment that seems to have been favoured by the Swiss in preference to freespringing, which was generally considered as the best arrangement by English makers. In addition to minute repeating, chronograph and phases of the moon mechanisms, this watch has a 'perpetual' calendar. Perpetual calendars took into account leap years and have considerably more favour with collectors than those watches which might have every other complication, but have a

Plate 174
Camerer Kuss & Co., London, hallmarked 1903

Bahne Bonnisksen (1859-1935) took out patent number 1421 in 1894 for a mechanism that revolved the escapement on a carriage with the purpose of ironing out positional errors. Called the 'karrusel' it was commercially more viable than tourbillon, required less skill to manufacture and is more robust in wear. The karrusel carriage has a wheel fixed with screws to its underside and this is normally driven off the third wheel pinion. Without this wheel the carriage would not revolve but the escapement would still be driven. This is not so with the typical tourbillion, however, as the escapement is on a carriage fixed to the fourth wheel arbor, the escape wheel pinion being driven by and revolving around the fixed fourth wheel. Most karrusel carriages revolve once

every 52½ minutes as in this watch. The *ébauche* was made by Bonniksen in Coventry which was then finished by various makers. It is signed by the vendor with the address 56 New Oxford Street, London and is engraved, 'Class "A" Kew certificate especially good', (see Glossary). The bottom plate and carriage are spotted, a finish which is more commonly found on marine chronometers. The dial, hands and case are of a high grade, the latter being marked 'F.T. (Thoms)'. Karrusels are not that rare, but they have attracted the attention of collectors whose interest in late 19th century English work has rapidly increased in recent years. (53mm. diam.)

Plate 175
Ingersoll, 'Quaker', circa 1903

The potential for a really cheap mass produced watch was at first only fully recognised by the American market. In 1891 R.H. Ingersoll and his brother C.H. Ingersoll engaged the Waterbury Company to make watches for them, and by 1896, their mail order business was selling watches for one dollar. The Swiss G.T. Roskopf had manufactured the first successful cheap watch in 1867, and he had used an escapement which was of the lever type, using pins in place of pallets and the pin pallet escapement of this watch is similar. The dial is of paper and the case of base metal while the movement is marked, 'R.H. Ingersoll and Bro. New York U.S.A. Patented' and on the outside edge 'Dec 29 90 Jan 18 91'. The Ingersoll 'Quaker' was about the fifteenth in a series of cheap watches sold and it was priced $2.50. By 1898 the

274

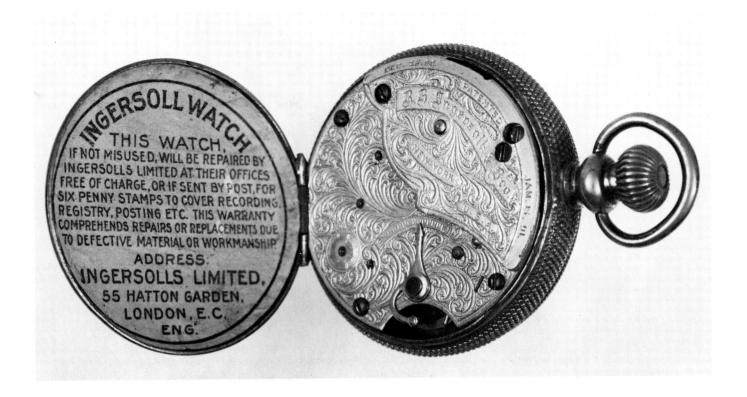

Waterbury Watch Company's name had changed to the New England Watch Company; in 1914 the Ingersoll Company absorbed it only to fail itself in 1922. The English branch of the firm however continued and is in business today. Large numbers of mass produced watches were made in both America and Switzerland, most particularly from the 1880's up to the First World War. Some were also made in Germany and France and there were also a few British attempts, including the 'John Bull' made by the Lancashire Watch Company in about 1905. There was a variety of designs, some of which were perfectly sound, while others incorporated eyecatching mechanical gimmicks which were not always conducive to reliability. Some of these watches were utterly reliable and were sincere attempts to produce a cheap and robust watch, but others were close to being fraudulent; for both financial failure was invariably the eventual result. Serious collection of such watches is in its infancy; it is largely an uncharted sea. (50mm. diam.)

Plate 176
Lancashire Watch Company, circa 1905

The 'John Bull' was a British attempt at a cheap mass produced watch to compete with those made by the Swiss and Americans. Although the watch was soundly made and of a good design, the company was in financial difficulties and the project was a failure. The dial is enamel and the movement, with pin lever and visible mainspring, bears the patriotic missive, 'British made by British labour'. (53mm. diam.)

Plate 177
Le Roy et Fils, Paris, hallmarked 1912

Up to 1900 only a very limited number of wrist watches were produced, although both before and after this date, some small 19th century lady's size pocket watches were modified with the bow removed and lugs fitted. The collection of wrist watches is centred around those which are either complicated or rare. Apart from repeaters (of which this is an example) those with calendar, moon phases and chronograph complications and early self winding mechanisms are of interest, while early electric watches also have a following. This elegant 18ct. gold double bottom cased watch has a minute repeating mechanism, club toothed lever escapement and bimetallic balance. The high grade movement was made in Switzerland where there was considerable competition to produce smaller and smaller minute repeating mechanisms between such firms as Le Coultre and the Piguets. This activity was centred in and around Le Sentier and Le Brassus in the Vallée de Joux. Repeating mechanisms vary greatly, and their history and development require a detailed study that is regrettably outside the scope of this book. However by the late 19th century the principle operating functions had become mostly standardised and the mechanism in this watch is typical. Very simply the time repeated when the slide in the case band is operated is governed by three rotating cams or 'snails' located in the centre of the movement. Racks operated by the slide drop on to that part of the snail faces that correspond to the time indicated on the dial. The movement of the slide also winds a subsidiary mainspring, and this produces the power by which, via a series of racks, the gongs on the reverse of the movement are sounded. (32mm. diam.)

Plate 178
Charles Frodsham, London, hallmarked 1920

The First War saw the real close of the English watchmaking industry, but it had long since failed to accept that degree of mechanisation or change in both design and organisation which would have made it viable. However to the last it was capable of high standards, which at least preserved some self respect. After the War there was still a residue of both unfinished and partly finished *ébauche* and small numbers were completed even into the 1930's. This minute repeater is signed by Charles Frodsham with the number 09819 together with the code AD Fmsz, which the company reserved for their better quality watches, while further engraving on the movement advertises royal patronage and the

successes of the past. Frodsham showed a new watch calibre engraved AD Fmsz in the 1851 Exhibition and it is thought that the letters in their name were taken to represent the numerals 1 to 8 consecutively with Z taken as 0, thus alluding to the date AD 1850. Generally speaking keyless hunters and half hunters tend to be more popular with collectors, but an open face watch of large proportions, with a dial and hands such as this one, must be an exception; it is certainly more practical. The proportions are quite superb. (57mm. diam.) See colour plate 8.

Plate 179
John Harwood, Swiss, hallmarked 1929

John Harwood granted his Swiss patent (106583) for a self winding wrist watch in 1924. The 15 jewelled Swiss lever movements were made in Switzerland to Harwood's design. Although he met with both mechanical and marketing problems he had considerable success and, while undoubtedly many have been thrown away, there are a fair number of surviving examples. Harwood was very interested in overcoming the problems of dirt and dust entering the watch movement through the winding and hand setting stem hole in the case. He therefore disposed of the winding button and devised an arrangement where the hands are set by rotating the bezel either forward or backward to obtain a similar motion to the hands. Having rotated the bezel in either direction, it is reversed half a turn to bring a red disc visible in the aperture in the dial to indicate that the hands are out of the hand setting position: while the hands are being set the red disc disappears. The winding weight, which is engraved 'Harwood Self-Winding Watch Co. Ltd.', is pivoted at the centre of the watch, and is provided with spring buffers which reduce the shock when it hits a block on one side of the movement, preventing rotation through 360 degrees. Unlike most modern mechanical self-winding wrist watches, the weights of which revolve a complete 360 degrees, winding is only effective in one direction. Some 14,000 were made for Harwood by Blancpain (who was succeeded by Rayville S.A.) and of these there are examples with silver cases with Arabic or Roman dials and gold cases with the same choice. These watches were preceeded by those of L. Leroy & Cie in 1922, which have oval weights covering almost the entire surface of the back, with very little movement, but enough to operate a click system in a very random fashion. (28mm. diam.)

Usher & Cole Ltd.

In 1861, Joseph Usher and Richard Wright Cole, the latter just out of his apprenticeship, decided to set up in business together as watch and chronometer manufacturers. But whereas Usher was one of the ten sons of the founder of Usher's Wiltshire Brewery, Cole was the third Richard of that name to follow the calling of watchmaker. The story of the firm of Usher and Cole might well begin, therefore, with the Coles of Ipswich, from whence they hailed.

The first Richard, grandfather of R.W. Cole, was born on 15th September, 1771, and was the son of another Richard, a miller of Shottisham, near Woodbridge, Suffolk. Richard Cole was apprenticed to John Wontner, watchmaker of the Minories, London, on 1st December, 1785, for seven years. Wontner was, according to Baillie's 'Watchmakers and Clockmakers of the World', 'a maker of repute'.

Richard Cole completed his apprenticeship at the end of 1792 when, presumably, he returned to Ipswich. The firm possesses a memorandum book of his which gives useful and interesting — and sometimes beguiling — information of the years 1793-99. The book begins with 'A list of Rich'd Cole's linen &c. on 15th day of September 1793 he being that day 22 years of Age'. See Fig. 1.

Reading on, we learn from the miscellany of receipts, payments and stock lists, not only about Richard Cole but also about what must have been a typical provincial watchmaker's stock of the period.

There are indications that young Richard was not at this time, married since he gives in the early pages what appears to be his household expenses. For example, a cucumber, 9d., porter, 2 days, 1/4, board &c., 21/-. A goose cost 1/- and a duck 6d. Postage of two letters cost 8d. There is also an item 'Hair Licence £1 1s.'. At that time there was a tax on hair powder; every person 'who shall use or wear any powder, commonly called hair powder, of whatsoever materials the same shall be made' had to take out a certificate which was charged with stamp duty of one guinea.

But the business entries are of more importance to us than his personal ones, and his stock lists are most fruitful of information. A silver plate licence cost £2 6s. 0d. This remained at the same rate, incidentally, until these licences were rescinded in 1949.

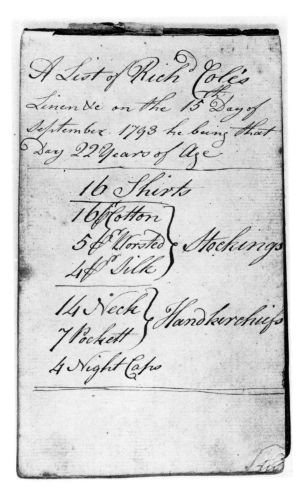

Fig. 1. Richard Cole's memorandum Book, 1793.

His stock was thoroughly comprehensive and included such items as women's buckles and knee buckles, smelling bottles, knives, forks, and spoons, spurs, bed hooks, patch boxes, punch ladles, tobacco stoppers and pipe tips, tooth picks, wist (sic) markers and pencil cases, pocket books and purses — most of these articles would have been either silver, silver-plated or silver-mounted — earrings and seals (steel, gilt or silver) the usual stock-in-trade of watchmakers such as watch keys, glasses and chains, clock cases ('4 Arch Wainscot Cases') clock dials, clocks and, of course, watches.

Joseph Usher, 1832-1903.

Such stock as seals, keys and chains he seems to have procured from Edward Hesketh of Birmingham.

The prices of some of these miscellaneous articles are interesting. For instance, a pair of silver buckles are listed at £1 5s. 0d. and a pap boat at 5/-. ½ grose (sic) keys are priced at £1 1s. 0d. and a similar quantity of springs at £1 16s. 0d., and of dials at £2 8s. 0d. Eight gross of glasses cost £5 12s. 0d. The four 'wainscot' clock cases cost £5 4s. 0d. An 8-day clock £5, a 'quarter spring clock' the same amount, a 30-hour clock £3 10s. 0d. and an alarm 17/-. A 'walnutree' clock case appears at £2 2s. 0d., two timepiece cases at £1 16s. 0d. and a movement at 10/6. Among clock dials we find two with 'moving ships' at £1 12s. 0d.

Most of the watches carried his own name, but he was unprejudiced in this matter for there are a number of other makers' names listed as well. Among these it is interesting to see the name of his master John Wontner, and also 'Rentnow' which is, as Britten notes, Wontner spelled backwards. 'Rentnow' was probably reserved for second

* An example from another source of the reversal of name-spelling is Wm. Terrag for Wm. Garret on a silver 'Dutch Market' watch of circa 1775.

284

quality watches. See Fig. 2*. Included in his stock list at Christmas 1798 is a watch numbered 1025 named 'Eloc', which is obviously his own name reversed; thus he followed in his master's footsteps. That he continued to have business dealings with Wontner is also plain from other entries in his book. For instance, in 1798 he notes a sum of £50 10s. 9d. as owing to his late master, and earlier in 1794, we read 'Box from Wontner & Co. 1/2'. We have noted that he sold watches bought in from other makers as well as those finished by his own hands; that he did actually 'make' watches we can be assured from such entries as 'one silver Rd. Cole for finishing' and a 'Silver Rd. Cole not finsht £3'.

The point is frequently made today that many of the large numbers of watch and clockmakers listed in Britten and in Baillie were not, in fact, makers at all, but merely had their own name inscribed on the work of others who supplied the trade, this being especially true after about 1750. There is little doubt that there is much truth in this contention, and Usher & Cole were themselves subsequently 'victims' of the practice. However, there is a danger of throwing the baby out with the bath-water; at any rate, Richard Cole can safely be claimed as a 'maker'. On 15th March 1793, he took out a patent (No. 1936) which reads as follows:

'An escapement, for beating, striking, and pointing seconds or parts of seconds. May be

Fig. 2. Verge movement, number 75034. Signed "Jno. Rentnow". Case hallmarked 1804.

either vertical or horizontal. The vertical wheel has fifteen teeth, and goes round twice in a minute. It acts on the verge, on which is fastened the pendulum spring and the verge wheel having ninety-six teeth; twenty-four of which, acting in a pinion of six teeth, turn the balance four times round every beat. In the horizontal escapement the horizontal wheel of fifteen teeth acts in a cylinder to which is fastened the regulating spring and the cylinder wheel of ninety-six teeth, which cylinder wheel acts as the verge wheel mentioned above. In both, the number of teeth in the wheels and pinion may be varied according to the number of beats required in one minute'.

Only in the 1798 stock list are watch numbers given. The earliest listed Cole number is 152 and the latest 1018 (extending to 1025 by 'Eloc'). If his numbering was strictly consecutive, it would mean that he completed over 1,000 watches in the six years from his apprenticeship. Fig. 3 illustrates a watch the silver hunting-type case of which is hallmarked for 1798. The movement carries his own name and the number 1068. An earlier movement and lower number (705) is shown in Fig. 4.

The cost prices of his watches were similar to those of the other makers whose products he stocked. A silver hunting watch of his own, number 996, cost £3 13s. 6d. A watch by Hedge in metal case, £1 11s. 6d., and a silver 'Rentnow' £2 14s. 6d. The most expensive watch is a metal 'jewelled Cole' at £5 5s. 0d. A P/C (pair-case) Cole watch cost £3 4s. 0d. and sold at £4. 4s. 0d., giving him a gain, as he calls it, of £1. He charged 1/8 for a silver thimble costing 1/- and 3d. for a watch glass costing 1½d. He charged 9d. for a watch paper which cost him 6d.! It is interesting to note that in those days one could charge for something which today we should regard as an advertisement.

The entry under 'Richard Cole' in Baillie states that Cole succeeded Bassett in circa 1795, but gives, as is usual in Baillie, no address other than Ipswich. The 'Ipswich Journal' of 23rd May, 1795, carries the two following announcements:

R. Cole.
Watch & Clock Maker, Silversmith, ec.
(from London)

Begs leave to inform his Friends and the Public in general, he has taken the shop late in occupation of Mr. Bassett in the Butter Market, where he solicits in continuance of the favours of Mr. Basset's friends; and where, by a steady and unremitting attention to business, he trusts he shall be supported by a liberal public.

Old gold and silver bought.

Bassett
Watch & Clock Maker, Silversmith, ec.
(from Ipswich)

Fig. 3. Verge movement, number 1068, silver hunter case, hallmarked 1798. Richard Cole, Butter Market, Ipswich.

Fig. 4. Verge movement, number 705. Richard Cole, Butter Market, Ipswich.

Respectfully informs the Ladies & Gentlemen and the public in general, of Melford & its environs, that he has opened a shop near the Cock And Bell, where he purposes carrying on the above businesses in all their various branches. Those Ladies, Gentlemen & others, who are pleased to favour him with their custom, may depend on being served on such terms as he hopes will not fail insuring him a continuance. Mourning & device rings neatly & expeditiously executed. Old gold & silver bought. Clocks attended to in the country at the distance of 12 miles. G. Bassett takes this opportunity to return his sincere thanks to his friends for the favours conferred on him while in Ipswich; at the same time wishes to solicit a continuance in favour of Mr. Cole.

The change of ownership of the shop in the Butter Market seems to have been conducted in a thoroughly gentlemanly fashion; and it is encouraging to know that the 12 miles Mr. Bassett was prepared to travel from Melford would not have impinged upon the activities of Mr. Cole in Ipswich.

But though Richard Cole was in business in the Butter Market in 1795, he must have moved to premises on Cornhill shortly after 1798. The watches illustrated in Figs. 3 and 4 bear the Butter Market address while Fig. 5 movement number 1734, gives the Cornhill address. The three watches cannot be separated by many years in date. Only Fig. 3 has a hallmarked case (1798). Turning to the 1798 stock list, some of the Cole watches are particularised as 'Butter Market', while others have no address added. It is possible that at this date he had the two addresses, and wished to indicate where his stock lay; possible, though not probable, since the two shops would have been in fairly close proximity. Alternatively, by Christmas

Fig. 5. Verge movement, number 1734. Richard Cole, Cornhill, Ipswich.

1798 he had already moved to Cornhill and merely wished to distinguish in his stock watches which bore his late address. A search of the Land Tax records has not shed any light on the problem, and the relationship of watch numbers to the addresses only serves to confuse the issue. It is certain, however, that the Cornhill shop was the final one, for it was there that his son, Richard Stinton Cole, traded. The Cornhill site must certainly have been more important than that of the Butter Market. Fig. 6 illustrates a later watch with the high number 22032. It is signed simply 'Richd. Cole Ipswich'. Presumably by that time no detailed address was considered necessary. Figure 7 is a view of Cornhill taken from a mezzotint dated 1790. What was later to be the Cole place of business is seen opposite the Market Cross. The tavern next door with the old Moot Hall adjoining, together with a corner of the old Corn Exchange across the way, illustrate clearly that the Cornhill area must have been the hub of Ipswich, with the future Cole business premises placed to the greatest advantage.

It is known that a few bracket and longcase clocks signed 'Richard Cole' still exist. An eight-day longcase clock by him can be seen in the state bedroom of Christchurch Mansion, Ipswich. It has an arched painted dial with a convex centre. Another in an oak case, has the arched painted dial which is shown in Fig. 8. The dial plate is stamped 'W. & H' — Walker & Hughes, Birmingham.

Richard Cole was 'free' of the Clockmakers Company in 1822 and was admitted to the Freedom of the City of London on 5th November of that year. His son, Richard Stinton Cole, was born 20th February, 1809, and on 16th April, 1823, was bound apprentice to him. See Fig. 9. Richard senior died on 16th August, 1833.

Richard Stinton Cole was 24 when he inherited his father's business on Cornhill. Fig. 10 shows the shop and its immediate environs in 1860-5. Compare with Fig. 7. The street name on the corner of his premises reads 'Cornhill' and the street name on the Corn Exchange opposite is 'King Street'. White's Directory of Suffolk 1844 gives Richard Stinton Cole, King Street, while for the year 1855 the address is Cornhill; as Fig. 10 makes clear the shop was in fact on the corner of Cornhill and King Street. King Street at that time, was the short street linking Cornhill with the Butter Market which is today Princes Street.

A few years ago there existed a pair of watchman's clocks from the old Ipswich gaol. Since they were signed 'R.S. Cole, Ipswich' on the dials he presumably supplied them. He certainly was clock-contractor to the gaol, a fact of which he was undoubtedly proud as it figures in his watchpaper, illustrated in Fig. 11. On the right will be seen the Market Cross, and the sailing ship

Fig. 6. Verge movement, number 22032, gilt metal case. Richard Cole, Ipswich.

Fig. 7. Messotint engraving, 1790, of Ipswich, showing the Market Cross, the old Moot Hall, and the Cole place of business, adjoining the tavern, on Cornhill. In the possession of Major R.C. Cole.

Richard Wright Cole, 1840-1919.

London where he met Richard Wright Cole while the latter was still serving his term with Worrall. On the completion of Cole's apprenticeship in 1861, they started that harmonious and successful partnership only ended by Usher's death in 1903. The firm they had initiated manufactured over 25,000 hand-made watches and marine chronometers, and achieved a high reputation for the quality of its products.

Information of the earliest days of the partnership can be gathered from the first catalogue they published. This catalogue or price list is addressed from 46 St. John's Square, the firm's first place of business. In 1873, they removed to 105 St. John Street Road, when the St. John's Square premises were required for the building of Clerkenwell Road. The second address was subsequently renamed and numbered as 339 St. John Street.

The first Usher & Cole price list provides as useful information of the 1870 period as Richard Cole's memorandum book did of his day. We quote the following trade prices:

A marine chronometer, of best quality, with rate, cost from £21. A pocket chronometer, in 18ct. gold case, cost £35.

further to the right is significant of the port of Ipswich. R.S. Cole also held the contract for the maintenance of the clocks on the stations of the old Eastern Counties Railway. According to his grand-daughter, her grandfather, wearing the long coat and tall hat of the period, was formally greeted by the station-master on these routine occasions. There is no doubt that he possessed a flourishing business when, in 1861, he was opposing the acquisition of his property for the extension of the Town Hall site and the improvement of King Street. A receipted account dated 1862 exists, representing fees and expenses to the Ipswich solicitors, Jackaman & Son, who conducted his case. He was unsuccessful in his opposition and the property was demolished in 1865-67 together with the Corn Exchange Tavern adjoining, and the second Town Hall, to make way for the present and third Town Hall.

R.S. Cole's son, Richard Wright Cole, was born 9th October, 1840. It is thought that he was apprenticed to Worrall of Goswell Road, London, in 1856. Before his son was out of his apprenticeship, therefore, R.S. Cole would have been aware of the threat to his ancient property in Ipswich. This may well have influenced the son in making his decision to commence business on his own in London.

Joseph Usher was born in Trowbridge in 1832 and served his apprenticeship there to William Bishop, watchmaker. Subsequently he came to

Fig. 8. Painted dial, 12in. x 17in. of 8-day long case clock. Steel hands. The case is oak, and has fluted pillars to hood, with brasss capitals and bases. Turned wood ball and spire finials.

This Indenture witnesseth, THAT

*Richard Stinton Cole son of Richard Cole of
Ipswich in County of Suffolk Watchmaker*

oth put himself Apprentice to *the said Richard Cole his father*

itizen and CLOCK-MAKER, of *London*, to learn his Art, and with him (after the Manner of an Apprentice) to serve from the
ay of the Date hereof, until the full End and Term of Seven Years, from thence next following, to be fully complete and ended.
uring which Term, the said Apprentice his said Master faithfully shall serve, his Secrets keep, his lawful Commands every where
gladly do. He shall do no Damage to his said Master, nor see it to be done of others; but that he, to the utmost of his Power,
shall let, or forthwith give Warning to his said Master of the same. He shall not waste the Goods of his said Master, nor lend
them unlawfully to any. He sha'l not commit Fornication, nor contract Matrimony within the said Term. He shall not play at
Cards, Dice, Tables, or any other unlawful Games, whereby his said Master may have any Loss. With his own Goods or others,
during the said Term, without License of his said Master, he shall neither buy nor sell. He shall not haunt Taverns or Play-
houses, nor absent himself from his said Master's Service Day nor Night unlawfully. But in all Things, as a faithful Apprentice,
he shall behave himself towards his said Master, and all his, during the said Term.

And the said Master (in Consideration of *Five Shillings*

being the Money given with his said Apprentice) his said Apprentice, in the same Art and Mystery which he useth, by the best
Means that he can, shall teach and instruct, or cause to be taught and instructed; finding unto his said Apprentice Meat, Drink,
Apparel, Lodging, and all other Necessaries, *according to the Custom of the City of London*, during the said Term.

And for the true Performance of all and every the said Covenants and Agreements, either of the said Parties bindeth himself
unto the other by these Presents. In Witness whereof the Parties above-named to these Indentures interchangably have put their
Hands and Seals, the *Sixteenth* Day of *April* in the
fourth Year of the Reign of our Sovereign Lord GEORGE IV. by the Grace of God, of the United Kingdom of
Great Britain and Ireland, King, Defender of the Faith, &c. and in the Year of our Lord One Thousand Eight Hundred and
twenty three

Sealed and delivered, being first duly stamped, in the Presence of

George Atkins Clerk   *Richard Cole*

This Indenture must be duly enrolled at the *Chamberlain's Office* in *Guildhall*, and on the Death or Change of Master, the Apprentice m
come to the *Clockmakers Company to be turned over* to the *Executor* or New Master, or he will lose his Freedom.

Fig. 9. Richard Stinton Cole's Indenture, 1823.

An 18ct. gold, 12 or 14 size full plate with six holes jewelled and compensation balance, is listed at £11 11s. 0d. With eight holes jewelled the price was £12 12s. 0d. The same watch, timed and rated in heat and cold, cost from £18 0s. 0d. This with single roller; with double roller escapement the price was £22 10s. 0d. These had double bottom cases and enamelled dials. Gold dials cost from 15/- to 25/- extra.

Silver verge watches were price listed as from £2 5s. 0d., and a small section was devoted to 'Geneva Watches'. As an example of the price of these, in 18ct. with gold dome and dial, the figure was £4 10s. 0d. These had cylinder, or 'horizontal' escapements as they were then usually termed.

Some repair charges were as follows: A duplex balance staff cost 8/6, or 14/- with roller, a duplex escape wheel 15/-. An English cylinder, pivoted-in, cost 7/- to 9/-. A cylinder escape wheel of 15 teeth cost 7/6 and a wheel with 13 teeth 12/-. An English lever balance staff 2/6 and 3/- for a staff for a three-quarter plate. A new escape wheel 2/6, and an escape wheel and pinion 4/6.

A new verge for an English movement cost 2/6, and a third or contrite (sic) pinion 1/9. It is interesting to note that balance or hair-springs are referred to as 'pendulum' springs.

A 'hard enamel dial' is listed at 1/6. A diamond end stone and setting 2/-.

A heading 'Geneva Watch Repairs' gives 'new cylinder pivoted in 5/6'. An escape wheel and pinion cost 7/6. A separate heading is given for case repairs, dials and jewel holes. The price list is thoroughly comprehensive and shows that Joseph Usher and R.W. Cole were offering a complete watch service to the trade.

The records and stock books of the firm — the latter running from 1870 until 1930 when watch manufacture virtually ceased — give the names of many men who were unknown outside a small

289

Fig. 10. The Cole shop with the Corn Exchange Tavern adjoining and the Corn Exchange. The shop and tavern, together with the Town Hall (not shown) were demolished to provide the site for the present third Town Hall.

circle, men who were, like the partners themselves, true craftsmen of the highest order. Such names as Costin, Harvey and Rome (escapement makers), Carswell, Meakin and Bird (finishers), Brown (complicated work), John Renn and Dring (examiners) were scarcely known to the outside world, and today they are forgotten. But these men stood at the head of their profession when the excellence of English watch-work, at its best, was unsurpassed. The firm itself never became universally known for its products since it was the general custom for the retailer to have his name engraved on the movement plate. Relatively few watches were turned out bearing the name of Usher & Cole; the stock books consequently read as a litany of the famous retailers of the day. Some of these firms are still in existence; others, like Barraud & Lunds, are names still remembered. Fig. 12 shows a stock book sheet. It is interesting to note that Usher & Cole made a number of watches for William Bishop & Son of Trowbridge over many years; Usher, it will be remembered, was apprenticed to William Bishop.

Watches, made up for stock, had the top plates and barrel bars stoned grey, so that when they were sold they could be finished off by engraving the name of the purchasing firm, and by gilding the plate or bar to match the rest of the movement. The movements in the rough, or grey (what we should now term the *ébauche*) were obtained from J. Preston or the Lancashire Watch Co.

In the earliest days the movements were mostly full plate, key-wind with fusee, but in the latter part of the nineteenth century, the three-quarter plate with going barrel and keyless work gradually ousted the time-honoured key-wind. The process of change was accompanied by much discussion in trade circles, and the 'Horological Journal' of January 1880, reported the first of a series of meetings under the title 'The Wisdom of Substituting the Going Barrel for the Fuzee in the English Watch Manufacture'. The industry was having the change forced upon it by the public demand, but as David Glasgow said, 'there is no watchmaker who would not rather wind three watches of ordinary construction than one keyless watch!' Ten years earlier J.A. Lund, of Barraud & Lunds, fought against the change and attempted to have the best of both worlds in his patent No. 914 of 29th March, 1870. This retained the virtues of the old fusee full plate, but provided a detachable key which was snapped into the pendant of case, so that with the key and its button in position, the

290

Fig. 11. Cole watch paper. The local gaol is shown on left where he maintained the clocks and, right, is the old Market Cross on Cornhill.

appearance of the watch was that of a keyless one. Usher & Cole made hundreds of these watches for Barraud & Lunds. But the three-quarter plate movement gave a more shapely watch and the old key-wind full plate was doomed.

The 'make-up' process, or manufacture, altered very little over the years. When the rough movements arrived from Lancashire (which was the centre of the movement trade) they were first taken to pieces and stamped with an identification number. The pillar plate was then sent to the dial maker. The movement, at this stage, consisted of plates, with centre and fourth holes drilled, train wheels and keyless work.

Back from the dial maker Willis — a Willis dial was the perfection of the dial maker's art — the dial and movement (frame) were then sent to the case maker, either Thoms* or the Woodman brothers†. The cases of the former have the stamp 'F.T.' with 'London' underneath and the latter 'P.W.' on gold and 'J.W.' on silver. For ladies size cases, Ball was employed, his punch being 'G.B.' Instructions specified, of course, whether the case was to be open face, half or full hunter. If either of the latter, the case was subsequently sent to the 'secret springer', as he was called, for the making and planting of the fly and lock springs. If a half

hunter was intended, the cover would have been first sent to the enameller.

Back again on the firm's premises, the movement was now in the escapement maker's hands. He selected a suitable escape wheel and pallets from stock, and then made and fitted the lever to the pallets, and shaped up and polished the escape wheel. The escape pinion and balance staff were next turned in. Mr. Cole having selected a balance, the escapement maker fitted the staff and roller, which he had made. Finally, he marked out and drilled the escape holes.

The movement was now sent out to the jeweller for the requisite jewelling to be done at that stage of manufacture. The jeweller supplied and fitted jewel holes and endstones and screws, as ordered.

---

* A.T. Oliver is the successor of Thoms. His mark for the Hall is A.T.O.

† No smaller quantity of gold could be purchased than £800 worth in bar. The sovereign being, of course, 22ct. it was the custom of the Woodman Bros. to buy £300 in gold sovereigns from the Bank of England. These were thrown into the melting pot with the appropriate alloy to produce 18ct. fineness for their watch cases!

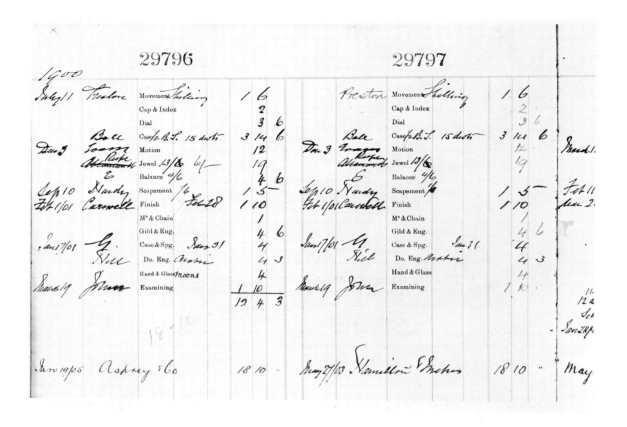

Fig. 12. An Usher & Cole stock book page. Both movements, Nos. 29796/7, were "shilling" size, and came from Preston. The names against some of the items, e.g. the dial, were not filled in, as these were almost invariably from the same source, or made by the same workman: the dials were made by Willis. Evans, who was responsible for the motion work in both instances, was an "indoor" workman, and a different man from the supplier of the rough balance, "E" standing for Evans. The jeweller Reepe had the first movement back a second time for extra jewelling after jewelling the escapement: hence the second cost of 6/-. "G" stands for Gardner. The examiner was John Renn, who was always known by his Christian name. The final entries indicate the purchaser of the watches. Some retailers had their own serial numbers given to the movements. In such cases, the Usher & Cole number, consisting of the last three figures of the serial number, are found on the pillar plate. Separate stock books were kept for Barraud & Lunds.

Once more at Usher & Cole, the finisher now took over. He marked off the third wheel hole, and turned and polished the pivots and hollows to the train wheel pinions and barrel; he also made the balance spring stud and screws to the balance cock, and checked the winding mechanism. If the holes were not to be jewelled, this craftsman finished a brass hole to fit each pivot, and turned the oil sinks in the plate. If, however, further jewelling had been decided upon, that is, the third, fourth and perhaps centre holes, the movement was sent to the jeweller a second time for this work to be done. The finisher next stoned the plates and train wheels, finished the steel work, blued the screws, etc., prior to the plates, and train wheels being sent out for gilding; excepting perhaps the top plate, for unless the retail

destination was known these particulars would yet have to be engraved thereon. The finisher finally completed assembly and passed the movement to the examiner. The hands had been made by Hood.

When the examiner and springer came upon the scene the final stage had been reached. This specialist tested the depths and end shakes. He put the stop work on the barrel, fitted the appropriate mainspring (made to the barrel by Cotton), and set up the stop work. He ran in the set square through the centre wheel pinion and turned on the balance spring collet and stud. He cut, trued and poised the balance. He pinned in the balance spring (in many cases made by Ganeval's to the balances) to the collet and stud, and turned up the coil for the Breguet spring. The now-finished watch was then timed in positions, and put through the ice box

292

and oven. In the process the examiner would select a proportion — according to the demand — to be put through the Kew and Greenwich Observatory Trials. Springing and timing were Joseph Usher's special province and no outside experts were employed for this the highest skill of the watchmaking art. Apart from being a springer and timer of unusual ability he was able to direct and supervise the springing carried out by the various examiners.

Marine chronometer manufacture followed similar lines. After the Lancashire movements had been numbered for identification, they were put out to the escapement manufacturers such as King or Mead, or were dealt with on the premises by Hope, in which case they were fitted with detents by Abbott. Fusee cutting was an outside speciality, and the fusee chains were obtained from Christchurch in Hampshire, or from Haswell's or Houghton's. The mainsprings were supplied by Cotton's. Finishing and spotting followed, and finally the balance was cut and the spring applied, and the instrument 'rated'. The balance springs were mostly made by Ganeval's. Jewelling was done by Claxton, and the brass work and gymballing by Ottway. The wood boxes were practically all made by the Marshall family. Apart from the Admiralty, Usher & Cole chronometers were sold to the Mercantile Marine. Many destined for the former had the name of the retailer engraved on them.

It is worthy of note that a hitherto, apparently, unrecorded arrangement of auxiliary compensation was applied by Chittenden of Epping to Usher & Cole chronometers, particularly to those instruments intended for the Greenwich Observatory Trials.

The sub-division of work at Usher & Cole which has been outlined in its order if not described in its complexity, was the normal practice in the trade. It was, in fact, a continuation and modification of the system employed in England since the days of Thomas Tompion. To the lay person it might appear complicated, but each craftsman was a specialist in his particular branch of the work and the system was efficient in its own context; the sub-division at Usher & Cole was not carried out for cheapness alone, but for more rapid production, and better results.

Usher & Cole received many interesting contracts, usually at one remove. For example (in this instance through Herbert Blockley of Duke Street, St. James's) the Royal Geographical Society equipped their Expeditions with watches made by Usher & Cole. These had a specially designed screw back and bezel and cap over the winding button which were leather-lined to withstand the rigorous climatic conditions encountered. The movements of these watches were

Fig. 13. Usher & Cole "Travellers Watch". Specially designed case with leather lined screw back, bezel and cap over pendant. Fusee keyless movement. Perhaps the first practical application of a water-resisting system to a watch. Woodman case, 1890.

fusee keyless, free-sprung, with 'up and down' mainspring indicator dials. Among other expeditions, these watches were used on the Jackson-Harmsworth Polar Expedition 1894-7. See Fig. 13.

Figs. 14 and 15, movement No. 26518, gives an example of complicated work: perpetual calendar, lunar work and minute repeater, in a 22ct. gold, chased case. The watchwork was done entirely on the premises in St. John's Street. The watch was sold in 1891 for £110. It was in the firm's hands for overhaul in 1960.

Fig. 16, movement No. 30459, gives an example of chronograph work turned out by Usher & Cole, and is a 1906 sample of Brown's craftsmanship. The same craftsman also made the repeating work for the all-English repeating watches. In some such watches, the movement as received from Lancashire was sent to Montandon

— Robert of Geneva who mounted the repeating work on it. The movement was then completed in the normal way by Usher & Cole.

Fig. 17 shows a watch, number 14579, of the St. John's Square period.

A silver medal was won by the firm at the Paris Exhibition of 1889. A silver medal was the highest award for a first exhibit. In 1900 Usher & Cole were to win a Paris Gold Medal and in 1910 a Grand Prix at the Japan-British Exhibition, but all through the years their products, watches and marine chronometers, were achieving quite exceptional results at Kew and Greenwich Observatories.

Mr. John Francis Cole entered the firm in 1892. He passed all the British Horological Institute examinations in 1895, winning the Bronze Medal, and when the Fellowship was inaugurated in 1908, Mr. Cole was one of the very first Fellows elected. He won the Clockmakers Company First Prize and Silver Medal of the City and Guilds of London Institute in 1899.

Mr. J.F. Cole was instructed in the art of springing and timing by Joseph Usher and he attended T.D. Wright's and F.J. Britten's lectures at the Horological Institute. In the 'Horological Journal' of March, 1899, (F.J. Britten at that time occupied the editorial chair) we read on page 99: 'Messrs. Usher & Cole occupy the premier position in the recent marine chronometer trials, as may be

Fig. 15. Dial and case of movement 26518. The 22ct. gold case weights over 5oz. and has the hallmark for 1890.

Fig. 14. Movement No. 26518. Minute repeater, perpetual calendar and lunar work. The rough movement was bought in 1888.

seen from the list on p.96. At least fifty of the instruments submitted have been purchased by the Admiralty. Of these Messrs. Usher & Cole sell five, and among other leading makers who have done well are Mr. Kullberg, Messrs. Johannsen & Co. and Mr. Robert Gardner. It is not often that an aspirant to Admiralty honours succeeds on the first attempt, but this good fortune attends Mr. J.F. Cole, son of Mr. R.W. Cole, who appears to be a young horologist of exceptional promise.'

In November, 1892, Bonniksen brought out his patent for his karrusel movement. Mr. J.F. Cole remembers his father and Mr. Usher consulting together with Mr. Bonniksen on the difficulties at first encountered on the introduction of the karrusel to centre second and chronograph movements. They also discussed the question of oil to the platform and decided that if the plates were gilt, no oiling was necessary. Usher & Cole probably made up more karrusels than any other firm, the majority, of course, for retail houses. A large proportion of these watches gained the 'especially good' certificate at Kew. In 1898 Usher & Cole headed the Kew list with 88.4 marks with a karrusel. In 1901 they removed the going barrel and fitted fusees and barrels to two of Bonniksen's movements, and made them up as fusee keyless with 'up and down' hands on the dials. These

Fig. 16. Free-sprung chronograph movement No. 30459.

watches gained 85.5 and 87.1 marks at Kew, and were probably the only two fusee keyless karrusels ever made. Mr. J.F. Cole spent much of his time in his younger days on the various stages of making karrusels into the finished article. Fig. 18 shows a karrusel movement in the partly finished state.

Early in his career, Mr. J.F. Cole suggested to his father that a reduction in the making costs might be achieved by omitting some of the 'finish' which it had always been customary to give. Mr. Cole senior agreed that this might be tried. Hollows were always turned in the pinions, and polished, the theory being that these hollows served as traps should oil run down the arbors. But experience had shown that rarely, if ever, was oil found in these hollows; they might well be omitted and the time saved. This operation, accordingly, was decided to be one of the items which could be dispensed with, as well as the polishing of the arbors, without detriment to the quality of the watch. But it proved to be unworkable. The men concerned continued to make these hollows with the lozenge-shaped gravers used for the work, and to polish the arbors, as had been their custom. The craftsmen knows only one method, strives after only one result: the best of which he is capable. If 'finish' and polish is where the eye cannot see, one can be certain that the quality is there too.

In spite of the fact that karrusels and tourbillons were sweeping the board in the years 1894-1910, in 1909 an Usher & Cole fusee keyless watch, with fixed escapement, movement No. 31052, obtained 91.2 marks at Kew, at that time the highest marks ever obtained by a fixed escapement.

To 'head the list' at Kew was a coveted distinction: to obtain the highest number of marks was a watchmaker's ambition. Thus, in an earlier year (1888) when the firm obtained 85.5 marks for watch No. 24329, and was informed that this was 'by far the highest number of marks yet obtained by a keyless centre seconds', it was cause for congratulations.

To give perspective to this matter it is necessary to give a summary of the conditions. The highest class of Kew certificate, an 'A' certificate, involved a 45 days test, divided into eight periods of five days each, and five intermediate and extra days in four of which the watch was not rated.

1st Period — Watch in vertical position with pendant up, at the temperature of the chamber (kept at 60°-65°).

2nd Period — Watch in vertical position with pendant to the right, at the same temperature.

3rd Period — Watch in vertical position, with pendant to the left, at the same temperature.

4th Period — Watch with dial up, in the Refrigerator, at a temperature of about 40°F.

5th Period — Watch with dial up at a temperature of 60°-65°F.

6th Period — Watch with dial up, in the Oven, at a temperature of about 90°F.

7th Period — Watch in horizontal position, with dial down, at a temperature of 60°-65°F.

8th Period — Same as the first, watch in vertical position, with pendant up.

The intermediate and extra days, during which the rate of the watch was not recorded, were at the commencement of the 4th, 5th, 6th and 7th Periods, which were extended one day each for that purpose.

Fig. 17. Three-quarter plate movement No. 14579. It has St. John's Square engraved on the plate: number 46 was the firm's first address.

To gain a Class A certificate, the performance of the watch was such that —

1. The average of the daily departures from the mean daily rate, during the same stage of trial, did not exceed two seconds in any one of the eight stages.

2. The mean daily rate while in the pendant up position differed from the mean daily rate in the dial up position by less than five seconds, and from that in any other position by less than ten seconds.

3. The mean daily rate was affected by change of temperature to an amount less than 0.3 second per 1°F.

4. The mean daily rate did not exceed 10 seconds while in any position.

The 100 Marks awarded to an absolutely perfect watch would be made up as follows: 40 for a complete absence of variation of daily rate, 40 for absolute freedom from change of rate with change of position, and 20 for perfect compensation for effects of temperature.

The Usher & Cole watch No. 31052, mentioned earlier, which obtained 91.2 marks, and which in its day held the record, scored 34.8 marks in respect of variation from daily rate, 36.9 in respect of change of rate with change of position, and 19.5 in respect of temperature compensation. In that same year (1909) Usher & Cole obtained an average of 81.5 marks on the watches submitted: a score of 80 marks earned the endorsement 'especially good'. (Note: The Kew Tests were discontinued in 1951.)

The Greenwich Observatory Trials were equally stringent, and rather more prolonged*, and Usher & Cole were similarly successful. According to their requirements, the Admiralty offered to purchase, at the end of each trial, those marine chronometers and watches standing at the head of the list.

Joseph Usher died in 1903. We quote from the March issue of the 'Horological Journal':

'To the deep sorrow of many friends, Mr. Joseph Usher, one of the most accomplished watchmakers of his time, passed away on Thursday, 5th February. Mr. Usher had remarkable ability as a springer and timer, and was also a recognised expert in complicated watch mechanism. In 1887 he was, as a representative of English watchmaking, called to give evidence before a Select Committee of the House of Commons which was sitting to consider the provisions of the Merchandise Marks Bill. Nearly three years ago, in failing health, he left London for Clevedon, Somerset, having previously initiated into the art of springing and timing Mr. J.F. Cole, who proved to be an apt pupil and worthy successor ... He was for many years a respected member of the Council of the Horological Institute, a position he occupied till his death.'

The firm's catalogue of the early 1900s illustrated a gold fusee keyless watch, half-plate movement fully jewelled, carefully adjusted (the description reads) for positions and temperatures, with 'up and down' indicator on the dial. The price in gold half hunter case was 'from £36 15s. 0d.' The catalogue stated: 'This is the highest class of watch it is possible to make'. Among other watches illustrated were chronographs, minute repeaters and minute repeaters with chronograph, the prices being, in hunter cases, from £34, £52 10s. 0d., and £65 respectively. Among ladies watches there was the famous 'shilling size' (movement) watch, the smallest English watch then made. The price of this, in gold crystal open face, was from £17 0s. 0d. A two-day marine chronometer 'ready for sea' cost £26. All these prices were 'trade' prices. Repair work was prominently featured and was stated to be a speciality.

The South African War was now to have its long-term effect on the watch market: it introduced the wrist watch to a receptive public. Small size pocket watches were converted to wrist watches by adding lugs to the cases to take a strap,

---

* In the early 20th century the duration of the trial was 29 weeks. For deck watches it was 16 weeks.

John Francis Cole.

and by reducing the winding pendant. The result was practical, if not elegant by later standards. The Swiss manufacturers were quick to realise the potential demand and the changing fashion.

The 1914-18 War was to give added impetus to the wrist watch demand, but for Usher & Cole as chronometer makers, the First World War had a different significance. A desperate situation arose for this country in its need for marine chronometers. The chronometer making firms numbered no more than five. Shipping losses had been enormous. The Government issued appeals to the general public to sell, loan or give chronometers, as the output of new instruments fell far short of the need. Those were, of course, pre-wireless days such as we have today, and practically every parsonage in the country had its chronometer. The instruments thus collected were then sent to firms like Usher & Cole for such overhaul and repair as was necessary to bring them to Admiralty standard. Usher & Cole undertook to turn out 20 chronometers per week.

Richard Wright Cole died in 1919. The following are extracts from his obituary notice in the May issue of the 'Horological Journal'. 'In Richard Wright Cole, who, on April 10, 1919, in his 79th year, passed quietly from these realms of Time to those of Eternity, the Horological trade, and particularly the Clerkenwell section of it, lost one who in a quiet and unobtrusive fashion did much to maintain its dignity and the high standard of its output and to support its charities . . .

The firm may be said to have specialised in the high class, hand-made Watch and Chronometer, and their work attained a degree of perfection, which is reflected not only in the reputation they acquired, but in the high places gained at the Kew and Greenwich trials as well as by the distinctions awarded at International Exhibitions at home and abroad. Their accurate workmanship has been selected for Polar research and Tropical expeditions.

Richard Wright Cole did not confine his activities merely to his firm, but devoted his energies to the best interests of the trade as a whole, always with a view to improvement in the standard of output.

For sixteen years he was a Vice-President of the British Horological Institute, and in 1906 became its Chairman.

His less successful brethren in the craft also found a warm corner in his sympathetic heart, and so we find him for forty-one years a member of the Committee of the Clock and Watch Makers'

Asylum now merged in the National Benevolent Society of Watch and Clock Makers . . .'

Like his father before him, Mr. J.F. Cole was active in his younger days in trade affairs. We find both his name and his father's among the subscribers when the British Horological Institute became limited by guarantee in 1913. In 1912 and 1913, like his father in earlier years, he served as Chairman of the Institute, and he acted as the Institute's Treasurer for 30 years. During the 1914-18 War years he was acting editor of the 'Horological Journal' and his energy in Institute matters is shown by his membership of the following committees: Northampton Polytechnic Institute Joint Committee; Finance Committee; Journal Committee; Class Examination Committee. Among his colleagues on these committees were T.D. Wright and James and Eric Haswell.

The 1914-18 War administered, perhaps, the *coup de grâce* to the English watch manufacturer of that era. The sands had been slowly but surely running out for a number of years, no matter how fine the work which had been produced by a select band of makers. In fact, the prophecy given by Henry Ganney in his lecture to the British Horological Institute in 1869 had been fulfilled: 'In my own mind I am fully convinced that the watches of the future will be machine made . . .' However, those who had introduced machinery into watchmaking in this country had fared no better. Switzerland had captured the trade of the world.

Usher & Cole, although still producing the hand-made watch up to 1930, were concentrating more and more on high class watch and chronometer repair work, keeping up to the same high standard set in their manufactured products. It was Mr. J.F. Cole's task to guide the firm through those days of change. That Usher & Cole

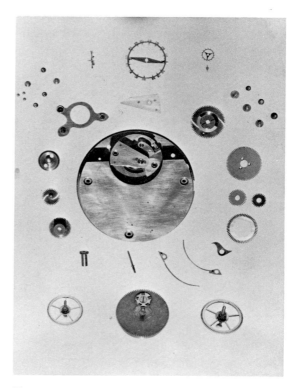

Fig. 18. A Bonniksen Karrusel movement. Apart from some jewelling, still in the rough.

were still 'making' in 1925 is illustrated by the certificate of Honour won at the British Empire Exhibition at Wembley. The firm continued to trade as repairers, servicing many of its own products and marine chronometers in particular. In 1958 it was finally absorbed by Camerer Cuss & Co. and Mr. J.F. Cole retired.

298

Glossary

This glossary includes some terms not used in the main text, but which are likely to be met with by those interested in the technical aspect of watches

ADJUSTED. A watch is said to be 'adjusted in 5 positions' if it has been rated in the two horizontal and three of the possible vertical positions — i.e. dial up, dial down, pendant up, pendant left, pendant right and pendant down. 'Adjusted for temperature' means that the compensation has been observed in at least three temperatures.

ADJUSTABLE POTENCE. See fig. 1. See **POTENCE**.

AFFIX. A small bimetallic blade, one end of which is fixed to the rim of the balance: used to correct the temperature compensating properties of the main compensating arrangement.

'ALL-OR-NOTHING' PIECE. In a repeating watch, a device which ensures that the striking is released only if the lever or push-piece for the repeating action is fully depressed. Without this mechanism, if the actuating lever or push-piece is insufficiently depressed an incorrect number of hours is sounded. With this improvement, the watch has to strike *all* or *nothing*. Both Tompion and Quare incorporated it, though Julien Le Roy is often credited with the invention.

AMPLITUDE. The maximum angle by which a balance swings from its position of rest. By observing the arms of a balance it is possible to estimate this angle. See **ARC**.

ANTI-MAGNETIC. Unaffected by magnetism. If those parts of a watch most affected by a magnetic field (balance, balance spring and escapement) are made of non-magnetic materials the watch is termed 'anti-magnetic', although more strictly 'anti-magnetic' upto a specified strength of field. The earliest non-magnetic balance springs were gold as used by John Arnold. Subsequently palladium alloy was invented by C.A. Paillard in 1877.

APPLIQUE. Applied ornament to a case, or applied chapters, numerals or decoration to a dial.

ARBOR. The spindle, shaft or axle upon which the wheels of a watch train are mounted.

ARC. The arc of a balance is twice the amplitude (q.v.). A balance with an amplitude of 270 degrees has an arc of 540 degrees (1½ turns of the balance).

ATTACHMENT. The 'point of attachment' or 'pinning-point' is the point at which the balance spring is pinned to the collet on the balance staff.

AUTOMATON WATCH. A watch with animated figures, actuated by the going, striking, musical or repeating train. See **JACQUEMART**.

AUTOMATIC WATCH. A watch which is wound by the movement of the wearer. Also known as a 'self-winding' watch. John Harwood patented a self-winding wrist watch in about 1928. Patent No 218,487 of 1923.

AUXILIARY COMPENSATION. An additional and subsidiary compensation sometimes fitted to a bimetallic balance to eliminate the middle temperature error (q.v.).

Fig. 1. Movement plate showing adjustable potence and adjustable bearing for crown wheel. From repeating movement by Romilly, Paris. *Circa* 1765.

BACKPLATE. See **TOP PLATE.**

BALANCE. A plain wheel with two or three spokes known as 'arms'. Coupled to its spring, the balance of a watch is the controlling device; its oscillation, its to and fro swinging properties, regularise the movement of the train powered by the mainspring, and hence the timekeeping ability of the watch.

A plain balance, or a monometallic balance, is an uncut ring, with or without timing screws. It may be made of brass, steel, gold, nickel or palladium. A modern alloyed metal such as 'Invar' or glucydur produces a balance which for all practical purposes is unaffected by temperature changes.

A 'compensated', cut bimetallic balance has its rim made of two metals of different coefficient of expansion (brass and steel) fused together. The rim is cut near each arm of the two-arm balance, the other end, the free end moves inward or outward on a rise or fall (respectively) in temperature, thus altering the moment of inertia of the balance by shifting the mass of the rim closer to or away from the centre. This counteracts the effect of temperature changes upon the elasticity of the steel balance spring. Brass has a higher coefficient of expansion than steel, and is on the outer side of the rim. Screws or weights on the balance rim enable the compensating property to be adjusted.

An 'unsprung balance' is a balance without a spring — i.e. before the introduction of the balance spring in 1675. See also **FOLIOT** and **'S' BALANCE.**

BALANCE COCK. See **COCK.**

BALANCE SCREWS. See **TIMING SCREWS.**

BALANCE SPRING. Both Robert Hooke and Christian Huygens have been credited with the invention of the balance spring as the controlling agent for watches. The Abbé de Hautefeuille also claimed priority, though it seems fairly certain that his conception was for a straight as opposed to a spiral spring. It also appears that Hooke's original idea of 1658 was a straight spring. It is certainly established beyond doubt that Huygens devised a practical means of applying a spiral spring and employed Thuret of Paris to make a watch with such a spring in 1675. Hooke had in 1664 propounded the first law relating to springs: *ut tensio sic vis* ('as the tension is, so the force'). Put more simply: The force which a spring exerts depends upon the amount it has been wound up.' Hooke's Law is only partially true as applied to a watch balance spring.

A balance spring is a weak spiral spring attached at its inner end to the balance staff and at its outer end to the balance cock or movement plate. The sprung balance regulates the timekeeping, the period of each swing depending upon the ratio of the moment of inertia of the balance to the stiffness or elasticity of the spring. The elasticity of any given spring depends basically upon the material from which it is made and upon its effective length. See **ISOCHRONOUS, COMPENSATED BALANCE** and **COMPENSATION CURB.**

The earliest balance springs were sometimes made of copper but mostly of steel. Gold springs were occasionally used in the later 18th and 19th centuries. C.A. Paillard invented a palladium spring — which is non-magnetic — in 1877, and of recent years alloys of nickel steel, chronium, manganese and other elements have rendered balance springs impervious to temperature changes, magnetic fields and damp. Dr. C.E. Guillaume did the original research on nickel steel alloys in 1896. 'Elinvar' (*'elasticité invariable'*) was the name given to his springs.

The earliest springs (with the verge escapement) had three or four coils; with the later escapements about fourteen are general.

A helical spring is one formed into a helix and is normally found with the chronometer or detent escapement. In about 1782 John Arnold discovered by empirical methods that isochronism could be achieved by a helical spring with the two terminal coils or ends incurved.

A.L. Breguet introduced a spiral spring with an overcoil as an aid to isochronism. The overcoil spring has the outer coil raised and turned in towards the centre, which ensures the concentric development of the spring as the balance oscillates. In 1861, Edouard Phillips gave the theoretical conditions for end curves for both helical and spiral springs to render them isochronous. Jules Grossman and L. Lossier took these investigations further.

A steel spring will lose its elasticity in heat and become more 'springy' in cold: hence the need for temperature compensation.

BALANCE STAFF. The spindle or arbor upon which the balance is mounted.

BANKING PIN. With the verge escapement, a pin protuding from the outer edge of the balance. The extreme arc of balance swing is limited by stops on the balance cock, against which the pin would 'bank' if the arc were excessive.

In later escapements, an equivalent provision is included and in the lever escapement the device of two banking pins is used to limit the angular movement of the lever. Occasionally, instead of two pins, banking takes place against walls forming part of the movement plate or of the pallet cock.

BAR. Bridge as distinct from a cock which has a foot by which it is secured to the movement plate.

BARREL (GOING). A cylindrical box (barrel) with a toothed disc (a wheel) on the outer edge. The disc is the 'great wheel' and the box contains the mainspring. The barrel (box) turns freely on its arbor, the mainspring being hooked to the barrel at its outer end and to the arbor at its inner end. The great wheel meshes with the first pinion of the watch train. In a watch movement with going barrel, the fusee (q.v.) is dispensed with. The barrel in fusee watches is a plain barrel without teeth.

In winding a going barrel, the barrel arbor is turned round, drawing the spring away from the rim of the box and coiling it round the arbor. A click and ratchet prevent the arbor from recoiling while the mainspring is being wound and when it is fully wound. The tensioned spring, in striving to 'unwind', expends its force in turning the barrel, this same force being utilised to drive the watch train via the great wheel. The barrel makes as many turns in unwinding, of course, as were given to the arbor in winding. See also **STOP WORK** and **SET UP**.

BARREL (HANGING). A going barrel, fixed to the movement only by its upper portion. Also known as 'standing barrel'.

BARREL (RESTING). The great wheel is mounted on an arbor, the power transmitted to the wheel by ratchet and click. The spring is enclosed in a barrel which is screwed to the plate.

BARROW REGULATOR. An early form of regulator of balance spring watches. Two pins (curb pins) held upright in a slide embrace the end section of the balance spring which is straight, not coiled. The slide moves along a worm (endless screw) which has a squared end to take a key. An index engraved on the movement plate indicates the amount the slide may be moved with the aid of a key, as the effective length of the spring is altered for regulation. A watch still retaining its Barrow regulator is very rare.

BASSE-TAILLE ENAMEL. Translucent enamel laid over a ground engraved to enhance the pictorial effect.

BASSINE. A type of watch case that is rounded on the edge and smooth.

BEAT. The multiple sound of the escapement action heard as the 'tick'.

BEETLE HAND. The type of hour hand faintly resembling a stag beetle. See **POKER**.

BEZEL. The rim holding the glass.

BIMETALLIC. Formed of two metals, brass and steel, whose different coefficients of expansion are utilised for compensating the effects of temperature changes on a steel balance spring. See **BALANCE.** Mostly in the early eighteenth century alternatively, a bimetallic strip, formed by riveting or fusing, was utilised, which bent under the influence of temperature changes. This strip was known as a compensation curb (q.v.).

BOTTOM PLATE. See **TOP PLATE**.

BOUCHON. Also 'Bush'. Hard brass tubing inserted into watch plates to form pivot holes — i.e. bearings for pivots.

BOW. The metal ring hinged, pivoted or looped to the pendant (q.v.) of the watch case, by which the watch may be attached to a chain or fob.

BREGUET BALANCE SPRING. See **BALANCE SPRING**.

BREGUET HANDS. Hour and minute hand slightly tapered, the end a disc eccentrically pierced to form a crescent. Also called 'moon hands'.

BREGUET KEY. A watch key in which the upper and lower portions of the shaft are connected by a ratchet clutch kept in gear by a compressed spring, so that the upper part will turn the lower part in the correct direction for winding, but if the upper part is turned in the opposite direction, the ratchet slips without moving the lower part. This ensures that no damage will result from turning the key in the wrong direction. This key is also called a 'tipsy' key, presumably since it ensured a watch against damage when owned by inebriates! A similar form of key was patented in England in 1789 by S.B. Harlow.

BREGUET OVERCOIL. See **BALANCE SPRING**.

BREGUET STOP-WORK. This form of stop-work (q.v.) has two toothed wheels, one of eight teeth fixed to the barrel arbor and one of ten teeth fixed to the barrel itself. Projections on the two wheels meet after four turns, thus limiting the extent to which the mainspring is wound.

BRISTLE. See **HOG'S BRISTLE**.

BULL'S EYE GLASS. A flattened dome glass in shape, but with a small circular flat ground in the centre. Popular in England between about 1685 and 1750 and for inexpensive watches in the first half of the 19th century.

BUSH. See **BOUCHON**.

BUTTON, WINDING. Round, or rounded, knurled or milled button fixed to a shaft or stem by which a watch is wound or the hands set. Sometimes called a 'set-hand button'. Used in keyless watches.

CADRATURE. Under-dial work, viz. repeating work.

CALIBRE. The size and type of design of a watch movement. The term was used by Sully in about 1715 to denote the dimensions and layout of a movement; more recently the term has been used to indicate the shape of the movement or even the designer's name — e.g. Lepine calibre (q.v.) — or the origin of the movement.

CAM. A part shaped with an irregular contour so as to give the requisite reciprocal irregular movement to a lever in contact with it.

CANISTER CASE. An early form of case, drumshaped. Not dissimilar to a tambour case (q.v.), but not hinged.

CANNON PINION. A pinion, part of the motion work carrying the minute hand. Its hollow arbor, or pipe, is merely a friction fit on the centre wheel arbor, thus allowing the hand to be set.

CAP JEWEL. See **ENDSTONE**.

CAPPED MOVEMENT. A movement provided with a dust cap (q.v.).

CARTOUCHE DIAL. Found on continental watches, French in particular. White enamel plaques with blue or black numerals, the plaques being fired on to the metal dial. On *champlevé* dials, the maker's name is usually engraved on a cartouche which has been polished in contrast to the matted centre of the dial.

CENTRE PINION. The pinion in the going train (see **TRAIN**), driven by the great wheel. Normally it is centrally placed in the movement.

CENTRE SECONDS. A seconds hand pivoted in the centre of the dial concentric with the hour and minute hands, and traversing the dial in one minute. Sometimes called a 'sweep seconds'. The hour and minute hands may be on a subsidiary dial.

CENTRE WHEEL. The wheel, centrally planted, the arbor of which carries the cannon pinion and minute hand.

CHAFF-CUTTER. See **ORMSKIRK** and **DEBAUFRE ESCAPEMENT**.

CHAISE-WATCH. A large watch used for travelling. Not to be confused with a carriage clock.

CHAMPLEVE. An area of metal which has been hollowed out with a graver to take enamelling: *champlevé* enamel. '*Champlevé* dial' is a metal dial with portions removed to leave others standing proud of the main surface — i.e. the hour numerals and minute markings. The hollowed-out numerals are then filled with black or coloured wax, or pitch.

CHAPTER RING. The ring upon which the hours and minute graduations or half and quarter-hour divisons are engraved. An alternative name is 'the hour ring'.

CHASING. Engraving in relief.

CHATELAINE. A chain for suspending watch or piece of jewellery. In addition to the watch, the winding key, seals or other trinkets were often attached. Normally the decoration on the watch case is *en suite* with the decoration on the châtelaine. See also **FOB CHAIN**.

CHINESE DUPLEX. A form of duplex escapement invented by C.E. Jacot in 1830. It was commonly used for watches exported from Fleurier to China. The locking teeth are double, thus resembling a fork. After the first prong of the fork passes the roller, the escape wheel is immediately locked again, so that a second swing of the balance is necessary to unlock the whole tooth or 'fork' before impulse can be given. A second elapses between each complete unlocking, but the intermediate stage is detectable by a slight movement of the centre seconds hand: otherwise, the watch *appears* to beat seconds.

CHRONOGRAPH. A watch which, in addition to the time-of-day hands, has a centrally mounted seconds hand. This can be started, stopped and returned to zero by means of a push-piece or slide. A subsidiary dial is provided which records the number of revolutions (each of a minute) made by the centre seconds or chronograph hand. A more correct term would be 'chronoscrope'. See also **SPLIT-SECONDS**.

CHRONOMETER. Among English watchmakers and collectors, a chronometer is understood to be a watch or portable clock (hence a ship's, marine or box chronometer) which has a detent escapement (q.v.) although the use of the word preceded the detent escapement. Of recent years there has been a tendency — regretted by many — to use the word in the French or Swiss sense to indicate a watch which has obtained an official rating certificate issued by the observatories at Geneva or Neuchâtel. Etymologically, any instrument for measuring time.

CHRONOSCROPE. See **WANDERING HOUR DIAL**.

CLICK. A pawl or lever with a 'beak' which engages in the ratchet-shaped teeth of a wheel, it being under the tension of a spring, and pivoted. The usual purpose of a click, its spring and the ratchet wheel is to allow the wheel to turn in one direction only. On watches the ratchet wheel is fixed to the arbor of the mainspring barrel, thus enabling the mainspring to be wound; the tension of the mainspring is held up against the tensioned click.

CLOCKMAKERS' COMPANY. The Worshipful Company of Clockmakers was granted its Royal Charter in 1631, with David Ramsay as its first Master. Prior to its incorporation, the craft of clock and watchmaking was controlled by the Blacksmiths' Company, and it would seem that boys were apprenticed as Blacksmiths in the earlier years. In the City of London apprentices were admitted through the Guilds, and after they had served their term they were granted the freedom of the craft. The Clockmakers' Company had the right to regulate the manner, order and form in which the craft should be conducted within the realm of England. It had powers to make laws and ordinances for all persons using the Art within a ten-mile radius of the City of London and had wide powers touching the 'Trade, Art or Mystery'. The Company had the right to make a general search and view all productions made in this country or brought in from abroad: it had powers to seize and to destroy unworthy work or cause it to be amended. None but admitted members might sell their wares within the City or ten miles thereof. An apprentice was bound for seven years and, after admittance as a Freeman, served a further two years as journeyman and then produced his masterpiece before being admitted as a workmaster. A Brother was allowed to engage only one apprentice, a Warden or Assistant Warden two only.

CLOCK-WATCH. A watch which strikes the hours at the hours. Not to be confused with a repeating watch. Clock-watches were made from the earliest period.

CLOISONNE. Divided into 'cloisons' or compartments by means of flat metal wires, forming a design in outline on a flat or curved surface. In *cloisonné* enamel, the partitions are filled with coloured enamels, and then fired. After polishing, the metal strips show off the design inlaid in the enamel. The metal used is mostly gold.

CLUB-FOOT VERGE. A frictional-rest dead-beat escapement, derivative of that invented by Debaufre *circa* 1704. Sometimes referred to as the 'dead-beat verge', or 'Ormskirk escapement.' after the town in Lancashire where watches with this escapement were made in the early 19th century.

CLUB-TOOTHED LEVER. A lever escapement with the form of escape wheel usually found in continental lever watches, as opposed to the English form of pointed-tooth escape wheel. In the club-tooth escape wheel the 'lift' is divided between the pallet stones and the impulse faces of the teeth. In the English form the impulse is taken entirely by the pallet stones.

COCK. A bracket, one end of which is fixed to the movement plate, the other end supporting the pivot of a wheel. The balance cock supports the top pivot of the balance staff and is mounted on the top plate of the watch movement. The earliest form was a simple S-shaped support. The cock was gradually given greater and more elaborate decoration to both foot and table, the former being that part of the cock which is fixed to the plate and the latter that part over the balance and providing the bearing for the top pivot of the balance staff. The English form of balance cock, as above described, is sometimes found on Dutch, German and Swiss watches of the early 18th century. Apart from this, the French and continental form of cock is round or oval with lateral lugs to take the fixing screws. In this form it is strictly speaking a bridge rather than a cock. Both English and continental cocks underwent changes, the finest quality being found between about 1625 and the early 18th century. Balance cocks are a useful guide to dating a watch.

COLLET. A cylindrical collar. An example is the small ring of metal which is fitted friction-tight to the balance staff to secure the inner end of the balance spring. A 'hand collet' is a dome-shaped washer to render secure the fitting of the hands.

COLOURED GOLD. See **TINTED GOLD.**

COMPENSATED BALANCE. A watch or chronometer balance that compensates for the effects of heat or cold. Airy showed, in 1859, that a chronometer with an uncompensated brass balance and steel spring lost on its rate 6·11 seconds in 24 hours for each degree (Fahrenheit) rise in temperature. It was known in the 18th century that changes in temperature affected the rate, and during the last half of that century various attempts were made to combat it. Pierre Le Roy was the first to attempt compensation by means of the balance which culminated in the cut bimetallic balance of Thomas Earnshaw. The same form of balance, only slightly modified, is used in modern marine chronometers, though it has been superseded in modern watches by a metal alloy monometallic balance coupled with an alloyed balance spring which is unaltered by temperature changes. See **BALANCE.**

COMPENSATION CURB. A laminated bar (or bimetallic strip) composed of brass and steel fixed at one end and free at the other, the later end carrying the curb pins (q.v.). It was first employed by John Harrison. The effect of a rise or fall in temperature causes the strip to bend, thus moving the curb pins in relation to the balance spring. The more usual form of the strip is an elongated U with one curb pin fixed to the free end of the strip, which is caused to move away from (in cold) or closer to (in heat) the other pin, thus varying the play of the spring between the pins and roughly compensating the effects of temperature on the steel balance spring and the balance itself. The U form of compensation curb is associated with Breguet and was fairly common in the earlier part of the 19th century. It was fixed to the index (q.v.). See also **SUGAR TONGS** and **'S' BALANCE.**

COMPLICATED WORK. A mechanism other than timekeeping — e.g. repeating, calendar work, chronograph work. La Vallée de Joux, Switzerland, became the centre for such work in the second half of the 19th century.

CONICAL PIVOT. A misleading term. 'Shoulderless pivot' would be more accurate. The pivot itself is straight, the 'shoulder' slightly conical. Breguet used conical (pointed) pivots to the balance staff of his shock-proofed watches. These give added strength, but they are not conducive to a close rate.

CONSULAR CASE. A double-bottom watch case fitted with a high rounded glass. Named in honour of Napoleon; at the time of their introduction he was Consul of France. The back of the case is hinged and when opened, a second back (or 'bottom') is revealed in which are the two holes for winding and hand-setting. The movement itself swings out from the front when the bezel is opened.

CONSTANT FORCE ESCAPEMENT. An escapement in which impulse is imparted by a spring which is itself tensioned by the going train. 'Constant' because the force or impulse delivered is unaffected by any irregularities arising from fluctuations in the power delivered by the mainspring. See also **REMONTOIRE**.

CONTRATE WHEEL. A wheel the teeth of which are at right angles to the plane of the wheel. In a watch with a verge escapement, it is the wheel which drives the escape wheel pinion.

CONVERSION. A watch is said to have been 'converted' if an escapement of one kind has been substituted for another. Thus a verge escapement may have been converted to a lever, and the escapement is a conversion. See also **ESCAPEMENT CONVERSION**.

COQUERET. A steel end-plate. After about 1735, a coqueret is found on French watches to give a bearing for the top balance staff pivot. it is screwed to the balance cock. By 1770 it was in general use on the continent for better quality watches until the introduction of jewelling from England. The underside was highly polished to give a good bearing for the pivot.

COUNT WHEEL. A wheel in the striking train that controls the number of hours struck. It consists of a series of eleven notches cut on the periphery of the wheel at increasing distances between each corresponding to the hours struck. A detent or L-shaped lever rides over the raised portions and drops into the slots as the count wheel revolves, which it is allowed to do at each hour when the detent is raised. The striking train is free to run when the detent is lifted, and the watch strikes for as long as the detent is held raised by the projections. There is no projection for 1 o'clock since the detent is merely lifted for a sufficient interval for one blow to be struck, and dropped again. Similarly, if half-hours are struck, the notches are sufficiently long to allow the detent to lift once and drop again before the next projection is reached. The system, though simple, has the disadvantage that the hours are struck in regular progression without reference to the positions of the hour hand. The alternative name for the count wheel is 'locking plate'. 'Rack-striking' superseded it.

COUNTERPOISE-PALLETS. In some high-quality Swiss levers of the 19th century a counterpoise to balance the pallets and fork was provided, the pallet arms, fork and counterpoise being filed out of one piece and highly polished.

'CRANK LEVER' ESCAPEMENT. A detached escapement sometimes referred to as the 'crank roller', or more recently as 'Massey's escapement'. This escapement, as designed by Edward Massey in 1814, appears in some respects to be a derivative of Litherland's rack lever (q.v.). The rack has

disappeared and substituted for the pinion is a roller mounted on the staff and having an impulse pin resembling a single leaf of a pinion; this projects from the circumference of the roller. The impulse pin acts in a square notch cut in the end of the lever, the notch being at right angles to the pallets. Two fork-like prongs extend either side of the notch and these provide the safety action, preventing the lever getting out of engagement until either of them enter slots cut on each side of the impulse pin. From about 1815, the acting surface of the pin was invariably a jewel — i.e. a jewel held between upper and lower sections of the 'pinion leaf', and a little later the entire pin became a jewel. There are thus three types of the crank lever. In the first form, draw seems to be absent, but in the later variants it was introduced. The crank lever led in due course to the single table roller (q.v.). Edward Massey died in 1852 and is buried in St. John's, Islington. He also invented a form of keyless winding.

A true cranked roller — i.e. where the roller is a separate entity to the balance staff — was used by Emery, the roller being pivoted, before 1800.

CRANK ROLLER. See **CRANK LEVER ESCAPEMENT**.

CROWN-WHEEL ESCAPEMENT. Another name for the verge escapement (q.v.). The name derives from the form of the escape wheel which somewhat resembles a medieval crown.

CRESCENT. The crescent-shaped hollow cut out of the roller in a lever escapement to permit the guard pin or dart to pass.

CURB COMPENSATION. See **COMPENSATION CURB**

CURB-PINS. Two pins which embrace the balance spring at its outer end near to its attachment. The pins are fixed to the regulator or index; 'index-pins' is an alternative term. The time of vibration of a balance is adjusted by altering the position of the pins. If the pins are moved towards the outer attachment point, the effective length of the spring is increased and the watch is made to lose; if the regulator (and therefore the curb-pins) is moved the opposite way, the reverse takes place. A similar effect to lengthening the spring is achieved by increasing the distance between the curb pins. See fig. 8.

CUT BIMETALLIC BALANCE. See **BALANCE**.

CUVETTE. An inside cover to protect the movement, hinged and sprung, often of brass even in good quality gold continental watches. The cuvette is sometimes provided with holes for the winding and set-hand squares, and is frequently engraved with the maker's name and movement number and often with the type of escapement and the number of jewels embodied in the movement.

CYLINDER ESCAPEMENT. See fig. 2 and 3. The escape wheel teeth in this escapement, unlike the verge, lie in a horizontal plane. The escape wheel usually has fifteen wedge-shaped teeth, standing above the rim of the wheel, the pointed end of the 'wedge' leading. Mounted on the balance staff is a polished steel tube or hollow cylinder — which gives the escapement its name — nearly one half of which is cut away allowing the teeth to enter as the balance swings back and forth and the wheel rotates. As each tooth enters the cylinder it impulses the balance on the entry lip of the cylinder wall. The tooth rests within the cylinder while the balance completes its oscillation (the 'supplementary arc') and begins its return journey. In due course the tooth escapes from within the cylinder, again giving impulse as it leaves. The succeeding tooth drops against the outside wall of the cylinder and the balance makes its excursion and return, after which the tooth enters the cylinder, and the process is repeated.

The diagram (fig. 2) shows the cycle of operation. Position 1 shows a tooth the instant before it enters the cylinder. 2 shows a tooth entering and giving impulse by sliding motion. At 3, the tooth has dropped on to the inner wall and the escape wheel is locked while the balance completes its excursion and begins its return journey, as seen in 4. 5 shows the position reached when the tooth escapes from the cylinder giving impulse as it does so to the balance in its back swing. Immediately it does escape, the next tooth following drops on to the outer wall of the cylinder, as seen in 6. As there is no 'recoil' (q.v.), the escapement is a 'dead-beat' type. It is also

classed as a 'frictional rest' escapement as opposed to a 'detached' one (q.v.). See also **RUBY CYLINDER** and **CYLINDER PLUGS**.

CYLINDER PLUGS. Plugs fitted into the top and bottom of the cylinder, the ends of which form the pivots for the balance staff.

DART. 'Guard-pin' is the alternative name for this safety device in the lever escapement. The dart is located on the end of the lever nearest the balance. It is also known as the 'safety pin', and its purpose is to prevent the escape wheel being unlocked except by the impulse pin.

DEAD-BEAT ESCAPEMENT. An escapement in which the escape wheel does not 'recoil' (q.v.). The cylinder escapement is a 'dead-beat' one.

DEAD-BEAT VERGE. The escape wheel is like that in the ordinary verge. Two bevelled-edge pallets are located on the balance staff. These receive impulse in each direction from the tip of an escape wheel tooth successively. This escapement would appear to have been derived from the Debaufre escapement (q.v.).

DEBAUFRE ESCAPEMENT. This escapement, like the cylinder, is a dead-beat, frictional rest escapement. It was invented by Peter Debaufre in 1704. There are two escape wheels, on the same axis, the teeth being saw-cut, and each set alternately in relation to each other, or 'staggered'. The balance staff is equidistant between them and at right angles to their axis. Fixed to the balance staff is a pallet, a semi-circular disc with an

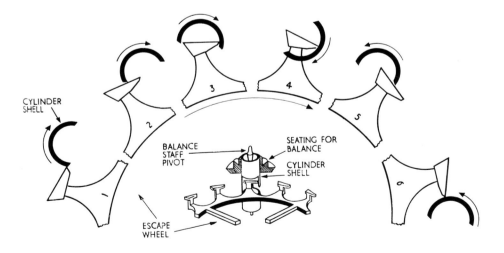

Fig. 2. Cylinder escapement.

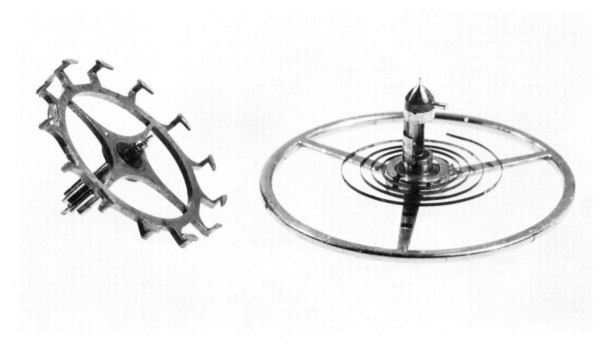

Fig. 3. Cylinder escape wheel, arbor and pinion. Balance, balance spring and cylinder. Also showing cylinder plug, banking pin, and lower pivot. These parts are from a movement by George Graham. Hallmarked 1739.

inclined plane cut on its edge. One tooth of the escape wheels alternately rests on the flat surface of the pallet while the balance oscillates, until the slope of the inclined plane is presented to it when it escapes, giving impulse as it slips down the inclined plane. Thus a succession of teeth, first one wheel and then its fellow, rest upon the pallet and then give impulse to the balance. There is no recoil.

Escapements known as the 'club-foot verge', the 'chaff-cutter' escapement (from the shape of the escape wheel teeth) or the Ormskirk escapement are derivatives. During the early 19th century the last enjoyed a mild popularity and a number were made at Ormskirk in Lancashire.

Henry Sully invented a similar escapement, and Paul Garnier's carriage clock escapement has similarity to the Debaufre form.

DEAF-PIECE. See PULSE-PIECE.

DECK WATCH. A large-sized and accurate watch used on board ship when making observations to find the ship's position, and to check the marine chronometer with an alternative time source.

DEPTH. If the meshing of two gears is excessive, the depth is said to be too great; if it is insufficient, the depth is too shallow. Bad gearing can have very adverse effects on timekeeping. general, depth is a term used by watchmakers for the degree of intersection or penetration between two parts. See also **END SHAKE.**

DETACHED ESCAPEMENT. An escapement in which the controller is free (or nearly so) from interference by the train. The lever escapement was often called specifically the 'detached escapement' or the 'detached lever' in its early history to distinguish it from the rack lever.

DETENT. A mechanism, or part, which prevents another part from operating at certain times or at one point in a cycle of operations. Two most common forms are those detents which cause a movement to stop in one direction only, and those which cause a movement to stop in both directions. It is, therefore, a locking device.

DETENT ESCAPEMENT. A detached escapement in which the escape wheel is locked on a stone (jewel) carried in a detent. Impulse is given by the teeth of the escape wheel — when a tooth is unlocked — to a pallet on the balance staff in every alternate swing of the balance.

The detent is a blade spring or alternatively a pivoted lever, that was used mainly by the Swiss from the middle of the nineteenth century. The detent or chronometer escapement is the most delicate and accurate of escapements used in portable timekeepers. The reader is referred to *The Marine Chronometer,* by R.T. Gould, for this specialised branch of watchmaking. See fig. 4.

DIFFERENTIAL DIAL. The centre of the dial is a revolving disc, with the hour numerals I to XII. This disc revolves $\frac{11}{12}$ of a full circle in an hour. An ordinary minute hand, centrally placed, revolves once an hour, and is thus always passing over the current hour. A few were made *circa* 1700, but later examples are known.

DIVIDED LIFT. If the impulse angle is divided between the impulse faces of the pallets and the teeth of the escape wheel, the lift is said to be divided. In the English form of lever escapement, all the lift is on the pallets. With the Swiss or French club-toothed escape wheel the lift is divided. An example of all the lift being on the teeth is S. Mairet's form where the pallets are pointed.

DOME. The second or inner cover of a later 19th-century watch case. This cover is hinged. The dome was a subsititute for the earlier dust-cap or the double-bottom case.

DOUBLE-BOTTOM CASE. A form of case in which the inner section is in one piece with the band of the case, the movement being attached to the case by joint and bolt. With the bezel opened, and the bolt pushed back, the movement hinges out of the case. The double bottom has a hole in which the key is inserted to wind the watch when the back is opened. A common form of watch case in England from the early 1800s to well past 1850. See **CONSULAR CASE.**

DOUBLE ROLLER. A lever escapement in which a second roller is used for the guard action.

Fig. 4. Spring detent from Earnshaw pocket chronometer, plate showing detent, wheel and roller.

Fig. 4. Late 19th century Swiss movement with pivoted detent showing detent staff with its cock removed. The coiled return spring is clearly visible as is the counterpoised extended arm of the detent.

DOUBLE 'S' BALANCE. An early form of bimetallic compensation balance used by John Arnold in 1779-82. The bimetallic 'strips' were formed into two elongated 'S' laminated pieces whose purpose and effect was to move inwards or outwards (in heat or cold) two weights situated on opposite sides of the balance rim.

"DOUBLE T" BALANCE. A compensated balance introduced by John Arnold which he used between 1778 and 1780. The plain steel circular rim is dissected by a flat steel bar on which the balance staff is mounted. The rim is also dissected by two bimetallic strips on either side and parallel to the bar. Attached to the centre of each of these strips and at right angles to them (thus making a "T") are steel rods that extend to the balance rim and pass through it with weights attached.

DRAW. The very slight recoil action of the lever escapement during unlocking to ensure that the lever is drawn to the banking pins while the balance is turning through its supplementary arc (q.v.). It is a safety action which counteracts the tendency of the lever to leave the banking before being impelled to do so by the impulse pin. In an escapement without draw, a jolt may cause the fork of the lever to move away from the banking pin during the supplementary arc so that the guard pin comes into contact with the roller's edge, thus creating friction.

Draw is achieved by the relative angles between the escape wheel teeth and the locking faces of the pallet stones. These are so formed that the pressure of a tooth on the locking face of the pallet produces a drawing-in motion of the pallet towards the wheel.

DROP. The free travel of the escape wheel after impulse and before locking.

DUMB-REPEATER. A repeating watch, the hammers for the hours and quarters striking upon a block in the case, or the case itself, instead of a bell or gongs. It was introduced by Julien Le Roy in about 1750.

DUPLEX-ESCAPEMENT. An escapement with two wheels on the same arbor, or — and this is far more commonly found — an escape wheel with two sets of teeth; one set for locking and one for giving impulse. It is a single-beat, frictional rest escapement. See figs. 5 and 6.

Long pointed teeth on the periphery of the escape wheel lock or rest against a hollow ruby cylinder fitted to the balance staff, and planted so that it arrests the teeth in their path. Cut in this cylinder or roller is a notch through which a tooth may pass (escape) when the balance is travelling in the opposite direction to that in which the escape wheel rotates. As a tooth is unlocked and escapes, a long finger (the impulse pallet) mounted on the balance staff above the roller receives an impulse from one of the shorter teeth which stand up from the face of the wheel and which are in the same plane as the impulse pallet. Impulse completed, the next pointed tooth drops on to the roller where it rides while the balance completes its swing — the supplementary arc. On the return swing, the roller notch slips past the tooth at rest on the roller without allowing it to escape. Hence

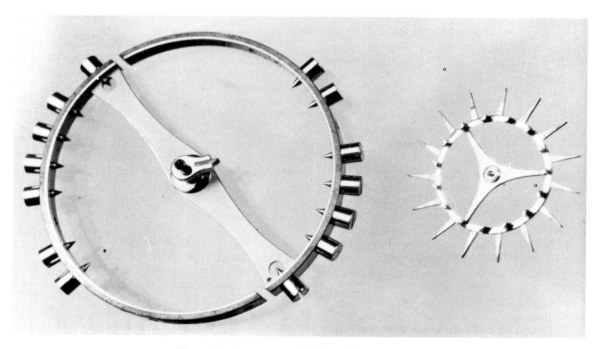

Fig. 5. Duplex escape wheel, staff and balance.

308

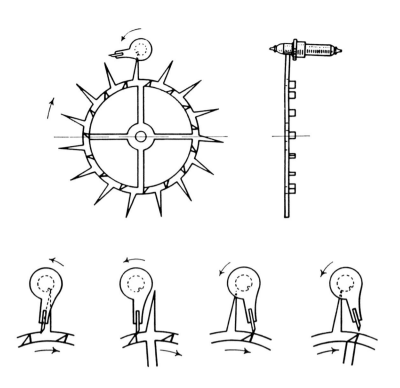

Fig. 6. Duplex escapement.

there is impulse in one direction only — when escape wheel and balance are travelling in opposite directions. Jean-Baptiste Dutertre (1715-42) invented the duplex escapement in its first form, Pierre Le Roy giving it the form in which we know it in about 1750. Thomas Tyrer patented it in England in 1782, No. 1311. It was particularly popular in England for high grade watches during the first three decades of the 19th century.

DUST-CAP. A cap to exclude dust fitted over the movement of pair-cased watches where the movement is hinged to the case. Dust-caps came into use in about 1715, and may have been introduced by George Graham. They are usually made of brass though occasionally of silver. Dust-caps are confined mainly to English watches.

DUTCH FORGERIES. Following the investigations of Mr. J.H. Leopold of Groningen, our ideas regarding the so-called 'Dutch forgeries' must be recast. It appears certain that during the second half of the 18th century there was a large export trade organised in Geneva which supplied inferior quality watches, many with spurious English names — and some even with forged English hallmarks — to England, Holland, Germany and other countries. Since many of these watches had dials with an arcaded minute band which had become popular among Dutch makers in the earlier part of the century, such watches have for long been thought to have originated in Holland, thus earning for that country the unenviable reputation which truly belongs to the city of

Geneva. The situation is however further confused by the possibility that enamel dials made in Geneva were exported and fitted to movements that are apparently genuinely English. Similarly *repoussé* cases — some very inferior — were exported and used in the importing country. Further Swiss movements were fitted into hallmarked English cases in Holland. The whole complex, therefore, was one of merchandising rather than watchmaking.

The watches in question are often recognisable by inferior workmanship, a bridge rather than a balance cock, a curious maker's name without a Christian name or initial, and an arcaded minute band to the dial.

EBAUCHE. Movement blank, or rough movement in the incomplete stage — 'in the grey'. In the early 19th century the *ébauche* was made up of two plates with pillars and bars, barrel, fusee, index, click and ratchet wheel and assembly screws. The parts were roughly filed and milled. In England during the 19th century, Lancashire became the centre of the movement trade. One of the best known makers was Joseph Preston & Sons of Prescot, founded in 1829. Their movements were stamped J.P. The work was much sub-divided.

END SHAKE. Axial play, or necessary clearance between the ends or shoulders of an arbor and the bearing surfaces.

ENDSTONE. An end-plate made of a jewel. A jewel set in a ring upon which a watch pivot rests, particularly for the balance staff pivot. It is generally fixed to the balance cock by means of screws. In continental watches, the end-plate was a polished steel plate screwed to the balance cock. It is called a 'coqueret' (q.v.). Endstones are also referred to as 'cap jewels'. English makers often used diamonds for the balance staff endstone.

ENDLESS SCREW. Also called a 'worm' or tangent screw.

ENGINE TURNING. Decoration performed by an engine-turning lathe, producing a variety of patterns on a metal surface. It is also known as *guilloché*. It was a very popular method of decorating watch cases from about 1770, often being overlaid with transparent or translucent enamel.

ENGLISH LEVER ESCAPEMENT. A lever escapement in which the escape wheel teeth are pointed, and the lift is entirely on the pallets. See also **LEVER ESCAPEMENT.**

ENTRY PALLET. The receiving pallet, which receives impulses from the escape wheel teeth as they enter. The exit pallet, or discharging pallet, receives impulse as the teeth leave.

EQUATION OF TIME. Adding to or subtracting from true solar (sun) time the amount necessary to obtain mean time, mean time being the average length of all the solar days in the year, which is therefore a mathematical division. The 'equation' was worked out by John Flamsteed in about 1670. He tabulated the difference between noon mean time and true solar noon. The tables were used to check a watch against a sun dial. A few watches have been made to show the equation on a subsidiary dial. Watch papers were sometimes printed giving the equation.

ESCAPEMENT. That part of the movement which controls the release of the motive power. The escapement both controls the release of the driving force and also imparts energy (impulses) to the balance to maintain it in oscillation. The regularity with which this dual action takes place is controlled by the balance and its spring. The *timekeeping* properties of an escapement, therefore, depend essentially upon the balance and spring.

Escapements may be classified as:

(1) Frictional rest, in which the balance is constantly in contact with a part of the escapement — e.g. (a) recoil escapements in which the locking faces are eccentric, causing a recoil of the escape wheel; (b) dead-beat escapements, with concentric locking faces, which give no recoil.

(2) Detached escapement, in which the balance is detached from the escapement except at the time of locking and receiving impulse. The verge escapement is an example of 1(a). The cylinder is an example of 1(b) and the lever an example of 2.

A single beat escapement gives a single impulse for each double swing of the balance. The duplex and the chronometer detent escapement are examples. A constant-force escapement employs an intermediate spring, a 'remontoire', wound periodically by the train, which spring impulses the balance.

ESCAPEMENT CONVERSION. Watches that had verge, cylinder, duplex and other escapements are to be found converted to lever. Very often there is an extra cock between the movement plates, see fig. 7, while at the same time the balance together with its spring is normally replaced and occasionally the cock. The new escapement required fresh pivot holes in the plates, leaving the original ones empty and these were nearly always filled and the plates regilded. Conversions were mostly carried out in the last three quarters of the 19th century to improve reliability. Modifications from early to later forms of the same escapement are also found.

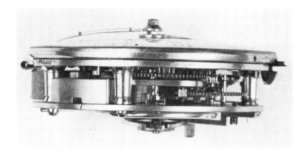

Fig. 7. Escapement conversion. Late 18th century movement with escapement converted in the 19th century to lever. A new cock, balance, balance spring and an extra cock between the plates have been fitted as well as an escapement.

ESCAPE WHEEL. The last wheel in the going train, which permits 'escape' of the motive power, giving impulse to the balance. It is alternately locked and released.

EXIT PALLET. See **ENTRY PALLET**.

FALSE PENDULUM. Also called a 'mock pendulum'. A small disc on one arm of a balance, visible through a slot or aperture in the dial or balance cock. The motion of the arm with disc attached gives the appearance of a pendulum, the second arm and the rim of the balance not being visible. The type was popular around 1700, particularly in Holland where the balance bridge type continued well into the century. If provided with a glass over the slot and a rim round the bridge, this type affords protection to the balance.

FIGURE PLATE. See **REGULATION**.

FIVE-MINUTE REPEATER. A repeating watch which gives the hours and a blow for each five minutes past the hour. In some cases the quarters are given in addition. A number were made in the second half of the 18th century and a few a hundred years later, but they are comparatively rare. They first appeared about 1710.

FLAGS. The pallets of the verge escapement are so called.

FLIRT. A lever or other device for causing a sudden movement of mechanism.

FLOATING HOUR DIAL. See **WANDERING HOUR**.

FLY. A two-bladed fan, acting as an air brake or governor to regulate the speed of striking or repeating.

FLY-BACK HAND. In split-seconds chronographs (q.v.) a centre seconds-hand that can move while remaining superimposed on the first hand, but which can be stopped independently and then made to fly back (or forward) to join the first hand as it moves round the dial.

FOB CHAIN. A short chain (or ribbon with metal attachments) fixed by swivel or bolt ring to the bow of a watch, and hanging outside the pocket.

FOLIOT. The earliest form of escapement controller, and applied to the verge escapement. It was first used in clocks. In a watch it takes the form of a cross bar with weighted ends — giving it a dumb-bell shape — carried at the upper end of the verge. It is found mostly on early German stackfreed watches, though it was being supseded by a plain two-arm ring or balance before 1600. The word probably derives from Old French 'folier', to dance madly.

FORGERIES. Forgeries of famous makers' work were most flagrant in the earlier part of the 18th century and again in the early 19th. In the former period, famous makers such as Tompion, Quare and Graham were the main victims, and in the latter, Breguet. See **DUTCH FORGERIES**.

FORK. The fork-shaped end of the lever in the lever escapement within which is the notch.

FOURTH WHEEL. The wheel in a watch that drives the escape wheel pinion, to the arbor of which the seconds hand is often attached.

FORM WATCH. A watch the case of which is made in the form of a cross, star, skull, flower bud or other bizarre shape. A number were made in the early 17th century and again 200 years later, when musical instruments were the most popular form.

FOUR-COLOURED GOLD. See **TINTED GOLD**.

FRAME. The movement plates.

FREE-SPRUNG. A balance spring unfettered by curb pins. Used in marine chronometers, pocket chronometers and very high grade watches. The rate of a watch so sprung can be adjusted by the timing screws on the balance.

FRICTIONAL REST ESCAPEMENT. An escapement in which the balance is never free from the escapement — e.g. the verge, cylinder and duplex escapements. It is therefore inferior to a detached escapement — e.g. the detent and the lever escapements.

FULL PLATE. A watch calibre in which the top plate (that furthest from the dial), as well as the pillar plate, is a circular plate, with the balance mounted above the top plate.

A three-quarter plate movement has a section of the upper (top) plate cut away to allow the balance to be mounted in the same plane as the plate, the balance and the escape wheel having separate cocks. In a half-plate movement, the fourth wheel, escape wheel and balance have separate cocks.

FUSEE. A mainspring-equaliser. A spirally grooved, truncated cone with the great wheel mounted upon it. A length of gut — after about 1670 a chain — connects the fusee to the mainspring barrel, one end being attached to the barrel and the other to the fusee. The winding key fits over the squared end of the fusee arbor, and the act of winding draws the chain from the barrel on to the fusee, starting at the wide end of the 'cone' and taking it up the spiral groove. As the chain is taken off the barrel, the mainspring is wound. The mainspring when fully wound exerts a greater torque than when it is only partially so. In unwinding, the chain is, of course, drawn off the narrow end of the fusee first, where it is acting with less leverage and this compensates the greater pull of the mainspring. Greater leverage comes into play as the chain is drawn towards the thicker end of the fusee; thus the tapering fusee matches the diminishing strength of the spring. This ensures a relatively constant motive force. The early long, tapering fusees were only moderately effective, but as time went on, and by empirical methods, a form with correct hyperbola curves was evolved.

A stop is fitted to the upper end of the fusee.

As the chain coils round the last groove of the fusee, it lifts a lever which comes up against a cam on the fusee and stops the mechanism. The mounting for the fusee stop lever or arm was given decoration after about 1650. The fusee was known — it appears in early manuscripts — in about 1450-70.

A fusee with maintaining power is known as a 'going fusee'.

FUSEE CHAIN. A steel chain as a substitute for a gut cord was invented in about 1635, but some years elapsed before it was made small enough for watch movements. It is rarely found in watches before 1670, and those on earlier watches are frequently conversions from gut to chain. The groove in a fusee intended for gut are rounded. It is probable that fusee chains were at first imported for English watches. From the early 19th century Christchurch in Hampshire specialised in fusee chain making. For the first quarter-century the work was done by young women and children in the Christchurch workhouse, but it later developed into a cottage industry.

GADROONING. Ornamentation found on the edges of late 18th and early 19th century watches. The decoration consists of either hammered or cast radiating lobes of curved or straight form.

GATE. The name given to the decorative piece covering the fusee stop finger. More correctly, the piece over the locking detent of the striking chain.

GATHERING PALLET. Part of the rack-striking mechanism; a finger which makes one revolution for each stroke of the hour and gathers one tooth of the rack.

GIMBALS SUSPENSION. Two independent concentric rings free to turn round their respective axes. Gimbals are used in marine chronometers to maintain the instrument in a horizontal position regardless of the pitching and rolling of the ship. Girolamo Cardano (1501-76) — 'cardan joint' — is credited with the invention.

GOING BARREL. See BARREL.

GOING FUSEE. A fusee with maintaining power (q.v.).

GOING TRAIN. See TRAIN.

GONGS. Coiled wire used for striking or repeating watches in place of a bell. Possibly introduced by Julien Le Roy (1686-1759).

GRANDE SONNERIE. A watch which strikes both the hours and quarters at each quarter.

GREAT WHEEL. The first wheel in the train. In a going barrel watch it is on the going barrel. See BARREL.

GUARD PIN. See DART.

GUILLOCHE. See ENGINE TURNING.

HAIRSPRING. A common name for the balance spring (q.v.).

HALF PLATE. See FULL PLATE.

HALF-QUARTER. A repeater which, in addition to repeating the hours and quarters, also gives an additional single stroke if 7½ minutes or more have elapsed since the last quarter. Introduced in about 1695.

HALLMARK. The mark made by punches on gold or silver, consisting of the standard mark, the mark of the Hall (e.g. the Goldsmith's Hall, London, the Birmingham mark, etc.), the quality of the metal, the date letter and the maker's mark. Other countries have assay marks.

HAND-SETTING. Also set-hand mechanism. Mechanism for altering the position of the hands. In the earliest watches this was done by pushing the hour hand directly to the right time. With two-hand watches, this was first done by fitting the key on to the hand-set square (the arbor carrying the hands). With the introduction of keyless work (q.v.) the hands can be set through the winding button. Also see MOTION WORK.

HANGING BARREL. See STANDING BARREL.

HEART PIECE. A heart-shaped cam used in chronograph work to cause the chronograph hand to fly back to zero. Patented by A. Nicole in 1844, No. 10348.

HELICAL SPRING. See BALANCE SPRING.

HOG'S BRISTLE. A bristle or flexible hair. Found on early German watches, where two upright, short bristles mounted on a pivoted arm act as banking pins to limit the supplementary arc of the foliot or balance, each end of the foliot striking against a bristle in turn. By moving the pivoted arm a degree of regulation can be effected, a shorter arc giving a faster rate and vice versa. A much rarer form is where a long bristle, fixed at one end, is flexed at its free end by two pins standing upright on the rim of the balance; reducing the length of the bristle causes a faster rate. Both forms give a certain amount of elasticity to the action of the balance.

HOOKE'S LAW. Hooke's Law relating to springs. See BALANCE SPRING.

HORIZONTAL ESCAPEMENT. See CYLINDER ESCAPEMENT, which is the alternative and now more usual name.

HORNS. The horn-shape extremity of the fork in the lever escapement. The two 'prongs' extend on each side of the notch.

HOUR RACK. Part of the striking mechanism that is moved one tooth for each hour. The rack — which is a pivoted toothed sector — has a tail which drops on to the snail (q.v.) and its position in relation to this determines how many teeth are to be gathered by the gathering pallet (q.v.) which in turn determines how many hours are struck. A quarter rack acts similarly for the quarter-hours. Rack striking was invented by Edward Barlow in 1676.

HOUR WHEEL. The wheel which carries the hour hand.

HUNTER. A watch the case of which has a front as well as a back cover, thus affording protection to the glass. The front is opened by means of a push-piece. A half-hunter has a small thick glass (a 'pebble glass') fitted into the front cover allowing a portion of the dial and hands to be seen.

IMPULSE. The energy or 'push' derived from the mainspring via the train and the escapement and imparted to the balance to maintain its oscillations. In the Swiss lever escapement, for example, the impulse is the action of the escape wheel tooth on the impulse face of the pallet, and the lever fork on the impulse pin.

IMPULSE ANGLE. In the Swiss lever escapement, it is the angle through which the lever moves between the first contact of the tooth of the escape wheel on the impulse face and the last.

IMPULSE PALLET. The pallet which receives impulse.

IMPULSE PIN. Alternatively called the 'ruby pin'. In the lever escapement it is fixed into the roller and works in the notch of the fork. On entering the notch it unlocks the escape wheel, receives impulse from the lever and passes out of the notch on the opposite side of the fork. The impulse pin is made of ruby or sapphire — nowadays synthetic — and may be elliptical, semi-circular or half-moon, or triangular in shape.

INDEPENDENT SECONDS. A watch having a seconds hand driven by a separate train. Attributed to J.M. Pouzait, in 1776. The seconds hand in such a watch may be stopped without interfering with the normal functioning of the watch.

INDEX. Regulator. A small lever, the shorter end of which carries the curb pins (q.v.), the longer end passes over a scale to serve as an indicator of any alteration made in the position of the curb pins when regulating the watch by moving the index forwards 'S' or 'R' ('slow' or *retard*) or 'F' or 'A' ('fast' or *avance*). See fig. 8.

ISOCHRONOUS. Occurring in equal periods of time. A balance would be truly isochronous if the duration of the oscillations were the same whether the arcs were long or short, if the duration of the arcs were independent of the amplitude of swing. The arcs are affected by — among other factors — the position of the balance (i.e. whether vertical or horizontal) and by the impulses delivered by the escapement. The technique of timing consists in achieving the isochronism of the oscillations of the balance. The chief factors that impair isochronism are: the escapement, the play of the balance spring between the curb pins, faulty poising of the balance and its spring. Pierre Le Roy was the first watchmaker to investigate the supposed isochronal

properties of the watch balance and spring in 1760. John Arnold found by experiment that a helical spring can be made isochronous, or very nearly so, by 'incurving' the terminal coils. See **BALANCE SPRING.**

JACQUEMART. Also called 'Jack'. Strictly, the model figure or automaton which strikes or appears to strike a bell at the hours or quarters. In watches the term is generally applied to repeating watches where figures appear to strike bells but where, in fact, normal repeating work causes hammers to strike gongs. Such watches were popular in France and Switzerland during the early 19th century. Some, not strictly speaking jacquemarts, depict unedifying subjects.

JEWELS. Bearings in a watch movement made of ruby, sapphire, crystal or garnet; in modern watches synthetic jewels are used. Their purpose is to reduce friction and to 'trap' the oil. See fig. 9. A 'jewel hole' is a stone pierced to take a pivot of a wheel. The chief types of watch jewels are: a flat jewel hole, the hole being cylindrical for a shouldered pivot; a domed jewel with endstone for a conical pivot, the tip of the pivot resting on the endstone; the pallet stones; the impulse pin. In the cylinder escapement the cylinder shell is sometimes a jewel, and is then referred to as a 'ruby cylinder'.

Nicholas Facio de Duillier in conjunction with

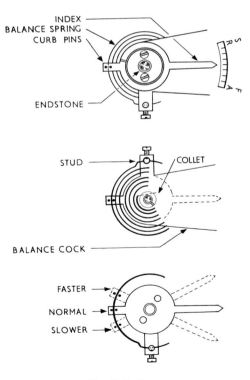

Fig. 8. Index.

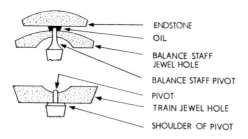

ENDSTONE
OIL
BALANCE STAFF
JEWEL HOLE
BALANCE STAFF PIVOT
PIVOT
TRAIN JEWEL HOLE
SHOULDER OF PIVOT

Fig. 9. Jewels.

Peter and Jacob Debaufre took out a patent (No. 371) in 1704 for a method of piercing jewels. These watchmakers were French immigrants working in Soho, London. Train jewel holes are exceptional until about 1800, and then only on high grade work.

JUMP-HOUR. An hour hand which jumps forward at the hour, not moving in regular progression. Often used by Breguet in his repeating watches.

JUMPING-HOURS. Hour numerals that appear through an aperture, and change at each hour. A number of such watches were made on the continent in the earlier part of the 19th century. The idea was revived in wristwatches before the Second World War.

JUMPING-SECONDS. A hand which every second completes one revolution of a subsidiary dial, or which does so in four- or five-second jumps.

KARRUSEL. A type of watch incorporating a device to eliminate errors of rate in the vertical positions. The escapement is mounted on a carriage or cage, the carriage being driven by the third wheel pinion, revolving once in 52½ minutes. Invented by Bonniksen and patented in England in 1894. Also see **TOURBILLON.**

KEYLESS WATCH. A watch which can be wound and the hands set without the aid of a key. Keyless mechanism was perfected at the end of the last century.

KEYLESS WINDING. A watch which can be wound without a key. A variety of systems were evolved during the 19th century, among the first that of Thomas Prest, who took out patent No. 4501 in 1820. See also **PUMP-WIND.**

LEPINE CALIBRE. A watch movement in which the top plate is replaced by bars or bridges. Introduced by J.A. Lepine in about 1770. This layout made possible a much thinner watch, particularly with countersinks in the dial plate and a hanging going barrel.

LEVER ESCAPEMENT. Basically, an escapement in which impulse is imparted to the balance by means of a lever, having at one end a pair of pallets which engage with the teeth of the escape wheel,

and at the other a fork with a notch, into which the impulse pin on a roller fixed to the balance staff enters, receives impulses from the lever, and exits.

The lever escapement can be divided into two main forms: the English with pointed escape wheel teeth, and the continental or modern Swiss form with club teeth. In the former the lift is on the pallets, and in the latter it is divided between pallets and teeth. The action of both is fundamentally the same.

Fig. 10 shows the right-angled English form with single or table roller. In the last quarter of the 19th century the double roller was used on high quality watches, the safety action provided by the dart taking place on a separate and smaller roller located below the impulse roller. The Swiss form has two rollers as seen in fig. 11.

Here, A designates the escape wheel. B and C are banking pins: two vertical pins which limit the travel of the lever in either direction. D is the dart or guard pin. E is the impulse roller mounted on the balance staff (not shown) and F, located on E, is the impulse or ruby pin. Below E is the second or safety roller, also mounted on the staff, with a crescent cut away at G. H and H are the horns of the lever. Neither the balance staff, balance nor balance spring are shown. The impulse pin F projects downwards from the underside of the roller E and engages in the rectangular notch of the fork between the horns H and H. The dart D, attached to the lever, is at a lower level than the horns being in the same plane as the safety roller and crescent G.

Position 1 in the diagram shows a tooth of the escape wheel, which revolves in a clockwise direction, at rest on the locking face of the entry pallet. The escapement is locked. The impulse pin has just entered the notch in the lever fork. The balance must be imagined, at this moment, to be swinging in an anti-clockwise direction taking, of course, the rollers and the impulse pin with it as it swings. The lever is at rest on the banking pin B. As the balance continues its swing, it causes the impulse pin F to move the lever and pallets over from left to right, so releasing the tooth from the locking edge of the entry pallet. As the tooth leaves the locking edge of the pallet it moves along the impulse face of the pallet, giving impulse to the lever as it pushes the pallet out of its path. This is shown in 2. The impulse given to the lever is transferred via the notch to the impulse pin, and thus to the balance. 3 shows the position reached after this motion is completed.

By the time the tooth whose movement we have been following is clear of the impulse face of the entry pallet, the second tooth in advance of it drops on to the locking edge (on the inner side) of the exit pallet, and the escape wheel is again momentarily held; the lever is now at rest on

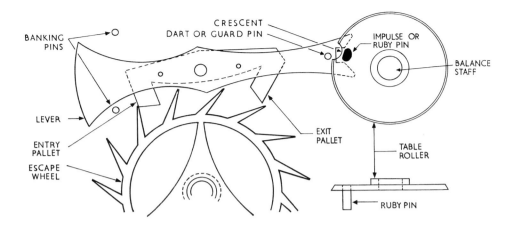

Fig. 10. English lever.

banking pin C while the balance completes its oscillation, still in the anti-clockwise direction but detached from the escapement.

When the energy delivered by the impulse and the momentum of the balance is expended, the balance spring exerts itself by 'uncoiling', reversing the motion of the balance. In due course the impulse pin again enters the notch, from the opposite direction from that in which it left it, as shown in 4, and the operation just described is repeated; this time, however, the exit pallet is unlocked, and impulse is given to that pallet to assist the balance in its clockwise motion by 'pushing' the lever over from right to left. Position 5 shows the final stage reached in the cycle, with a tooth again locked on the entry pallet and the balance completing its swing in a clockwise direction, and detached from the escapement.

The escape wheel teeth are so formed in relation to the pallets that the pressure of a tooth on the locking face produces a drawing-in motion of the pallet towards the escape wheel. This is the important device of 'draw'. Its purpose is to counteract the tendency of the lever to leave the banking pins before it is impelled to do so by the ruby pin acting within the notch.

The purpose of the banking pins is to limit the supplementary travel of the lever, in either direction, after locking has taken place.

The object of the dart is to prevent the escape wheel being unlocked while the balance is oscillating free of the escapement; if this were to happen, the impulse pin would come into contact with the outside of the horn and the watch would stop. It *cannot* happen because if the lever is jerked by some outside cause while the balance is free, the dart comes up against the edge of the safety roller and prevents further movement of the lever. The crescent is cut in the safety roller to allow the dart to pass freely while the impulse pin is within the fork.

The horns of the fork are an additional safety device and may come into play while the dart is passing through the crescent and the impulse pin is within the fork. The horns are there to act in place of the dart at that stage.

LEVER NOTCH. In the lever escapement, the opening in the fork into which the impulse pin pentrates.

LIFT. The angle through which the lever travels (in the lever escapement) during the impulse and escaping action. Lift may be divided between the pallets and the escape wheel teeth (the club-tooth) or be all on the pallets (pointed wheel teeth) or all on the teeth (with pointed pallets).

LIGNE. Also Line. A French and Swiss unit of measurement for indicating the size of a movement. A ligne = 2.25 mm.

"LIVERPOOL" JEWELS. Inordinately large but impressive movement jewels, popular with Liverpool makers in the second half of the 19th century.

LOCK(ING). The period between impulse when the train is locked and the balance is completing its oscillation, in either direction — i.e. during its supplementary arc (q.v.).

LOCKING PLATE. See **COUNT WHEEL.**

LUNETTE. A rounded watch glass, only slightly domed.

MAINSPRING. The spring which provides the driving power for the going or striking sides of a watch movement.

MAINTAINING POWER. A device for driving a fusee movement by means of a ratchet and click during the action of winding when the power is otherwise taken off.

MALTESE CROSS. A wheel of that shape forming part of a stop-work (q.v.). It is associated with the 'Geneva' stop-work.

MARINE CHRONOMETER. See **DETENT ESCAPEMENT.**

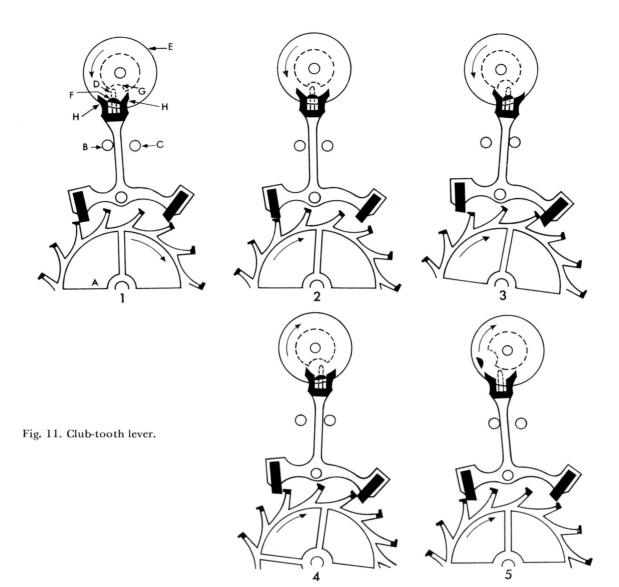

Fig. 11. Club-tooth lever.

MASSEY LEVER ESCAPEMENT. See **CRANK LEVER ESCAPEMENT.**

MEAN TIME. The time recorded by a watch; that is the average of all the solar days in the year is the ordinary day of 24 hours.

MIDDLE TEMPERATURE ERROR. The elasticity of a balance spring does not vary with temperature changes in the same proportion as the compensating effects of the bimetallic balance (q.v.). A watch with such a balance will only be accurate in its rate for two given temperatures. The inaccuracy between the two extreme temperatures (the M.T.E.) may be corrected by auxiliary compensation.

MINUTE REPEATER. A watch which not only repeats the hours and quarters, but also the minutes which have elapsed since the last quarter. A very few were made in the last quarter of the

18th century and they are not common until the end of the 19th.

MOCK PENDULUM. See **FALSE PENDULUM.**

MOON HAND. See **BREGUET HAND.**

MOTION WORK. The gearing under the dial which causes the hour hand to travel twelve times slower than the minute hand. It consists of the cannon pinion, minute wheel and pinion and hour wheel.

MOVEMENT. The main assembly of a watch comprising the power, transmission, escapement, regulating, winding and handsetting mechanisms. In short, the 'works' without the case, hands or dial. Also see **EBAUCHE.**

MUSICAL WATCH. A watch with separate mechanism, set in motion at each hour or at will, which produces a tune on the steel comb and pinned barrel principle. Introduced in Switzerland at the end of the 18th century.

NIELLO. A process similar to *champlevé* enamel but using a black metallic filling of silver, lead and sulphur.

NOTCH. See LEVER NOTCH.

NUREMBERG EGG. A misnomer for early South German watches, which in fact were not oval in form but spherical or drum-shape. The term arose from a misreading and mistranslation of 'Uhrlein' into 'Eierlein': 'little watch' — 'little egg'.

OIL SINK. A small cavity turned in the outside surface of the movement plates around the holes for the pivots to retain the oil. Introduced by Henry Sully in about 1715. Jewels, too, have a sink for oil retention.

OIGNON. The popular name given to the large and rather bulbous French watches of the late 17th and early 18th centuries.

OPEN FACE. An 'open face' watch is one without a front cover — i.e. neither a hunter nor a half hunter.

ORMSKIRK. A town in Lancashire. In the early 19th century, a number of watches with a type of Debaufre escapement were made there, and these are known as 'Ormskirk' watches. See DEBAUFRE ESCAPEMENT and DEAD-BEAT VERGE.

OUTER CASE. The outside case in a pair-case watch. Such cases were often embellished.

OVERCOIL. The last coil of a Breguet balance spring. See BALANCE SPRING.

PAIR-CASE. The standard form of case for English watches from 1650 to 1800 and beyond. Also widely used on the continent during the earlier years. The inner case, which houses the movement, is generally without decoration unless the watch is a repeater, alarum, or a striking watch when it is pierced and sometimes given minor decoration. The outer case normally is decorated; *repoussé*, engraved, enamelled, or hollowed agate or some other hard stone, or decorated in some other way according to the fashion of the period. Sometimes the outer is left plain, particularly at the end of the period.

PALLET. In particular, the part or parts through which the escape wheel teeth give impulse to the balance. In the club-tooth lever escapement a tooth locks on the outer edge of the pallet after impulse has been given by the preceding tooth. In general, the pallets are jewels and termed 'pallet-stones'.

'PARACHUTE'. A device invented by Breguet in which the endstones of the balance staff are supported in short arms of spring steel: hence 'sprung jewels', which give a cushioning effect to the staff pivots should the watch be dropped. It is the earliest form of shock-resisting device. Also *suspension élastique*.

PASSING CRESCENT. See CRESCENT.

PASSING SPRING. Also known as the 'gold spring', out of which metal it is usually made. It is mounted on a detent in the chronometer escapement. The discharging pallet on the staff unlocks a tooth in one direction. On the return swing it passes the detent without disturbance due to the flexibility of the passing spring.

PEDOMETER WATCH. Sometimes understood to mean a watch and pedometer combined. Ralph Gout took out patent No 2351 for such a watch in 1799.

PEDOMETER-WIND. See PERPETUAL WATCH.

PENDANT. A neck, fitted to the case of a watch, to which the bow (q.v.) is fitted. In a keyless watch, the winding button is at the top of the pendant, the winding button stem passing through the pendant.

PENDULUM WATCH (DIAL). A watch in which a 'mock' or 'false' pendulum (q.v.) appears through an aperture in the dial or is visible through a slot cut in the balance cock or bridge. See also FALSE PENDULUM.

PERPETUAL CALENDAR. A calendar watch which takes into account not only the short months, but leap years, without manual adjustment.

PERPETUAL WATCH. The English translation of the French *'montre perpétuelle'* is the name given to a watch which is wound by the oscillation of a pivoted weight during the movements of the wearer. Also called a pedometer-winding watch. Its invention by A.L. Perrelet in about 1770 is generally now accepted. Breguet made a number of such watches. Recordon took out patent No. 1249 for a pedometer-winding watch in 1780.

PILLARS. The pillars of a watch movement are the 'distance pieces' which serve to keep the two plates in their relative positions. The earliest were of plain square section. Later, spiral or round baluster forms were introduced. After about 1600, types became diverse: vase-shape, pyramidical (so-called Egyptian), tulip-form, pierced foliate, lyre-shaped, square section baluster, and finally cylindrical.

PILLAR PLATE. The plate, nearest the dial, to which the pillars are fixed. The pillars are merely *pinned* to the top plate — i.e. that furthest from the dial.

PINION. A small toothed wheel. The 'teeth' are spoken of as 'leaves'. In watch work the wheel is the driver and the pinion is the follower, except in the motion work.

PINCHBECK. An alloy of zinc and copper — named after its inventor, Christopher Pinchbeck, about 1730 — which resembles gold in colour. The term is used rather indiscriminately for gilded brass.

PIN WORK. See PIQUE.

PIQUE. Or 'pin work'. Pins of gold, silver or brass, the purpose of which is to secure the leather, shagreen or tortoise-shell covering to the outer cases of watches. The practical purpose also served decorative ends in that the heads of the pins were arranged in a decorative pattern. Indeed, more pins were inserted than was strictly necessary in order to form a decoration.

PIROUETTE. A balance staff with integral pinion, thereby causing the balance to swing through a large arc.

PIVOT. The extremity of a rotating arbor on which it is supported.

PIVOTED DETENT. The pivoted detent performs the same function as the blade spring. See **SPRING DETENT.** John Arnold used this form of detent on his early chronometers. It was favoured more on the continent than in this country.

PLATES. The flat discs between which the wheels and pinions are pivoted. They form the foundation of the movement.

POISE. A balance is in poise if it has no heavy point; if its equilibrium is unaffected by change of position.

POKER HAND. A minute hand somewhat resembling a poker in form. Usually associated with the beetle hour hand (q.v.).

POSITIONAL ERROR. Changes in the rate of a watch arising from the different positions — i.e. the horizontal and the vertical.

POTENCE. Also spelled 'potance'. A hang-down bracket supporting a pivot; in particular (in watchwork) the underslung bracket supporting the lower pivot of the balance staff in full plate watches.

In the early balance spring verge, the verge was pivoted between the balance cock and an extended piece (to give a bearing) of a bracket extending between the movement plates. Later, as a flatter watch became the fashion, this bracket (the potence) was reduced in length and the crown wheel reduced in size.

A second extended block on the potence — rather less than mid-way between the top plate and the bearing for the lower pivot of the verge — gave the bearing for the inner pivot of the crown wheel arbor, the other pivot being carried in a second block with an endpiece mounted on the underside and at the edge of the top or potence plate. Julien Le Roy introduced an improvement to make this second block or bearing for the crown escape wheel adjustable as well as the bearing for the inner pivot, i.e. an adjustable potence which enabled the action of the escapement to be adjusted without dismantling the movement. The use of a screwdriver or key will move the inner pivot, and thus the crown wheel across the verge to bring it into beat. The adjustable steel endpiece on the outer pivot enables the depth of the engagement to be varied, and thus the arc of escapement (see fig. 1).

POTENCE PLATE. An alternative name for the top plate to which the potence is fixed.

POUZAIT ESCAPEMENT. J.M. Pouzait, 1743-93, introduced a form of lever escapement in 1786 which has been named after him. It was perhaps the first lever escapement with divided lift (q.v.). The thirty escape wheel teeth stand up from the plane of the wheel. The steel pallets are rather claw-like in appearance and the notch imparts impulse to the balance acting upon a steel impulse pin located on the balance staff. The balance diameter is almost that of the movement plate and the escapement beats seconds. An upright pin on one arm of the lever, acting on the outside of a safety ring on the balance staff in one direction, passes through an opening in the ring in the other direction, then being within the safety ring; this provides the safety action.

PULL-WIND. See **PUMP-WIND.**

PUMP-WIND. An early form of keyless winding. The watch is wound by moving a shaft, located in the pendant, in and out: a pushing or pulling action. Edward Massey and Viner are associated with forms of pump or pull winding.

PULSE-PIECE. A pin projecting from the edge of a repeating movement and through to a hole in the bottom edge of the case. The finger, held against the pin, receives the blows of the hammer when the watch is striking instead of the bell. Also called a 'deaf-piece' or by the French name 'sourdine'.

PURITAN WATCH. A simple form of English watch, oval in shape, without decoration and usually in silver. They were made between about 1625 and 1650.

QUARTER RACK. See **HOUR RACK.**

QUARTER REPEATER. A watch which repeats the hours and quarters when a push-piece is depressed or a slide-piece moved.

RACK. A toothed segment. See **HOUR RACK.**

RACK LEVER ESCAPEMENT. See fig. 12. A form of lever escapement patented by Peter Litherland in 1791, patent No 1830, but an earlier escapement embodying the same principle was invented by the Abbé de Hautefeuille in 1722. The lever terminates in a rack which meshes with a pinion on the balance staff. The balance is never detached. It was made in large numbers in Lancashire in the early 19th century.

RACK STRIKING. See **HOUR RACK.**

RATCHET WHEEL. Saw-toothed wheel. The fronts of the teeth of a ratchet wheel are radial and the backs straight lines. Used in conjunction with a click (pawl) and spring and fixed by a square hole to the barrel arbor. The click prevents

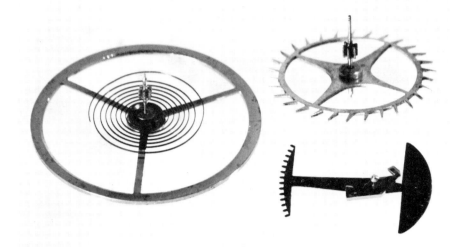

Fig. 12. Rack lever. Balance staff with pinion. Lever with rack, jewelled pallets and counterpoise. Brass escape wheel. Thirty inclined teeth.

the wheel turning in the unwinding direction. Ratchet wheel set-up was the first form of regulation of the fusee watch.

RATE. The timekeeping performance of a watch. Thus 'daily rate' is the term used to denote the difference between two states of a timekeeper separated by an interval of 24 hours.

RECOIL. Backward movement of the escape wheel during the unlocking process. It occurs when the exit pallet presses a tooth of the escape wheel backward. In a watch escapement that has draw (q.v.) the escape wheel recoils at the instant of unlocking.

RECOIL ESCAPEMENT. An escapement in which recoil takes place, as opposed to a dead-beat or frictional rest escapement.

REGULATION. In pre-balance spring watches regulation depended primarily upon altering the set-up of the mainspring. In addition, on some early German watches the supplementary arc could be varied by altering the position of two upright hog's bristles against which the arms of the balance, or the foliot, banked. As a rare alternative to this, a long bristle, which could be adjusted as to length, lay across the balance, two upright pins on which flexed the bristle on each swing of the balance.

The earliest form of adjustable set-up is the ratchet and click, found on fusee watches up to about 1640, when it gave place to the tangent screw and wheel, although the two forms overlap in period. After the introduction of the balance spring, the set-up was transferred from the top plate (where it was readily accessible for regulation) to between the plates, regulation now being possible by altering the effective length of the balance spring. Tompion's form of regulator was universally adopted. It consists of a segmental rack, which follows the outer coil of the spring, and is geared to a small wheel carrying a key

square and an index dial. Using a key, the position of the curb pins where they embrace the balance spring can be altered, either by shortening or increasing the effective length, thus causing the watch to gain or lose on its previous rate. The index dial known as the 'figure plate' or 'rosette' gives a guide to the alteration made, although the numbers engraved on it are arbitrary. The only other form of regulation dating from this period has been accredited to Nathaniel Barrow although with no good reason. This consists of a worm with squared end to take a key. This worm carries a slide on which are mounted two curb pins embracing the straightened outer end of the balance spring. The slide has a pointer which moves across an index engraved on the movement plate, thus indicating the amount the slide has moved when regulating. Very few watches with this form of regulation have survived. In 1755 Joseph Bosley patented 'A new-invented slide, which slide has no wheel attached to it'; that is, he dispensed with the Tompion segmental rack. Bosley's consisted of a small lever, the shorter end of which carries the curb pins which embrace the balance spring, the longer end (by which it is moved) travels across a scale which served to indicate the alteration to 'fast' or 'slow' in the position of the curb pins. A 'free-sprung' watch can only be regulated by altering the timing screws on the balance.

REGULATOR. See INDEX.

REMONTOIRE. A spring (or other device) which is wound by the train and discharged at regular intervals.

REMONTOIRE ESCAPEMENT. An escapement employing a remontoire which is interposed between the escape wheel and the balance to ensure constant force to the balance. The distinction between a remontoire and a remontoire escapement lies in the point at which the remontoire is introduced. In the former it is interposed between the mainspring and the escape wheel, and in the latter between the escape wheel and the balance. In both cases the purpose is to secure a more constant torque than is delivered by the driving train. Such an escapement is also known as a 'constant force escapement'.

REPEATER. A repeating watch in which mechanism can be set in motion to denote the approximate time by hammers striking bells, gongs or a block within the watch case. This last is known as a 'dumb repeater'. Repeating work was invented by Daniel Quare between 1680 and 1686. Matthew Stogden introduced improvements about 1725.

REPOUSSE. Decoration achieved by hammering metal from the back into a shape or pattern resulting in relief decoration. A similar effect is given by casting.

REPUBLICAN CALENDAR. Introduced in France in 1792, and in use until January, 1806.

RESILIENT ESCAPEMENT. A form of lever escapement in which the impulse pin, when pressing on the outside of the lever, causes the lever to yield and allow the pin to pass.

ROBIN ESCAPEMENT. Introduced by the 18th century French watchmaker of that name. It is a single beat escapement, impulse being given by the escape wheel in one direction only and which relies on the balance to help run the lever to banking. A rare escapement of which Breguet made a number.

ROLLER. In the lever escapement, the disc fitted on the balance staff and carrying the impulse pin, the latter receiving impulse via the pallets. This is the single or table roller. In later lever escapements, with double rollers, a smaller, safety roller was introduced which has a crescent or passing-hollow cut in it for the guard pin. Also see **TABLE ROLLER** and **CRANKLEVER ESCAPE-MENT.** In the duplex escapement (q.v.) the roller is a hollow ruby cylinder against which the teeth of the escape wheel are locked.

ROSKOPF. G.T. Roskopf manufactured the first cheap and successful watches in 1867. The Roskopf escapement is basically a lever, but the impulse pin and pallets are steel pins. The modern form is called a 'pin lever'. The pin-pallet is not exclusively Roskopf.

RUBY CYLINDER ESCAPEMENT. A cylinder escapement in which the cylinder shell is made out of ruby. It was probably introduced by John Arnold in 1764, though not used to any extent for some years. The second John Ellicott used it in his later cylinder watches, but it was very popular with Breguet.

RUN-TO-BANKING. In the lever escapement, the movement of the lever towards the banking pins after a tooth has given impulse to the pallet. This is a safety factor to ensure the passage of the escape wheel teeth. See **DRAW.**

'S' BALANCE. See DOUBLE 'S' BALANCE.
SAFETY ROLLER. See ROLLER.
SAFETY DART. See DART.
SAVAGE TWO-PIN. A form of lever escapement named after George Savage in which the roller carries two pins which unlock the escapement via the fork. A third pin, mounted upright at the end of the lever, acts as the impulse pin, passing into a narrow notch cut in the roller, when the escape wheel has been unlocked. This third pin also serves as the guard pin for the safety action during the supplementary arc. Savage introduced his escapement about 1814, certainly before 1818 when he emigrated to Canada. There he founded the firm of Savage & Lyman. Very few watches signed by Savage have survived. He made for Edward Bracebridge of Red Lion Street, 1805-15.

SAVONNETTE. A watch with a front cover to give protection to the glass. See HUNTER.

SECONDS PINION. The extension of the fourth wheel arbor to which the seconds hand is attached.

SECRET SIGNATURE. A device used by A.L. Breguet to combat the forgery of his work. The name and the number of the watch were engraved with a pantograph on the dial, and these can only be seen when examining the dial with the light falling across it. Subsequently, makers other than Breguet used the idea.

SECRET SPRING. The fly and lock springs of a hunter watch case.

SELF-COMPENSATING SPRING. A balance spring made of an alloy impervious to temperature changes.

SELF-WINDING. See PERPETUAL WATCH.

SET-UP. The degree of tension to which a main-spring is set when the watch is fully run down. The use of stop-work enables a going barrel watch to be 'set-up' so that only the middle turns of the main-spring are in use, thus providing more even torque. By altering the set-up, a degree of regulation was effected in the fusee, pre-balance spring watch.

SHIP'S CHRONOMETER. See DETENT ESCAPE-MENT.

SINGLE ROLLER. See TABLE ROLLER.

SIX-HOUR DIAL. A watch dial of the late 17th century period in which the chapter ring is marked in Roman numerals I to VI and superimposed on these are arabic numerals 7 to 12. The single hand revolves once in six hours. Due to the larger spacing between the numerals (only six instead of twelve) the divisions between them can be legibly calibrated into two-minute divisions, and the time read to two minutes from the one hand.

SKELETON DIAL. A dial from which metal has been cut away leaving only the hour and minute ring, thus exposing the movement.

SKELETONISED MOVEMENT. A watch movement in which all the spare metal has been cut away from the top movement plate, thus exposing the wheel work.

SNAIL. A cam shaped like the profile of a snail; part of the striking mechanism in the rack-striking layout. The snail determines — owing to the steps cut thereon — how far the rack may fall when it is released, and hence how many blows are struck, each step corresponding to an hour.

SOUSCRIPTION (MONTREA). The cheapest possible Breguet watch of the highest possible quality, subscribed for in advance and made by him in batches.

SPLIT-SECONDS. A form of chronograph in which there are two centre seconds hands, one over the other. When the chronograph is started, the hands travel together, but with a secondary push-piece the under one is halted while the other continues. The stationary hand can be made to rejoin its fellow, that can also be stopped independently. Once together and stationary both can be returned to zero.

SPRING BARREL. The barrel containing the main-spring.

SPRING DETENT. In the chronometer escapement a blade spring carrying the locking jewel. A detent mounted on a spring. It is sometimes called a 'footed detent'. Patented by John Arnold in 1782.

STACKFREED. An eccentric cam or snail serving as a main spring-equaliser. It is mounted on a wheel geared to a pinion on the main spring arbor, making rather less than one revolution on one winding or in the going time of the watch. Pressing against the edge of the snail is a strong spring which terminates in a roller, the roller thus setting up friction between itself and the edge of the snail or, more correctly, between the stackfreed wheel and the post upon which it revolves, the friction varying with the radius of the snail. The wheel upon which the snail is mounted has a short section on which no teeth are cut. This, in conjunction with the pinion on the main spring arbor, provides stop-work. When the watch is run down, the roller lies in a notch or depression between the highest and lowest portions of the snail. In this position the roller-spring is not tensioned. Also, the uncut section of the snail-wheel butts against a leaf of the pinion mounted on the main spring arbor. On winding the watch, the 'stop' position is reached when the pinion comes up against the uncut section of the snail-wheel, approaching it from the contrary direction. Also, on winding, the roller is lifted out of the notch on to the snail at its highest point where it exerts greatest pressure. As the main-spring runs down, less and less pressure is exerted to match the decreasing force of the main spring until, right at the end of the run, the roller starts to enter the notch, and for a short

time actually 'helps' the main spring.

The stop-work arrangement not only prevents over-winding, but — and this is important — can be arranged to allow only a portion of the main spring to be used; that is, the middle portion, thus avoiding the two extremes. (see **SET-UP**.)

The stackfreed was almost certainly invented in Nuremberg, probably fairly early in the 16th century. It would appear that Henlein's watches with a 40-hour duration employed neither the stackfreed nor fusee. A few watches with a wedge-shaped cam and without a notch exist. In this type — which is the late form of stackfreed — the main spring was given 'assistance' rather sooner than on the snail-type. The profile of the cam altered over the years, starting from a simple curve, with the notch, and becoming more 'snail'-like. The form of the cam probably altered as it became possible to make thicker (consequently shorter) springs which would produce a different torque-curve. The final form (*circa* 1585-1620), before the 'wedge', was kidney-shaped. The stackfreed seems to have been confined to southern Germany. Its only advantage over the early, crude fusee was that it occupied less height and so enabled a flatter watch to be made.

STANDING BARREL. Hanging barrel is the alternative name for a going barrel whose arbor is supported at the upper end only.

STOP-WORK. A device to prevent over-winding of a main spring, and to enable the spring to be set-up. (See **SET-UP**). A form of stop-work was used on the earliest Nuremberg watches. See **STACKFREED**.

STRAIGHT LINE LEVER. A lever escapement in which the escape wheel arbor, the pallet staff and the balance staff are planted in a straight line.

STRIP COMPENSATION. See **COMPENSATION CURB**.

STUD. A small piece of metal pierced to receive the end of the outer coil of a balance spring.

'SUGAR TONGS'. The name given to the compensation curb used by Thomas Earnshaw, its shape roughly resembling a pair of tongs.

SUN AND MOON DIAL. A popular dial in the late 17th and early 18th century. A sun is depicted on one half and a moon on the other of a disc revolving once in 24 hours. Each is visible in turn through a semi-circular hole cut in the dial plate. Above the hole a segment of the dial is marked from VII to XII and from I to VI. The sun indicates 6 a.m. to 6 p.m. and the moon 6 p.m. to 6 a.m. The minutes are indicated in the normal way.

SUPPLEMENTARY ARC. The arc described by an oscillating balance outside the function of escapement, after the impulse and before unlocking.

SURPRISE PIECE. A device fitted to the quarter-snail of a repeater to prevent incorrect striking just prior to the next hour.

SWEEP SECONDS. See CENTRE SECONDS.

SWING WHEEL. The escape wheel used to be so called.

SWISS LEVER ESCAPEMENT. The lever escapement now in universal use. It is distinguished by the form of the escape wheel teeth — i.e. club-toothed.

TABLE ROLLER. The roller of a lever escapement which carries the impulse pin. The term 'table' was originally applied to distinguish this kind of roller from the part carrying the impulse pin in Massey's escapement, or the so-called 'crank lever'. The impulse pin on the table roller is a jewel and protrudes downwards from the table in contradistinction to the crank roller where the impulse piece protrudes from the circumference. The table roller came in shortly after 1825-30.

TACT. A '*montre à tact*' has a stout external hand fitted over the back cover of the watch, and not connected directly with the movement. If the hand is moved by one's finger in a clockwise direction, it moves freely until it is, in fact, indicating the correct time, when it comes up against a stop. The time is then 'read off' by feeling the hand's position relative to pins on the exterior of the case at each hour position. It is thus possible to ascertain the time in the dark. The *montre à tact* is thus in fact a form of 'repeater'. There is usually a normal dial with two hands visible if the front cover is opened. Breguet made a number of such watches. It is a mistake to think of them as being intended primarily for use by blind persons.

TAILLE DOUCE. Fine line engraving.

TAMBOUR CASE. An early form of watch case, pill box in shape, with hinged cover.

TANGENT SCREW. An endless screw, or worm gear. Tangent screw and wheel were used rather before the mid-17th century, replacing the ratchet wheel method, as a means of setting up the main-spring and as a means of regulation. A small dial mounted on the top plate served as an index. After 1675 the worm and wheel were mounted between the plates.

TEMPERATURE COMPENSATION. Any device to counteract the effects of temperature changes on the rate of a watch; in particular, the effect on the steel balance spring which loses some of its elasticity for a rise in temperature with the contrary effect for a fall. See also COMPENSATION BALANCE and COMPENSATION CURB. 18th century watchmakers usually referred to the 'thermometer'.

TERMINAL CURVES. The curves at the two ends of a cylindrical or helical balance spring, or the outer curve of an overcoil balance spring. In 1858 Edouard Phillips began his investigations into the geometry of the balance spring and into the theoretically correct terminal curves which render it isochronal. Prior to that, watchmakers had used empirical methods, though John Arnold's patent of 1782 referred to the ends of the spring as being 'incurvated'. Briefly, the condition necessary for isochronism is that the centre of gravity of the spring should lie on the axis of the balance. The method adopted to arrive at this condition is to fix the inner and outer ends of the spring in a certain relationship to one another.

THIRD WHEEL. The wheel between the centre and fourth wheel.

THREE-QUARTER PLATE. See FULL PLATE.

TIMING IN POSITIONS. The art of adjusting the balance and its spring so that the watch keeps time in different positions. Also see ADJUSTED.

TIMING SCREWS. Properly, only those screws at the ends of the arms of a cut, compensated balance which are used to bring the watch to time; hence 'mean time screws'. In a chronometer balance there are two timing screws or nuts: one at each end of the arm. Timing screws should not be confused with those balance screws used for adjusting the compensation.

TINTED GOLD. Also called 'coloured gold'. A form of decoration applied to watch cases and dials. The gold is coloured by alloys to produce a reddish, greenish, silvery or yellowish hue. Introduced in the last half of the 18th century, it was known as '*or à quatre couleurs*', though four colours were not necessarily used. Coloured gold was also used effectively with gems in case decoration.

TIPSY-KEY. See BREGUET KEY.

TOMPION REGULATOR. See REGULATION.

TOP PLATE. That furthest from the dial. Also known as the 'potence plate'. The movement plate seen from the back, the other plate being the 'bottom' or 'dial plate'. 'Back plate' is the equivalent plate in a clock movement and is so called.

TOUCH PINS. Pins were usually inserted at the hour positions in 16th century watch dials to enable the time to be read with the aid of a finger during darkness.

TOURBILLON. A.L. Breguet's invention (patented in 1801) for neutralising the positional (vertical) errors inherent in a watch. The escapement is mounted in a revolving carriage or cage with the result that the positional errors are repeated (with a cancelling-out effect) in every revolution of the carriage. The speed of revolution of the carriage depended on the layout. In some instances the escape wheel pinion turns about the

Fig. 13. Crown (escape) wheel, arbor and pinion. Balance, balance spring and verge. One flag (pallet) can be clearly seen on the verge.

fixed fourth wheel, but whose arbor is free to turn the carriage mounted on it once in a minute. In others the revolution is made in two, four or six minutes. A 'tourbillon watch' is not a watch with a special kind of escapement.

TRAIN. The wheels and pinions which connect the going barrel or fusee with the escapement. In watch work, the wheel is the driver and the pinion the follower, except in the motion work. The 'going train' concerns the timekeeping part of the mechanism, the 'striking train' that side concerned with the striking. In the case of a fusee watch the great wheel, and in a going barrel watch the teeth round the barrel, drive the centre pinion, to the arbor of which is attached the centre wheel. This drives the third wheel pinion, the third wheel driving the fourth wheel pinion, the fourth wheel driving the escape wheel pinion. The number of teeth in the various wheels and pinions in general is determined by the following considerations (among others): the minute hand, being fixed to the centre wheel and pinion arbor, must make one revolution in an hour; the fourth wheel, to the arbor of which the seconds hand is fixed, must make one revolution in a minute.

TRIAL NUMBER. A symbol used to express the relative excellence of chronometers and watches in competitive trials. The Greenwich Observatory method was to multiply the difference between the greatest and the least variation by twice the difference between one week and the next.

TRIPLE-CASED. A watch, usually made for the Turkish market, which has an additional case to the outer case of pair-case watch.

TRIPPING. The accidental passing of two teeth of the escape wheel instead of one. This may occur in the duplex and detent escapements.

TURKISH MARKET WATCHES. Watches made for export to Turkey and provided with a dial with 'Turkish' numerals. Such watches normally had three cases; that over the movement being plain, the second with some engraving to the rim and the third or outer tortoiseshell-covered or occasionally shagreen. A fourth case, either of stiffened leather or silver, of native craftsmanship, is sometimes found. Watches were exported to Turkey in the 17th century, but large quantities were made in London for this market at the end of the 18th and early 19th centuries.

TWO-PIN ESCAPEMENT. See SAVAGE TWO-PIN.

UNDER-DIAL WORK. Complications such as calendar, lunar or repeating mechanism in addition to motion work, situated on the dial plate under the dial.

UP-AND-DOWN DIAL. A subsidiary dial indicating the state-of-wind of the main-spring, usually found on marine chronometers or pocket chronometers and on some high-class watches between about 1880 and 1910.

VERGE. In the limited sense the verge is the rod or spindle upon which the balance or foliot is mounted. It carries two 'flags' or pallets. In the wider sense the word implies a watch with the verge or crown wheel escapement.

VERGE ESCAPEMENT. See figs. 13 and 14. Sometimes called the crown-wheel escapement, it was used in the earliest watches; its inventor is unknown. It consists of a crown wheel (the escape wheel), the arbor of which carries a pinion driven by the train. A vertical arbor (the verge) is at right angles to the crown wheel and has two pallets or 'flags' separated by a distance approximating to the diameter of the crown wheel and at an angle of approximately 100 degrees to each other. The verge carries at its upper end a balance and is pivoted at its two extremities. The teeth of the

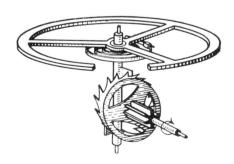

Fig. 14. Verge escapement.

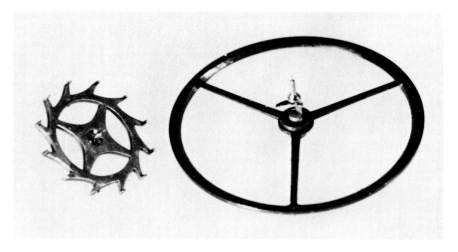

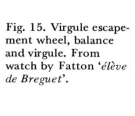

Fig. 15. Virgule escapement wheel, balance and virgule. From watch by Fatton '*élève de Breguet*'.

crown wheel act upon the pallets alternately and cause the balance to oscillate.

The eleven or thirteen teeth of the crown wheel are very approximately a sloping triangle in shape and the wheel itself somewhat resembles a medieval crown. A tooth of the crown wheel comes into contact with one pallet, thrusts upon it (gives it impulse) and imparts circular motion to the balance, which motion moves the pallet away from the tooth until this is free to slip past the pallet which has been pressing upon it. The crown wheel is momentarily free to advance, but almost immediately a tooth on the opposite side of the wheel comes into contact with the other pallet, the circular motion of the balance having brought it down into the path of the wheel. In order to free itself (escape) this tooth thrusts the second pallet out of its path, thus giving the balance an impulse in the opposite direction. The continued process results in the oscillatory movement of the balance and a tooth by tooth advancement of the crown escape wheel.

The verge is a recoil escapement. There is a supplementary arc of balance swing — i.e. the balance continues its gyration after it has been impulsed, and the teeth of the crown wheel are undercut to free the face of the pallet during the resulting recoil. The inclination of the teeth is about 30 degrees. Figs. 13 and 14 show a verge escapement with balance spring.

VIRGULE ESCAPEMENT. See fig. 15. Also known as the 'hook escapement', deriving both names from the part which receives impulse, this being somewhat like a comma in shape. Like the cylinder escapement (to which it has some similarity) it is a frictional rest escapement, usually credited to J.A. Lepaute, and it was used in France in the last quarter of the 18th century and during the early years of the 19th. This escapement appears also to have some resemblance to the

horizontal escapements considered by Tompion and his associates towards the end of the 17th century. The patent they took out in 1695 implies a cylinder more than a virgule but it reflected only part of their deliberations.

The virgule escape wheel has teeth standing up from the plane of the wheel. The teeth may be described as pins. These lock on the outside edge of the rounded part of the 'comma' or small cylinder and give impulse when entering and passing along the inner side of the downward curve of the 'comma'. The balance, therefore, receives impulse in one direction only, and not in both as occurs in the cylinder escapement. J.A. Lepine employed this escapement in conjunction with his bridged movement: the Lepine calibre (q.v.). The double virgule, invented by Beaumarchais, is exceedingly rare.

WANDERING HOUR DIAL. Sometimes called a 'Floating Hour Dial'. A semi-circular slit opening in the upper half of the dial reveals Roman hour numerals, appearing one at a time and in ordinary succession. On the outer edge and beyond the slit are the minute graduations occupying the corresponding half-circle to the inner slit for the hour numerals, and marked 0-60 minutes. The hour numeral travels from left to right, indicating the minutes in its passage. On reaching the 60 minute mark, it disappears beyond the slit and is succeeded by the next hour numeral following in its wake. A third, and innermost semi-circle, is marked off in quarter-hours.

Wandering-hour watches were quite popular during the last quarter of the 17th century and during the earlier years of the 18th. A few were also produced at the end of the 19th and early 20th century. They are also called 'chronoscopes'.

WARNING. The preparatory operation of the striking mechanism occurring a few minutes before the striking is released on the hour. A wheel in the striking train (the 'warning wheel') carries a pin which is arrested and then released by the 'warning piece'.

WATCH PAPER. Embroidered cambric or muslin or printed papers that were placed in the backs of the outer case of pair-case watches. These served to prevent the back of the inner case becoming scratched and also took up any slackness between the two cases. Towards the end of the 18th century they also served as advertisements of the watchmaker or repairer. Many have sentimental rhymes or admonishing proverbs, and some gave the equation of time.

WINDING SQUARE. The squared end of the barrel or fusee arbor on which the key is fitted in order to wind the watch. A similar squared end is on the arbor carrying the hands, by which the hands may be set in key-winding watches; this is called the 'set-hand square'.

WORM WHEEL. See **TANGENT SCREW.**

"Z" BALANCE. A balance consisting of two steel arms and two bimetallic terminal curbs. Introduced by John Arnold in about 1791 and seen on watches as late as 1818.

Index

This index includes makers' names from the Glossary, but not technical terms. References to the Clock-makers' Company, descriptions of gold and silver cases and pair-cased watches are so numerous in the text to the plates that they have not been included in the index. Many references to enamel dials and pendants also fall into this category.

Makers' Marks referred to in the text

AD	178
AR	115
ATO	*see* Oliver, A.T.
CH G	163
CW	*see* Caspar Werner
FF	115
FT	*see* Thoms
GB	*see* Ball
IH	208
IW	116, 117
JB	202
JM	181
JP	*see* Preston (John) & Sons
JW	*see* Woodman Brothers
MB	51
ND	*see* Delaunder, Nathaniel
PW	*see* Woodman Brothers
RP	144
TP	99
VW	157
WM	171
WS	112

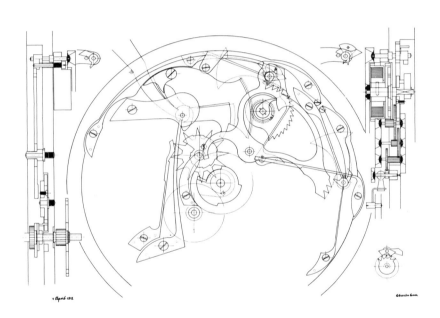

4 April 1988   Charles Ross

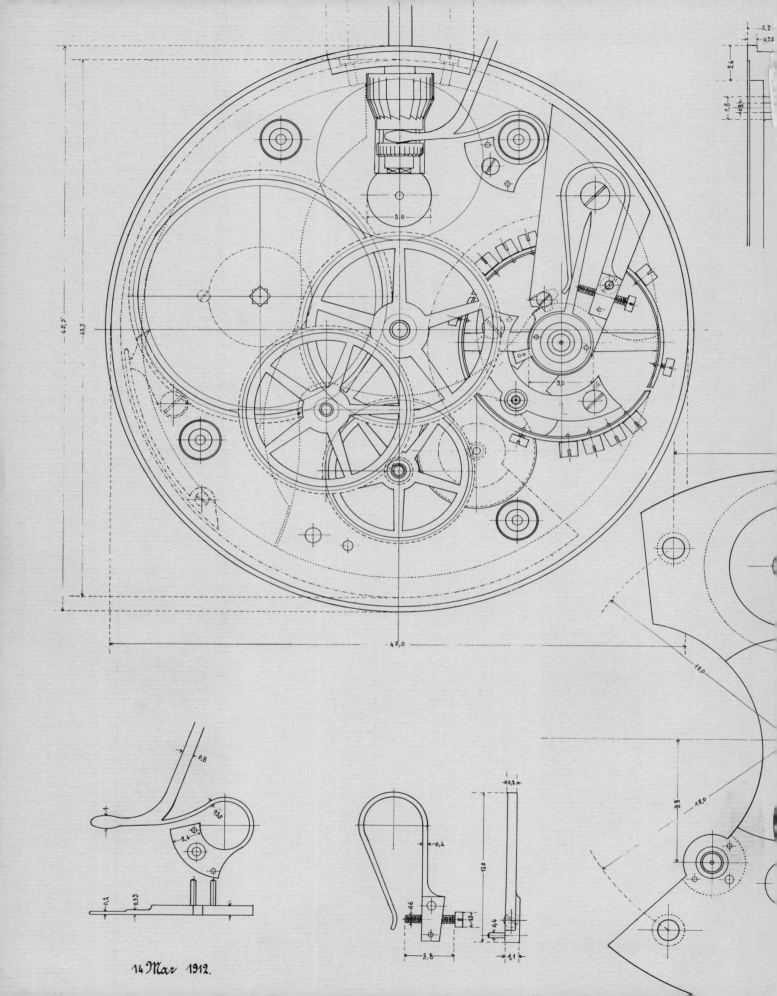

14 Mar 1912.